THE CHINESE LEARNER:

CULTURAL, PSYCHOLOGIC
— and —
CONTEXTUA
INFLUENCES

Edited by **David A. Watkins and John B. Biggs**

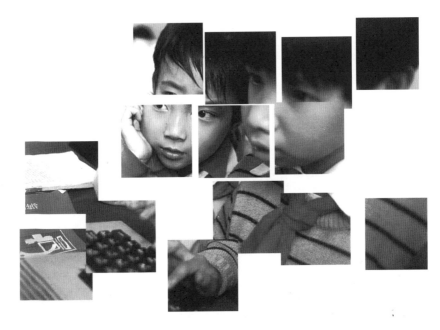

CERC & ACER

First published 1996 by
Comparative Education Research Centre
Faculty of Education
University of Hong Kong
Pokfulam Road
Hong Kong
and
The Australian Council for Educational Research Ltd
19 Prospect Hill Road
Camberwell, Melbourne
Victoria 3124
Australia

Design by Michael Lau
Printed by The Central Printing Press Ltd, Hong Kong

ISBN 0 86431 182 6

The Chinese Learner:

Cultural, Psychological, and Contextual Influences

David Watkins & John Biggs (Editors)

Chapter Titles and Authors

ABOUT THE AUTHORS

John Biggs was Professor of Education at the University of Hong Kong from 1987 until his retirement in 1995. He is now an educational consultant based at the University of Sydney, NSW. His research interests are in the conditions of effective learning and teaching, and students' approaches to learning, particularly in students from Confucian heritage cultures.

Gloria Dall'Alba has worked within the field of educational development since 1988, first in Australia and then in Sweden. She currently has responsibility for research on higher education within the Department for Research and Development in Medical Education at Karolinska Institute in Sweden.

Lyn Gow is a Senior Scientist at the University of New South Wales coordinating large research projects in the areas of Aboriginal Affairs and Disability. At the time this chapter was written, she was the Chief Investigator of an Action Learning Project funded by the University and Polytechnics' Grants Committee in Hong Kong.

Keith Johnson is a Reader in Education at the University of Hong Kong, having previously taught in Zambia and Papua New Guinea. He has published extensively in the areas of bilingual education, curriculum development, the use of English as a second language medium of instruction, literacy, and the development of reading strategies.

David Kember is the Coordinator of the Action Learning Project. This is an inter-institutional project which aims to encourage and support academics in all seven universities in Hong Kong to participate in action research projects concerned with aspects of their own teaching. The Project currently supports over 50 sub-projects which fit within the overall theme of enhancing the quality of student learning by improving the quality of teaching. The Project is funded by a grant from the University Grants Committee of Hong Kong. He has also published extensively in the areas of student learning and conceptions of teaching.

John Kirby is a Professor of Education at Queen's University in Ontario, Canada. He is the coauthor of six books and has published about 50 journal articles in the areas of simultaneous and successive processing, reading and cognitive strategies.

W.O. Lee is a Senior Lecturer in Education and Director of the Comparative Education Research Centre at the University of Hong Kong. His teaching and research interests cover educational philosophy, values education, and comparative study. He has published extensively on educational development in Asian countries from philosophical and social perspectives, and is now working on the implications of Asian values on education and development.

Yamin Ma completed her BA in English Language and Literature at Shanghai Teachers' University, and a Master of Education at Queen's University, where she specialized in adult Chinese learners' communicative competence in English. She is now teaching at an international school in Hong Kong.

Ference Marton has been Professor of Education in the Department of Education and Educational Research at the University of Gothenburg in Sweden since 1977. Together with a number of colleagues and students, he has been engaged since the early 1970s in exploring the qualitatively different ways in which people experience and are aware of phenomena in, and aspects of, the world around them. These differences are arguably the most critical features of variation in learning within and between individuals.

Jan McKay is a Course Leader, BS Radiography at the Hong Kong Polytechnic University. She has recently completed her PhD. The action research study included the development and implementation of the Radiography degree.

Peter Renshaw is a Senior Lecturer in Education at the University of Queensland. His research is based on a sociocultural theory of development, and has included studies of early literacy, collaborative learning, peer group interaction, and university student learning. He is currently Honorary Secretary of the Australian Association for Research in Education.

Farideh Salili is a Senior Lecturer in Psychology at the University of Hong Kong. Her PhD is from the University of Illinois. She is currently the Coordinator of the Master of Social Science in Educational Psychology Programme. She is the author of over 30 journal articles specifically in the area of achievement motivation and its attributions.

Catherine Tang has been involved with the education of student physiotherapists at the Hong Kong Polytechnic University for 15 years. She is currently the University's Assistant Director of Educational Development. Her research interest is in student learning, and particularly in the effects of assessment on student learning.

Tse Lai Kun is a Language Instructor in the English Centre at the University of Hong Kong.

Simone Volet is a Senior Lecturer in Educational Psychology at Murdoch University in Western Australia. Her research interests are in the area of tertiary student learning, with particular reference to study goals, cognitive and affective processes in the management of learning, and metacognitive instruction.

David Watkins is a Reader in Education at the University of Hong Kong. He has published widely in the areas of student learning, self-esteem, and the evaluation of university teaching based on research in Australia and a number of Asian and African countries.

Sam Winter is a Lecturer in Education at the University of Hong Kong. He has published extensively in the areas of peer learning, applied behaviour analysis, and sociometric ratings.

Rosamund A. Woodhouse has a PhD from Queen's University and works in the Faculty of Medicine at the University of Toronto. Her research interests include bilingualism and student learning.

Agnes S.N. Yau is a Lecturer in Education at the Baptist University in Hong Kong. She previously taught English in a Chinese medium secondary school. Her main research interest is in the development of reading strategies in students whose first language is Chinese and second language is English.

PREFACE

Until recently it was commonly assumed that 'modern' practices in areas such as business, industry, and education utilized in Western countries were superior to the 'traditional' practices of the Third World. However, just as in the economic sphere, students in many Asian countries, and particularly those from Confucian heritage cultures, are now out-performing Western students in international comparisons of educational progress. What is their secret? Is it just hard work?

Over the last 20 years Western researchers have developed quantitative and qualitative research methods that further our understanding of the teaching/learning process. These approaches to research have now been extended to some Asian countries, such as Singapore, India, Nepal, Brunei, and the Philippines. However, over the last ten years, it is Hong Kong that has become the particular focus for both pure and applied research, and this work is revealing much about Chinese students' approaches to learning. The results, as reported in this book, paint a much clearer picture of how Chinese students and their teachers see the context and content of their learning, and help us to see how these students, from their own cultural background, cope so well with versions of Western-style education. These results also raise questions about the foundations of Western educational theory and practice.

This book is divided into four main chapter groupings as follows:

Setting the Scene. This section contains two chapters designed as a background for the research to follow. The first has two main functions: to introduce the reader to the theoretical framework and research methods typically adopted in the book, and then, because these theoretical and research orientations have been developed in Western countries, to examine their validity for investigating study learning in non-Western cultures. The second chapter examines conceptions of teaching and learning as construed in traditional Confucian texts and to what extent such notions serve as a cultural context for Chinese and other Southeast Asian learners today.

Perspectives on the Paradox of the Chinese Learner. The next four chapters focus on the 'paradox' which is at the heart of this book: how can Chinese learners be so successful academically when their teaching and learning appears to be so focused on rote memorization? Solutions to this paradox are sought in terms of personality and cognitive constructs based in their cultural context.

Coping with the Context of Learning. In the previous four chapters it is established that Chinese learners are very conscious of the learning context. The next five chapters, show that they also tend to be extremely able at adapting their learning strategies to cope with the problems of studying in a second language and varying assessment and teaching methods both in Hong Kong and overseas.

Intervention Strategies. The next two chapters discuss two intervention strategies which have been implemented and work well in Hong Kong. The first complements Chapter 10 in demonstrating that peer teaching seems to be particularly suited to a relatively group-oriented, collectivist society such as Hong Kong. The second illustrates how the Action

Learning approach can be used to help teachers understand their students better, leading to improved learning outcomes.

In the final chapter we as editors attempt to draw out the implications of the earlier chapters both for educational and psychological theorising as it may apply cross-culturally, and to Chinese and Western cultures in particular; and for assisting teachers, researchers, study skills counsellors, and staff developers both to understand and to interact with their Chinese students more effectively. We conclude that cross-cultural differences in the processes of teaching and learning, particularly with respect to the role of memorization and to the nature of motivation, resolve the so-called "paradox" of the Chinese learner, but more importantly, perhaps, show that the misconceptions and stereotyping of Western observers are without foundation.

We are grateful to many people for their assistance in producing this book:

- to Fanny Wong for her usual meticulous typing despite pressures from all her many other job commitments;
- to Leo Li for help with indexing;
- to William Pang for assistance with the figures;
- to Michael Lau for designing the cover;
- to Lee Wing On of CERC and Ian Fraser of ACER for their encouragement and advice; and
- to Rosalind A. Haddon for copy editing.

David Watkins & John Biggs

July, 1996

SETTING THE SCENE

1

Learning Theories and Approaches to Research: A Cross-Cultural Perspective

David Watkins

The purpose of this chapter is to set the scene for the investigations of the Chinese learner that are reported in this book. While the chapter writers espouse a range of theoretical positions there is a commonality of fundamental notions about the nature of learning shared by us all: one that can be referred to as the student approaches to learning (SAL) position (Biggs, 1993; Entwistle and Waterston, 1988). The approaches to research utilized by many authors also show certain similarities: basically by either using quantitative analyses of responses to structured learning process questionnaires; or a focused qualitative approach based on content analyses of in-depth interviews to aid their understanding of the Chinese learner.

This chapter introduces the reader to both these common theoretical and complementary research approaches. However, it is imperative to realise that both are the products of a century of Western research. Third world psychologists have actively warned against the assumption that Western theories and research methods are appropriate in other cultures, for some time now (Enriquez, 1982). So the second purpose of this chapter is to examine the applicability of the theoretical and research approaches adopted in this book for non-Western cultures, and the Chinese in particular.

Theories of Learning

Over the last 30 years educational psychology has been dominated by cognitive theories of learning where the processing of information is seen as the key to understanding the complex behaviour that human beings undertake everyday (Walberg and Haertel, 1992). Previously, under the influence of behaviourism, observable behaviour rather than the mind was seen as the only fit subject of study for a scientific psychology (Skinner, 1958; Watson, 1914). However, cognitive psychologists argued that the behaviourist approach, while being sufficiently adequate for explaining the learning of animals and simple human tasks, it was quite inadequate to explain the more sophisticated learning necessary to acquire language and to be used everyday in our schools. To understand such complex learning, cognitive theorists argued, it was necessary for the focus of study to be the structure and processes of the mind (Floden, 1981). The advent of the computer played a major role both as a model of the human mind and as a tool for describing and testing complex theories in the development of the information processing theories which dominated the 1970s. The importance of plans and goals in human thought were emphasized (Miller, Galanter, and Pribram, 1960). Complex behaviour was broken down into simple cognitive processes which were initiated and coordinated by higher order metaprocesses. Cognitive psychologists recognized the importance of the learner being active, the content of learning, and the method of instruction. They also highlighted the role that advanced organizers played aiding the learner to construct new knowledge structures through the assimilation of old and new information (Walberg and Haertel, 1992).

This principle that understanding is not just a matter of the accumulation but rather the construction and transformation of knowledge is a basic tenet of current educational thinking, including both approaches to investigating student learning discussed below (Blumenfeld, 1992). Knowledge is not seen as something external to the learner for which it is the teachers' job to transmit to their students:-

> ".... methods of teaching should be designed to stimulate students to construct meaning from their own experience rather than stimulating them to reproduce the knowledge of others." (Wittrock, 1977; p.180)

The information processing (IP) approach has been applied to the area of student learning in the work of American researchers such as Schmeck (1988) and Weinstein, Schulte, and Palmer (1987). These researchers have developed learning strategy questionnaires from this perspective. Biggs (1992a; 1993) has pointed out several problems with their approach. These arise because the IP approach focuses "too narrowly on the study processes of students as if that studying took place in a vacuum. In fact, the learning environment has profound effects on studying" (Entwistle and Waterston, 1988; p.264). The IP approach proposes a set of theoretical ideas about learning (focusing on processes such as rehearsing, elaborating, and imaging) which apply regardless of the context and content of learning, which are to be claimed universal (Moreno and DiVesta, 1991). Thus motivational and affective aspects of learning were deliberately excluded. However, researchers are now realizing that education does not take place in a laboratory but in a "soft, slimy swamp" (Schon, 1987; p.3). Any model which claims to be an adequate basis for understanding human learning cannot hope to statistically or experimentally 'control' away this complexity, but must try to take into account its usage of research methods necessary for analyzing this complexity (Salomon, 1991).

The Student Approaches to Learning Position

The student approaches to learning (SAL) position which is advocated in this book arose out of dissatisfaction with the above aspects of the information-processing approach. The SAL theory is derived bottom-up from the perspective of the student not the researcher. As most students recognize that affect and context influence their learning methods, this is reflected in SAL theory (Biggs, 1993). The SAL approach is thus consistent with the current advocacy of the notion of situated cognition (Brown, Collins, and Duguid, 1989). The impetus for the SAL approach was a paper by Marton and Saljo (1976), one of the most widely cited sources in the entire literature of educational psychology (Walberg and Haertel, 1992). That paper described a study where Swedish University students were asked to read an academic article and then explain what they had learned and how they had achieved that learning. These students generally expressed two major ways of tackling this task. Some tried to memorize details or key terms in order to be able to answer subsequent questions. They tended to focus on the reading at word or sentence level. Most of the other subjects tried to understand the message that the passage was trying to impart. They tended to focus on the themes and main ideas and generally tried to process the reading for meaning. These intentions and their associated reading strategies were called 'surface' and 'deep' approaches, respectively. The researchers reported qualitative differences in learning outcomes depending on the approach to reading that had been utilized. Students who had adopted a surface approach typically could not explain the authors' message and could only recall isolated factual fragments of the passage. Those adopting a deep approach were able to provide a more sophisticated overview of the authors' intentions and frequently used extracts from the reading to support their reasoning.

At this point the SAL literature proceeded in two contrasting but not incompatible directions. The Swedish researchers developed a qualitative approach to research which they called 'phenomenography' (Marton, 1981). The aim of this approach was to understand how students perceived the content and process (the 'what' and 'how') of learning. The underlying rationale was the phenomenological notion that people act according to their interpretation of a situation rather than to 'objective reality'.

The basic principle of the phenomenographic view of learning is that "learning should be seen as a qualitative change in a person's way of seeing, experiencing, understanding, conceptualizing something in the real world" (Marton and Ramsden, 1988; p.271). From this perspective there is no point trying to derive general principles of learning independently of the context and content of learning. The ways students learn is a function of how they perceive the learning task and the learning environment. Although phenomenography itself is seen as descriptive, rather than prescriptive, principles based on this approach, have been shown to lead to a higher quality of teaching and learning. In particular it is emphasized that the focus of learning is conceptual change and that teachers need to understand their students' conceptions of learning and how they can facilitate conceptual change (Bowden, 1988; Ramsden, 1992).

Phenomenography typically uses interviews to probe the students' conceptions of learning. Unlike most other qualitative approaches to research these interviews are highly focused. The interviewer is not wholly dependent on a preset set of questions, but commences with a question such as "What do you mean by learning?" and then uses the interviewees' own responses to encourage them to probe further and further into their own conceptions. From this perspective conceptions are "conceived as *relational* phenomena rather than inherent qualities in the minds of the thinker or in the objects/phenomena themselves" (Saljo, 1988; p.44) and can be stated in different ways like any abstraction of reality. The main task for the phenomenographer is to identify these different categories of description. Research has now identified six hierarchically ordered conceptions of learning commonly reported by different students (see Chapter 4). These six conceptions can be divided into quantitative and qualitative groupings. However, there is growing evidence that these conceptions may be more stable over time and less situationally affected than the phenomenographic literature might anticipate (Marton, Dall'Alba, and Beaty, 1993; see also Chapter 6). According to Marton et al. (1993), as could be logically expected, there is clear evidence that conception, approach, and outcome are linked by a chain of functional relationships. It seems that students who are only capable of conceiving a quantitative conception of learning can only achieve a surface approach to learning, and that awareness of a qualitative conception of learning is a necessary but not sufficient condition for the adoption of a deep-level approach. What some of these conditions might be is now being suggested by quantitative approaches to SAL research (see 3P model of learning in Chapter 3).

The quantitative SAL approach was founded by the work of Biggs in Australia and Entwistle in the United Kingdom (UK). Both researchers developed, relatively independently, learning process inventories which owe a debt to the paper of Marton and Saljo (1976), and later phenomenographic writing, by adopting the 'surface/deep' and 'approaches to learning' terminology. However, while these constructs were originally used to describe how a student went about a particular reading task, in the questionnaires these constructs were used to assess how a student would usually, or would prefer to, go about learning tasks in general. As Biggs (1993) explains, the way these terms are used either in the 'presage' or 'process' sense has led to some confusion.

Biggs (1987), in developing his Learning Process Questionnaire (LPQ) and its tertiary counterpart, the Student Process Questionnaire (SPQ), and Entwistle and Ramsden (1983) in developing their Approaches to Studying Inventory (ASI) added a third approach, 'achieving'. Students adopting this approach tried to achieve the highest possible grades by such strategies as working hard and efficiently, and being cue conscious. They would use any strategy, be it rote memorizing lots of facts, or understanding basic principles, that they perceived would maximize their chances of academic success.

Biggs' instruments are based on a neat 'motive/strategy' model of learning (see Table 1.1). He operationalizes the constructs of approach to learning in terms of this motive/strategy combination. Factor analysis of responses to the SPQ, LPQ, and ASI has generally supported the underlying structure of surface, deep, and achieving approaches to learning (Biggs, 1993). Biggs emphasizes that the motive/strategy model is related to the students' intentions and their perceptions of the learning context, and is therefore only meaningful in context. He has adapted a model of teaching proposed by Dunkin and Biddle (1974) to capture the relationships between characteristics of the learner and the learning context (Presage), student approaches to a particular learning task (Process), and outcomes of learning (Product) in his 3P model of learning (see Chapter 3). As explained in that chapter he now emphasizes the 'systemic' nature of this model. The variables involved in the 3P model do not form a simple linear path from presage to process to product. Rather each component of the system interacts with all other components until equilibrium is reached. Inspection of this model indicates why both simple general laws of learning have not been possible to validate, and attempts to improve learning outcomes based on the 'deficit' model are ineffective. To explain student learning requires an appreciation of the interactive, multi-dimensional nature of 'the swamp' of real life learning. General laws such as the Law of Effect (Thorndike, 1921) which focus on just one aspect of the learning situation, such as reinforcement, cannot achieve this. To try to improve the products of schooling by changing just one factor (be it the assessment system or the study methods of students) is likely to be counterproductive if other components of the system remain unchanged (Ramsden, Beswick, and Bowden, 1986).

Table 1.1
Descriptions of scales of learning processes and study process, questionnaires
(after Biggs, 1987; note underlying motive/strategy model)

Scale	

Surface Approach

| Surface motivation | Motivation is utilitarian; main aim is to gain qualifications at minimum allowable standard |
| Surface strategy | Strategy is to reproduce bare essentials often using rote learning |

Deep Approach

| Deep motivation | Motivation is interest in subject and its related areas |
| Deep strategy | Strategy is to understand what is to be learnt through inter-relating ideas and reading widely |

Achieving Approach

| Achievement motivation | Motivation is to obtain highest possible grades |
| Achievement strategy | Strategy is to achieve high marks by being a 'model' student, e.g., being punctual, doing extra readings, etc. or whatever else that is needed |

The Cross-Cultural Perspective

Psychologists are now well aware of the central role of learning in the socialization process and in the development of human behaviour:

> "The moment a child enters the world, he or she begins the task of learning the requirements of a particular family, cultural group and society." (Cushner, 1990; p.100).

"We are what we are because of culturally based learning" (Segall, Dasen, Berry and Poortinga, 1990).

However, until recently theories of learning have been unsuitable for understanding such learning. Both the behaviourist and cognitive (IP) theorists of the 1960s sought universal laws of learning which they "construed as something much more 'basic' than the 'trivial' particulars of how people actually make sense of the world around them." (Saljo, 1991; p.179).

Fortunately, as explained earlier in this chapter, the SAL perspective is one which wishes to take the context of learning seriously. Although developed to account for how students learn in Western cultures, the general approach may be suitable for studying learning from a cross-cultural viewpoint. However, psychologists from Third World countries have questioned the appropriateness of Western theories, constructs, and measuring instruments for non-Western cultures (Enriquez, 1982; Sinha, 1993).

Many of the early cross-cultural studies could certainly be criticized as being little more than the administration of a Western developed psychological test to non-Western subjects (after translation if necessary). The tests were then scored and the results statistically compared with Western norms and a 'conclusion' drawn about the relative level of whatever construct was being measured in each culture. Cross-cultural methodologists have consistently pointed out the pitfalls of such an approach to research. It assumed what Hui and Triandis (1985) refer to as 'scalar equivalence', i.e. that the construct of interest, is measured on the same metric scale in the different cultures. Such a level of equivalence is very difficult to justify, involving firstly the demonstration of conceptual, construct operational, and item equivalence. However, for many research purposes all that needs to be done is to demonstrate that our instruments measure equivalent concepts and that the relationships between variables are comparable. If it can be shown that a Western measure of learning processes, such as the LPQ, is embedded in the same network of constructs in different cultures, then we can be fairly confident that our constructs are conceptually and operationally equivalent in these cultures and are, therefore, in a much stronger position to claim scalar equivalence (Hui and Triandis, 1985). This involves testing the equivalence of both the internal structure of the constructs, perhaps through internal factor analysis, and of the relationships between the constructs and other variables. In the terminology of the well-known Campbell and Fiske (1959) treatise on construct validity, this involves testing both within- and between-construct portions of the nomological network. Validation in this sense not only supports the cross-cultural validity of the LPQ but also of the model of learning on which it is based (see Table 1.1).

Cross-cultural Validity of SAL Constructs and Measuring Instruments

Questionnaires such as the LPQ, SPQ, and ASI have now been completed by both school and university students from a wide range of cultural, socioeconomic, and religious backgrounds from a similarly wide geographical range, and the results are generally supportive of the cross-cultural reliability and validity of the instruments and their underlying model. The results are summarized below (the sources of the studies referred to are presented in Note 1).

Internal consistency reliability. Reliability is a necessary but not a sufficient condition for test validity. Table 1.2 summarizes the internal consistency reliability coefficients alpha for Biggs' SPQ and LPQ scales for university and Form 4 secondary school students from a number of countries in the Asia-Pacific region. In Australia, Nepal, and the Philippines, the original English language items were administered but in the other countries translations were made into the most appropriate language (Hong Kong students were given both the English and Chinese items; see Biggs, 1992b). From Table 1.2 it is clear that the SPQ may not be suitable for the Nepalese students, probably because of their inadequate English language competence (even though English is the language of instruction there). However, the qualitative analysis of Watkins and Regmi (1992; 1995) suggests that Nepalese students may have a different learning concept to that of students in Western cultures (see below). For all students, other than the Australian university sample, the two surface scales have rather low reliability, but the other scales seem quite acceptable for research purposes. Biggs (1993), in acknowledging the lack of unidimensionality of the surface scales, argues that this is due to a surface approach being adopted for two different reasons: fear of failure or the desire to obtain credentials. Similar generally adequate reliability estimates have been found for the LPQ with Nigerian and Lithuanian school students, for the SPQ with Nigerian university students, and the ASI with Filipino secondary school students (short version of the ASI), Hong Kong, Nepalese, and South African (both black and white) students.

Factor analysis. Factor analyses of the LPQ, SPQ and ASI, both at scale or item level, and using both exploratory and confirmatory methods with students from a range of cultures, generally support two underlying factors: deep and surface (see Biggs, 1993; Wong, 1995). Typical findings based on two factor oblimin solutions of SPQ and LPQ scales are shown in Table 1.3 (as we do not expect factors to be independent, oblique rather than orthogonal factor analysis is appropriate).

Table 1.2
Internal consistency reliability coefficients alpha of Biggs' questionnaires for Form 4 secondary school (LPQ) and university (SPQ) students from Australia and different Asian countries

Country Subjects	Australia		Hong Kong		Brunei	Indonesia	Malaysia	Nepal	Philippines
	1367 Sch.	823 Univ.	1331 Sch.	2338 Univ.	524 Univ.	90 Univ.	301 Sch.	342 Univ.	Univ.
Questionnaire Scales									
Surface motivation	.46	.61	.51	.53	.58	.37	.56	.40	.51
Surface strategy	.51	.66	.35	.65	.48	.30	.44	.25	.51
Deep motivation	.56	.65	.56	.60	.58	.67	.55	.44	.57
Deep strategy	.67	.75	.67	.75	.73	.70	.68	.47	.60
Achieving motivation	.68	.72	.65	.74	.64	.68	.69	.48	.57
Achieving strategy	.67	.77	.73	.69	.76	.74	.65	.56	.57

Table 1.3
Factor loadings from two factor oblique solutions of responses to LPQ and SPQ by country

| | LPQ | | | | | | | | SPQ | | | | | |
| | Australia | | Hong Kong | | Nepal | | Nigeria | | Brunei | | Indonesia | | Nigeria | |
	F I	F II	F I	F II	F I	F II	F I	F II	F I	F II	F I	F II	F I	F II
Surface motivation	.24	.35	-.07	.86	.04	.38	.01	.67	-.08	.71	.02	.69	-.10.	.78
Surface strategy	-.12	.82	-.07	.66	-.07	.64	.03	.67	.08	.67	-.08	.59	.22	.47
Deep motivation	.80	-.14	.79	-.13	.57	.08	.44	.20	.67	-.06	.67	.16	.51	.21
Deep strategy	.73	-.02	.83	-.02	.63	-.14	.69	.04	.85	-.07	.88	-.21	.91	-.14
Achieving motivation	.65	.00	.28	.58	.61	.07	.59	.17	.41	.23	.43	.50	.31	.44
Achieving strategy	.57	.15	.53	.17	.65	-.03	.91	-.24	.79	.02	.70	.01	.66	.09

Factors I and II in each country with the SPQ or LPQ clearly represent deep and surface level approaches to learning, respectively. The median cross-cultural coefficients of congruence (Wrigley and Neuhaus, 1955) were 0.92 and 0.85 for Factors I and II of the LPQ and 0.98 and 0.92 for Factors I and II of the SPQ. This indicates a high level of similarity between the factor loadings provided by subjects of these countries. However, the Achievement Motivation scale varies from country to country in terms of whether it loads principally on Factors I or II. As explained earlier (P.7), students with high achievement motivation tend to adopt whatever approach they feel will maximize their chances of academic success. So the differences in factor solutions evident in Table 1.3 suggest the Australian, Nepalese, and Nigerian school students and the Brunei university students believed that academic success comes through a combination of deep and achieving strategies. However, the Hong Kong school and Indonesian and Nigerian university students believed that success in their academic contexts requires principally a surface-level approach to learning.

Correlations with academic grades. It is predictable that students who adopt deep and achieving approaches to learning would be more successful academically than those who adopt a surface approach. Table 1.4 summarizes correlations between approach to learning and academic achievement in 16 studies with which the writer or his associates have been involved.

Over these 16 studies, with a total of 9,841 students from both school and university sectors from five different countries, and using a range of learning questionnaires, the trends of the correlations were in the expected direction. The mean correlations obtained from these studies were -0.11, 0.20, and 0.19 with the surface, deep, and achieving approach, respectively. That the mean correlation was somewhat less with the surface approach is not surprising, given the lower reliability of these scales (see Table 1.2). The means are pulled down by the two Nepalese studies which also tend to have the lowest-scale reliabilities. It should be noted that failure to find the predicted correlations with academic achievement may be a reflection that deeper approaches to learning are not always rewarded by academic grades (see Chapter 9). Indeed, research has found somewhat higher correlations between indicators of quality of learning outcomes and approaches to learning (see Chapter 9). However, as the review of academic correlates by Fraser, Walberg, Welch, and Hattie (1987) makes clear, correlations of the order of 0.20, while only explaining 4% of the variance of academic achievement, are not that common and well worth pursuing.

Table 1.4

Summary of research reporting correlations between learning approach and academic achievement

Country	Subjects	Questionnaires[*]	Correlations with grades		
			Surface Approach	Deep Approach	Achieving Approach
(1) Australia	181 university students	ASI	-.25*	.21*	--
(2) Australia	292 university students	ASI	-.28*	.23*	--
(3) Australia[b]	1,352 secondary school students	LPQ	-.13*	.18*	.22*
(4) Australia[b]	1,274 secondary school students	HIS	.14*	.23*	.25*
(5) Australia	249 university students	LPQ	-.25*	.24*	.18*
(6) Australia	249 university students	ILP	-.19*	.31*	.35*
(7) Hong Kong	3,770 secondary school students	LPQ	-.09*	.11*	.16*
(8) Hong Kong	127 secondary school students	LPQ	-.12	.13	.25*
(9) Hong Kong	314 secondary school students	LPQ	-.10	.14	.06
(10) Nepal	342 university students	SPQ	-.10*	.06	.06
(11) Nepal	509 secondary school students	LPQ	-.14*	.09	.09
(12) Nepal	202 secondary school students	HIS	-.11	.21*	.29*
(13) Nigeria	265 secondary school students	LPQ	.01	.20*	.28*
(14) Philippines	147 secondary school students	LPQ	-.14	.29*	.27*
(15) Philippines	445 secondary school students	ASI(S)	-.14*	.28*	.13*
(16) Philippines	123 university students	ILP	.16	.30*	.10
Overall mean correlations	9,841 students		-.11*	.20*	.19*

* Indicates correlation is significantly different from zero at .05 level of significance

[*] ASI = Approaches to Studying Inventory   SPQ = Study Process Questionnaire
   LPQ = Learning Process Questionnaire   ASI(S) = ASI (Short version)
   HIS = How I Study Questionnaire   ILP = Inventory of Learning Processes
   See source article for references to these questionnaires

[b] Indicates that the correlations were based on subject self-estimates of their school grades rather than actual academic performance

Correlates with self-esteem and internal locus of control. It was hypothesized that for students to want to adopt a deep-level approach to learning requires confidence in their own academic ability, and a belief that they should not rely too much on the teacher but accept responsibility for their own learning (see also Chapter 5, and Purdie and Hattie, 1995). Thus it was predicted that self-esteem and internal locus of control should be correlated with deeper and more achievement-oriented approaches to learning. Table 1.5 summarizes findings-relating approaches to learning, to self-esteem, and to locus of control from nine studies (involving 3,701 subjects from six different countries) and 17 studies (involving 10,543 subjects from eight different countries), respectively, with which either the writer or his associates have been involved.

The means of the nine correlations reported in Table 1.5 between self-esteem and approaches to learning are -0.03, 0.30, and 0.28 for surface, deep, and achieving approach, respectively. Thus there is quite a strong relationship as predicted, between self-esteem and both deep and achieving approaches.

The means of the correlations of the 17 studies reported in Table 1.5 between internal locus of control and the surface, deep, and achieving, approaches to learning are -0.22, 0.08, and 0.10, respectively. So, as predicted there is a trend for more superficial approaches to learning to be associated with an external locus of control.

Summary. The quantitative review of the studies the writer has been associated with reported in Tables 1.2 to 1.5 is generally supportive of the appropriateness of the LPQ and similar questionnaires in different cultures. While these studies cannot claim to be a representative sampling of relevant research, they do involve both school and university students from a wide range of countries and utilize a range of measuring instruments. The results do indicate that such questionnaires are moderately reliable and the underlying factors reflect surface and deep approaches to learning. Also, considering their limited reliability, these scales correlate with academic achievement, self-esteem, and locus of control in generally predictable ways. Thus the studies tend to support the within- and between-construct validities of questionnaires such as the LPQ for use in different cultures.

Table 1.5
Summary of research reporting correlations between approaches to learning and both self-esteem and internal locus of control

Country	Subjects	Questionnaires*	Correlations with approaches to learning		
			Surface Approach	Deep Approach	Achieving Approach
Self-esteem					
(1) Australia	1,274 secondary school students	HIS, HISM	.18	.33*	.34*
(2) Hong Kong	314 secondary school students	LPQ, SDQ	-.06	.24*	.16*
(3) Lithuania	222 secondary school students	LPQ, SDQ	-.12	.29*	.37*
(4) Malaysia	301 junior secondary students	LPQ, SDQ	-.03	.26*	.38*
(5) Nepal	302 university students	ASI, SRS	-.15*	.29*	--
(6) Nepal	398 secondary school students	HIS, HISM	.02	.54*	.30*
(7) Philippines	261 secondary school students	LPQ, FAS	-.11	.22*	.18*
(8) Philippines	445 secondary school students	ASI(S), FAS	-.12*	.12*	.16*
(9) Philippines	184 secondary school students	HIS, HISM	.16	.42*	.31*
Internal Locus of Control					
(10) Australia	1,353 junior secondary students	LPQ	-.18*	.12*	.17*
(11) Australia	979 senior secondary students	LPQ	-.22*	.13*	.22*
(12) Australia	744 university school students	ASI, IAR	-.21*	.11*	.23*
(13) Hong Kong	3770 secondary school students	LPQ	-.28*	.09*	.12*
(14) Hong Kong	244 secondary school students	LPQ	.06	.23*	.27*
(15) Hong Kong	314 secondary school students	LPQ	-.24*	.09	.08
(16) Indonesia	90 university students	SPQ, IAR	-.18	.16	.15

Table 1.5 (Cont.)

Country	Subjects	Questionnaires*	Correlations with approaches to learning		
			Surface Approach	Deep Approach	Achieving Approach
(17) Lithuania	222 secondary school students	LPQ	-.33*	-.22	-.15
(18) Malaysia	301 junior secondary students	LPQ	-.19*	.02	.17*
(19) Malaysia	301 senior secondary students	LPQ	-.49*	-.16	-.18
(20) Nepal	342 university students	SPQ, IAR	-.10*	.24*	.21*
(21) Nepal	509 secondary school students	LPQ	-.32*	.19*	.17*
(22) Nigeria	150 secondary school students	LPQ	-.29*	.02	.09
(23) Nigeria	195 secondary school students	LPQ	-.24*	-.14	-.16
(24) Nigeria	323 secondary school students	LPQ	-.32*	.11	.08
(25) Philippines	261 secondary school students	LPQ	-.07	.21*	.16*
(26) Philippines	445 secondary school students	ASI(S), IAR	-.08	.21*	.10
Overall Mean Correlations					
Self-esteem	3701 students		-.03	.30	.28
Internal locus of control	10,543 students		-.22	.08	.10

* Indicates correlation is significantly different from zero at .01 level of significance

* ASI   = Approaches to Studying Inventory   SDQ = Self-Description Questionnaire
ASI(S) = ASI (Short version)   LPQ = Learning Process Questionnaire
HIS   = How I Study Questionnaire   SRS = Self-Rating Scale
HISM   = How I See Myself Questionnaires   FAS = Filipino Academic Self Scale
IAR   = Intellectual and Academic Responsibility Scale
See source article for references to these questionnaires

Culture and gender differences. As argued earlier (p.9), the support for cross-cultural construct validity reported above is a necessary but not sufficient condition to justify the assumption of scalar equivalence required when comparing scale means across cultures. A major problem with cross-cultural comparisons at the mean level is the relatively unexplored area of cross-cultural differences in response sets (see, for example, Hui and Triandis, 1989; Watkins and Cheung, 1995). People from different cultures may tend to respond in different but consistent ways to questionnaire and rating scale response formats independently of the nature of the items. So we will proceed cautiously to report an analysis of culture and gender differences in responses to the LPQ by 14-16-year-old school children from six rather different countries (see Table 1.6).

Two-way (Country x Gender) Analysis of Variance (ANOVA) found significant ($p<0.01$) differences in the means of all six LPQ scales for Country and Country x Gender with effect sizes ranging from 0.32 to 0.57. However, only one relatively minor (effect size = 0.12) gender main effect was found to be significant at the 0.01 level. This was for Surface Strategy, with the males more frequently reporting utilizing superficial learning strategies. This trend was strongest with the Australian, Nepalese, and Filipino subjects. Examination of the LPQ scale means in Table 1.6 indicates that the Hong Kong and Malaysian students, relative to the Australians, were less likely to report surface level motivation and strategies but more likely to report trying to understand what they were learning. These trends were even more accentuated in the Nepalese sample, surprisingly given what is generally regarded as the low quality of education in that country (Watkins et al., 1991). The Filipino sample responded similarly to the Australians on the surface scales but tended to respond in a deeper, more achievement-oriented manner (the latter was another feature of the Nepalese data). That it was not just Asian learners who reported deeper level learning strategies than the Australians is shown by the Nigerian students who showed similar trends. That these findings are not due to an aberration of the particular sample or questionnaire is evident from similar findings with other Australian and Asian students at both school and university level using other learning questionnaires (Biggs, 1992b; Kember and Gow, 1990; Watkins et al., 1991). Data such as these are the basis of one component of the 'Paradox of the Chinese Learner' discussed in Chapter 3.

Table 1.6
Mean responses to Learning Process Questionnaire of 14-16-year-old secondary school students by country and gender

	Australia Male (n=653)	Female (n=713)	Hong Kong Male (n=701)	Female (n=792)	Malaysia Male (n=151)	Female (n=150)	Nepal Male (n=254)	Female (n=255)	Nigeria Male (n=113)	Female (n=119)	Philippines Male (n=147)	Female (n=126)	Overall Weighted Means Male (n=2,019)	Female (n=2,155)
Surface motivation	21.48	21.42	19.64	19.54	18.37	19.07	17.46	18.27	18.38	18.79	21.20	22.00	19.42	19.85
Surface strategy	18.29	17.08	15.73	15.29	15.92	15.57	15.30	13.89	18.12	17.86	19.10	17.90	17.08	16.27
Deep motivation	19.71	19.42	19.32	18.54	19.77	18.71	23.61	24.97	21.64	21.66	22.00	23.40	21.01	21.12
Deep strategy	17.21	16.73	18.46	17.49	19.56	18.03	23.40	24.42	22.32	21.79	21.40	21.30	20.39	19.96
Achieving motivation	20.82	19.66	20.16	19.15	20.52	20.07	24.12	26.23	21.64	22.45	21.30	20.00	21.43	21.26
Achieving strategy	17.31	18.02	17.64	17.60	19.30	19.35	25.19	25.87	24.42	24.72	21.10	20.80	20.83	21.06

Etic and Emic Approaches to Cross-Cultural Research

The data reported in the previous section is based on an 'etic' approach to research, where theory and measuring instruments developed to be meaningful for one culture are utilized to compare different cultures. Triandis (1972) warns about the dangers of 'pseudoetic' research, where concepts from one culture are imposed on another as if they are universal. That is why much of the focus of the previous section was on demonstrating construct validity of both the learning questionnaires and the underlying SAL theories for a range of students from different cultural, religious, socioeconomic, and philosophical backgrounds.

However, demonstration of a satisfactory degree of cross-cultural validity in this quantitative manner does not mean that culture-specific notions of concepts like 'learning' do not exist. Indeed, an appreciation of such culturally relevant concepts may greatly increase our understanding of learning within that culture. An alternative approach to cross-cultural research known as the 'emic' approach uses only concepts that emerge from within a particular culture and is associated with the traditions of anthropological research (see, Berry, 1989, for a fuller discussion of these issues). For example, qualitative methods have questioned whether Nepalese students hold a conception of 'learning as memorizing and reproducing' commonly found in Western students (Watkins and Regmi, 1992, 1995). This may help to explain the lower reliability and validity figures on Western questionnaires for Nepalese students reported earlier. In a related study, the quantitative, memorizing conception of learning and the conception of learning as understanding were identifiable in the responses of Nigerian secondary school children (Watkins and Akande, 1994).

The phenomenographic approach seems particularly suited to a rigorous investigation of emic conceptions of learning. The reader can judge the benefits of an emic research approach to help our understanding of the Chinese learner from a reading of Chapters 2, 5, 6, 9, and 10.

The ultimate test of the validity of any psychological theory is a demonstration that its implications work in the real world. Thus the ultimate test of the validity of the Western developed SAL approach is that it works in practice for Chinese learners in actual classrooms. The two 'intervention' chapters in this book address that issue.

NOTE

The source references for the data reported in Tables 1.2 to 1.6 are as follows:
Table 1.2 (Reliability): Australia (Biggs, 1987); Hong Kong (Biggs, 1992b); Brunei (Watkins and Murphy, 1994); Indonesia (Hotma Ria, 1993, personal

communication); Malaysia (Watkins and Ismail, 1994); Nepal and Philippines (Watkins, Regmi, and Astilla, 1991).

Table 1.3 (Factor Structure): LPQ: Australia (Biggs, 1987); Hong Kong (Biggs, 1992b); Nepal (Watkins et al., 1991); Nigeria (Watkins and Akande, 1994). SPQ: Brunei (Watkins and Murphy, op. cit.); Indonesia (Hotma Ria, op. cit.); Nigeria (Watkins and Akande, 1992).

Table 1.4 (Correlation with Grades): Data Set 1 (Watkins, 1982); Set 2 (Watkins, 1983); Sets 3 and 4 (Biggs, 1987); Sets 5 and 6 (Watkins and Hattie, 1981); Set 7 (Biggs, 1992b); Sets 8 and 9 (Wong, 1995); Set 10 (Watkins and Regmi, 1990); Sets 11, 12 and 14 (Watkins et al., 1991); Set 13 (Watkins and Akande, 1994); Set 15 (Watkins, Hattie, and Astilla, 1986); Set 16 (Watkins and Hattie, 1981).

Table 1.5 (Correlations with Self-Esteem and Locus of Control): Data Set 1 (Watkins and Hattie, 1990); Sets 2 and 15 (Wong, 1993, op. cit.); Sets 3 and 17 (Watkins and Juhasz, as yet unpublished research); Sets 4, 18 and 19 (Watkins and Ismail, op. cit.); Set 5 (Watkins and Regmi, in press); Sets 6, 7, 9, 21, and 25 (Watkins et al., 1991); Sets 8 and 26 (Watkins, Hattie, and Astilla, 1986); Sets 10 and 11 (Biggs, 1987); Set 12 (Watkins, 1987); Set 13 (Biggs, 1992b); Set 14 (Chan, 1990); Set 16 (Hotma Ria, op. cit.); Set 20 (Watkins and Regmi, 1990); and Sets 22 to 24 (Watkins and Akande, 1994).

Table 1.6 (LPQ Means): Australia (Biggs, 1987); Hong Kong (Biggs, 1992b); Malaysia (Watkins and Ismail, op. cit.); Nepal and Philippines (Watkins et al., 1991); and Nigeria (Watkins and Akande, 1994).

REFERENCES

Biggs, J.B. (1987). *Student approaches to learning and studying*. Hawthorn, Vic.: Australian Council for Educational Research.

Biggs, J.B. (1992a). From theory to practice: a cognitive systems approach. Keynote paper, Annual Conference, Higher Education Research and Development Society of Australasia, Gippsland.

Biggs, J.B. (1992b). *Why and how do Hong Kong students learn? Using the learning and study process questionnaires*. Hong Kong: Faculty of Education, The University of Hong Kong.

Biggs, J.B. (1993). What do inventories of students' learning processes really measure? A theoretical review and clarification. *British Journal of Educational Psychology, 63*, 3-19.

Blumenfeld, P.C. (1992). Classroom learning and motivation: clarifying and expanding goal theory. *Journal of Educational Psychology, 84*, 272-281.

Bowden, J. (1988). Achieving changes in teaching practice. In Ramsden, P. (ed.), *Improving learning: new perspectives*. London: Kogan Page.

Brown, J.S., Collins, A. & Duguid, P. (1989). Situated cognition and the culture of learning. *Educational Research, 18*, 32-42.

Campbell, D.T. & Fiske, D.W. (1959). Convergent and discriminant analysis by the multitrait-multimethod matrix. *Psychological Bulletin, 56*, 81-105.

Chan, I. (1990). The relationship between motives, learning strategies, attributions for success and failure and level of achievement among secondary school students in Hong Kong. Unpublished M.Soc.Sci. Dissertation, The University of Hong Kong.

Cushner, K. (1990). Cross-cultural psychology and the formal classroom. In Brislin, R.W. (ed.), *Applied cross-cultural psychology*. London: Sage.

Dunkin, M.J. & Biddle, B.J. (1974). *The study of teaching*. New York: Holt, Rinehart, & Winston.

Enriquez, V. (1982). *Decolonising the Filipino psyche.*. Quezon City: Philippine Psychology Research House.

Entwistle, N. & Ramsden, P. (1983). *Understanding student learning*. London: Croom Helm.

Entwistle, N. & Waterston, S. (1988). Approaches to studying and levels of processing in university students. *British Journal of Educational Psychology, 58*, 258-265.

Floden, R.E. (1981). The logic of information-processing psychology in education. *Review of Research in Education, 9*, 75-110.

Fraser, B.J., Walberg, H.J., Welch, W.W. & Hattie, J.A. (1987). Synthesis of educational productivity research. *International Journal of Educational Research, 11*, 145-252.

Hui, C.H. & Triandis, H.C. (1985). Measurement in cross-cultural psychology: a review and comparison of strategies. *Journal of Cross-Cultural Psychology, 16*, 131-152.

Hui, C.H. & Triandis, H.C. (1989). Effects of culture and response format on extreme response style. *Journal of Cross-Cultural Psychology, 20*, 296-309.

Kember, D. & Gow, L. (1990). Cultural specifity of approaches to study. *British Journal of Educational Psychology, 60*, 356-363.

Marton, F. (1981). Phenomenography - describing conceptions of the world around us. *Instructional Science, 10*, 177-200.

Marton, F., Dall'Alba, G. & Beaty, E. (1993). Conceptions of learning. *International Journal of Educational Research, 19*, 277-300.

Marton, F. & Ramsden, P. (1988). What does it take to improve learning? In Ramsden, P. (ed.), *Improving learning: new perspectives*. London: Kogan Page.

Marton, F. & Saljo, R. (1976). On qualitative differences in learning - 1: Outcome and process. *British Journal of Educational Psychology, 46*, 4-11.

Miller, G.A., Galanter, E. & Pribram, K.H. (1960). *Plans and the structure of behavior*. New York: Holt, Rinehart, & Winston.

Moreno, V. & DiVesta, F.J. (1991). Cross-cultural comparisons of study habits. *Journal of Educational Psychology, 83*, 231-239.

Purdie, N.M. & Hattie, J.A. (1995). The effect of motivation training on approaches to learning and self-concept. *British Journal of Education of Psychology, 65*, 227-235.

Ramsden, P. (1992). *Learning to teach in higher education*. London: Routledge.

Ramsden, P., Beswick, D. & Bowden, J. (1986). Effects of learning skills intervention on first year university students' learning. *Human Learning, 5*, 151-164.

Saljo, R. (1988). Learning in educational settings: methods of inquiry. In Ramsden, P. (ed.), *Improving learning: new perspectives*. London: Kogan Page.

Saljo, R. (1991). Introduction: culture and learning. *Learning and Instruction, 1*, 179-185.

Salomon, G. (1991). Transcending the qualitative-quantitative debate: the analytic and systemic approaches to educational research. *Educational Researcher, 20*, 10-18.

Schmeck, R.R. ed. (1988). *Learning strategies and learning styles*. New York: Plenum.

Schon, D.A. (1987). *Educating the reflective practioner*. San Francisco: Jossey-Bass.

Segall, M.H., Dasen, P.R., Berry, J.W. & Poortinga, Y.H. (1990). *Human behavior in global perspective*. New York: Pergamon.

Sinha, D. (1993). Indigenization of psychology in India and its relevance. In Kim, U. & Berry, J.W. (Eds.), *Indigenous psychologies: research and experience in cultural context*. London: Sage.

Skinner, B.F. (1958). Teaching machines. *Science, 128*, 969-977.

Thorndike, E.L. (1921). *Educational psychology*. New York: Columbia University Teachers College Press.

Triandis, H.C. (1972). *The analysis of subjective culture*. New York: John Wiley.

Walberg, H.J. & Haertel, G.D. (1992). Educational psychology's first century. *Journal of Educational Psychology, 84*, 6-19.

Watkins, D. (1982). Identifying the study process dimensions of Australian university students. *Australian Journal of Education, 26*, 76-85.

Watkins, D. (1983). Assessing tertiary study processes. *Human Learning, 2*, 29-37.

Watkins, D. & Akande, A. (1992). Assessing the approaches to learning of Nigerian students. *Assessment and Evaluation in Higher Education, 17*, 11-20.

Watkins, D. & Akande, A. (1994). Approaches to learning of Nigerian secondary school children: emic and etic perspectives. *International*

Journal of Psychology, 29, 165-182.

Watkins, D. & Cheung, S. (1995). Culture, gender, and response bias. *Journal of Cross-Cultural Psychology, 26*, 490-504.

Watkins, D. & Hattie, J. (1981). The learning processes of Australian university students: investigations of contextual and personological factors. *British Journal of Educational Psychology, 51*, 384-393.

Watkins, D. & Hattie, J. (1990). Individual and contextual differences in the approaches to learning of Australian secondary school students. *Educational Psychology, 10*, 333-342.

Watkins, D., Hattie, J. & Astilla, E. (1986). Approaches to studying by Filipino students: a longitudinal investigation. *British Journal of Educational Psychology, 56*, 357-362.

Watkins, D. & Ismail, M. (1994). Is the Asian learner a rote learner? A Malaysian perspective. *Contemporary Educational Psychology, 19*, 483-488.

Watkins, D. & Murphy, J. (1994). Modifying the Study Process Questionnaire for ESL students. *Psychological Reports, 74*, 1023-1026.

Watkins, D. & Regmi, M. (1990). An investigation of the approach to learning of Nepalese tertiary students. *Higher Education, 29*, 459-469.

Watkins, D. & Regmi, M. (1992). How universal are student conceptions of learning? A Nepalese investigation? *Psychologia, 35*, 101-110.

Watkins, D. & Regmi, M. (1995). Assessing approaches to learning in non-Western cultures: a Nepalese conceptual validity study. *Assessment and Evaluation in Higher Education, 20*, 203-212.

Watkins, D. & Regmi, M. In press. Towards the cross-cultural validation of a Western model of student approaches to learning. *Journal of Cross-Cultural Psychology*.

Watkins, D., Regmi, M. & Astilla, E. (1991). The Asian-learner-as-a-rote-learner stereotype: myth or reality? *Educational Psychology 11*: 21-34.

Watson, J.B. (1914). *Behavior: an introduction to comparative psychology.* New York: Holt.

Weinstein, C., Schulte, A. & Palmer, D. (1987). *Learning and study strategies inventory (LASSI).* Clearwater, Florida: H & H Publications.

Wittrock, M.C., ed. (1977). *The human brain.* Englewood Cliffs, NJ: Prentice-Hall.

Wong, N-Y. (1995). The relationship between Hong Kong students' perceptions of their mathematics classroom environment and their approaches to learning: a longitudinal study. Unpublished Ph.D. thesis, The University of Hong Kong.

Wrigley, C. & Neuhaus, J. (1955). The matching of two sets of factors. *American Psychologist, 10*, 418-419.

2

The Cultural Context for Chinese Learners: Conceptions of Learning in the Confucian Tradition

Lee Wing On

Introduction

The success of East Asian countries has attracted worldwide attention not only for their development strategies, but also on the ethos and cultural traits that could support their development. Recently, there has been a considerable focus on studying the Confucian ethic, in the hope of finding cultural keys to success in East Asian countries, vis-à-vis the Protestant ethic, which was believed to have supported development in Western capitalist countries. In the context of education, the fact that Asian learners have achieved high scores in international studies, and that students of Asian origin have been able to excel in Western countries has also attracted much attention (see Chapter 3). Many studies discovered that these Asian students are not only diligent, but they also have high achievement motivation. Invariably they have a high regard for education (Ho, 1986; Yang, 1986). Against this background, this chapter aims to uncover what underlies Asian people's positive attitude towards education, their achievement motivations, and their willingness to spend most of their free time in the pursuit of study. This chapter studies conceptions of learning in the Confucian tradition in order to provide a specific focal point for analyzing the Confucian ethic. It discusses the Confucian conceptions of learning in relation to such beliefs as human perfectibility and educability, and the emphasis on effort and will power, in the hope of demonstrating their learning motivations and achievement motivations.[1]

The Significance of Education

> Men, one and all, in infancy are virtuous at heart.
> Their natures are much the same, the practice wide apart.
> Without Instruction's aid, our instinct grew less pure.
> By aiming at thoroughness only can teaching ensure.
> ...
> To feed the body, not the mind - fathers, on you the blame!
> Instruction without severity, the idle teacher's shame.
> If a child does not learn, this is not as it should be.
> How, with a youth of idleness, can age escape the blight?
> ...
> Diligence has its reward; play has no gain.
> Be on your guard, and put forth your strength.

The above poem is part of the *Three Character Classic*, arranged in 356 alternately rhyming lines of three characters to each, and containing about 500 different characters in all. It prevailed in China over the last 600 years, being adopted as a major elementary guide to knowledge for school beginners. It begins with the significance of education, and ends with an exhortation on the significance of diligence (Giles, 1972; Wu, 1989).

Indeed, the significance of education stands out in the Confucian tradition. Education is perceived as important not only for personal improvement but also for societal development. *The Great Learning* constitutes one of the *Four*

---

1.   While elaborating the Confucian conceptions of learning as a cultural background for understanding the learning attitudes of Asian students, the author is aware of the complexities involved, such as the danger of overgeneralizing Asian learners under the Confucian aegis, and arguments concerning how far the Confucian ethics can serve as a deterministic explanation for the modern East Asian phenomenon. However, the present scope and focus of this paper does not allow for engaging in this kind of discussion. Moreover, given that most of the East Asian societies such as those of China, Taiwan, Hong Kong, Singapore, Korea and Japan share an obvious Confucian tradition, and that there has been a minimal attempt to explore the Confucian ethics from educational perspectives, the author believes that this study can provide a cultural background for understanding the Asian attitudes towards education and learning.

Books[2], and the opening sentence of Confucius's *Analects* (I.1) refers to the significance and joy of learning: "Is it not pleasant to learn with a constant perseverance and application?" In fact, close scrutiny of the *Analects* reveals that the term 'learning' pervades the whole literature, thus qualifying it to be called a book of learning. The way Confucius depicts his life-span development is characterized as a learning process: he began to set his mind on learning at the age of 15; began to take a stand at 30, became free from doubts at 40; was able to understand the principles of life and fate at 50; was attuned to the reception of truth at 60; and was free to follow his heart's desire without worrying about being wrong at 70 (*Analects,* II.4). Education is not only important for personal development, according to Confucius, society requires learned people to be officials: "The officer, having discharged all his duties, should devote his leisure to learning. The student, having completed his learning, should apply himself to be officer" (*Analects,* XIX.13) - a similar notion to Plato's philosopher king, who asserts that the country should be ruled by wise and learned people. As will be discussed below, the Confucian tradition is characterized by discourse and debate on learning - why learning is significant, and how it is to be carried out.

As recently as the late Qing dynasty when China was faced with crises, challenges and invasions, discussions on reform or revolution seldom excluded education. Zhang Zhidong's *Learn* was a seminal work on the notion of education for saving the nation. Invariably, such thinkers as Liang Shuming, Hu Shi, Chen Duxiu, and Cai Yuanpei pointed to the significance of education for saving the country, although the contents and contexts of education they referred to were quite different. Present day China is experiencing heated economic growth, and associated with it is the emergence of the concept 'education is useless', as educational qualifications are not positively correlated with income levels. Even so, higher institutes still report keen competition in entrance examinations, and there is no lack of parents expecting or pushing their children to pursue higher studies. As Cleverley (1991, p. *xii*) comments:-

"Traditionally the Chinese have placed a high valuation on education.... While modern schooling has been accompanied by far reaching attitudinal change, the Chinese people have not lightly discarded the patterns of thinking and action from their rich historical past whose values have permeated the new Marxist precepts."

Similar remarks about East Asian countries with a Confucian tradition are

2. When quoting the *Four Books*, the author freely adapts the translated versions of James Legge, D.C. Lau, Chai Chu, and Tu Wei-ming, plus his own interpretation.

numerous. For example, referring to Japan, Leestma and his associates (1987, p. 3) say:-

"Japanese society is education-minded to an extraordinary degree: success in formal education is considered largely synonymous with success in life.... The origins of the Japanese commitment to education lie in the Confucian and Buddhist heritage in which great respect is accorded to learning and educational endeavour as means to personal and societal improvement. Today, there is a clear consensus that education is essential for both individual and social development that it requires active, sustained commitment of energy and resources of all levels of society."

Referring to Korea, Bae (1991, pp. 56-7) says:-

"A great majority of Koreans are marked by an outstanding enthusiasm for education.... Koreans have traditionally regarded education as 'the most reliable property' ... although it must also be noted here that the long tradition of Confucian teaching firmly implanted in their minds the belief that education is of paramount importance in a man's life."

Educability for All and Perfectibility for All

That education enjoys special significance in the Confucian tradition rests upon the Confucian presumption that everyone is educable. Confucius himself set an example by never refusing to teach whosoever came with a nominal ceremonial tutorial fee (*Analects*, VII.7). Indeed, one of his most famous sayings refers to education without class distinction. This is exemplified by the mixed backgrounds of his students, varying from children of noble families and rich families to those of obscure origins (Zhu, 1992).

By saying that all are educable, it does not mean that Confucius ignored differences in intelligence and/or individual differences. He acknowledged the existence of the wisest and dullest people (*Analects*, XVII.3), and that there are four categories of people in the context of learning: those who are born with knowledge; those who attain knowledge through study; those who turn to study after having been vexed by difficulties; and those who make no effort to study after having been vexed by difficulties (*Analects*, XVI.9). In practice, very few (or even none) belong to the wisest group; Confucius himself explicitly disclaimed membership of the wisest group, and identified with the group(s) that liked studying (*Analects*, VII.19). Rather, he stressed that it does not matter whether you are born with knowledge, or you attain knowledge by learning, or you attain knowledge by taking pain to learn, once you attain knowledge, it is all the same (*The Mean*, XX.10). All this suggests that differences in intelligence, according to Confucius, do not inhibit one's educability, but the incentive and attitude to learn does. Therefore, although Confucius did not refuse to teach anybody who wanted to learn, he would have refused to teach a person who was not eager to learn (*Analects*, VII.8).

Confucius's view on human nature was most inclined towards the educability of human beings: "By nature men are nearly alike, but through experience they grow wide apart" (*Analects*, XVII.2). This statement implies the significance of environment, henceforth education, in personal development, and pushed Confucius to take the nurture side in the nature-nurture debate. While Confucius did not specify what human nature is precisely, his disciples have extremely diverse views. For example, Mencius claims that human nature is good, whereas Xunzi asserted that human nature is evil. But interestingly, both believed in the significance of the environment and education in the process of personal development.

Mencius argued that human nature is good, as everyone is born with a sense of compassion as the source of humanity (or benevolence), a sense of shame as the source of righteousness, a sense of respect as the source of propriety, and a sense of right and wrong as the source of wisdom (*Mencius*, VIA.6). This makes all human beings potentially educable, and based on this premise the notion that "everyone can become a sage" emerges. The impact of environment was put more strongly by Mencius than Confucius. For example, he referred to the difficulty of learning a language in an unfavourable linguistic environment (*Mencius*, IIIB.6), and the possibility of environmental 'pollution' to one's good nature. The parable of the Bull Mountain is most illustrative of the latter: "no matter how bountiful of trees the mountain is, if trees are hewn down day and night, it will turn out to be a barren rock" (*Mencius*, VIA.8). The reinstatement of the mountain's original beauty requires much nourishment. Likewise, the reinstatement of a person's good nature requires education (*Mencius*, VIA.11).

Although Xunzi, a critic of Mencius, held an opposing view on human nature, he shared the idea of human educability:-

"Mencius said: 'The reason why man is educable is that his nature is good.' I reply: 'It is not so. Mencius failed to understand human nature, failed to distinguish between what is congenital and what is acquired. Man's nature as conferred by Heaven cannot be learned and cannot be worked for; whereas the rule of rites and righteousness, as formulated by sage-kings, can be attained by learning and accompanied by work.'"

"... Sagehood is a state that any man can achieve by cumulative effort [of learning]. One may ask, 'Why is it possible for the sage and not possible for the mass of people to make accumulations.' My answer is that it is possible for anyone, but the mass does not use it (Collected in Chai, 1965, pp. 235-236)."

The idea that everyone can become a sage reflects a belief in human perfectibility (Tu, 1979), and this belief remains a characteristic of the Confucian tradition. For example, a clear statement is made by the Neo-Confucianist Wang Yangming: "The Teacher said, 'There is the sage in everyone'. Only because one falls short of self-confidence the sage is being buried (Cited by Tu, 1979, p. 141)." Inherent in the structure of the human, according to the Confucian tradition, is an infinite potential for growth and an inexhaustible supply of resources for development (Tu, 1979).

The concept that everyone is educable, everyone can become a sage, and everyone is perfectible forms the basic optimism and dynamism towards education in the Confucian tradition. And this explains why education is viewed to be wholly significant in such a tradition.

Learning, Effort, Will Power, and Human Perfectibility

The concept of the attainability of human perfectibility is expressed in terms of sagehood in the Confucian tradition, and is closely related to education. For Xunzi, sagehood can be attained through learning and effort:-

> "Now suppose a man in the street pursues knowledge and devotes himself to learning, by concentration of mind and singleness of purpose, thinking, studying and investigating, day in and day out, with persistence and patience. He accumulates goodness without ceasing, and then may be counted among the divinities, to form a triad with heaven and earth. Sagehood is a state that any man can achieve by cumulative effort..." (Collected in Chai, 1965).

Xunzi placed strong emphasis on the significance of effort in the process of learning. For Xunzi, the possibility of rectifying the evil of human nature came from deliberate effort and learning in human development. In contrast to Xunzi, the Mencian school believes that sagehood is inherent in the human. However, this does not preclude the necessity to employ self-effort in the pursuit of sagehood. As from the parable of the Bull Mountain, despite one's intrinsic sagehood, one must unceasingly learn how to become a sage in one's daily existence (Tu, 1979). The Neo-Confucianists emphasize the importance and indispensability of learning in the process of attaining sagehood. Concerning this, they argue that Confucius and Mencius were not born sages, they acquired sagacity by devotion to study. Sagehood has nothing to do with esoteric knowledge, it is attainable by reading and reflection (Chang, 1957). As Cheng Yi says, "When one begins to study and learns how to think, one will be on the road to sagehood." Cheng also says, "Subsequent generations ... thought that sagehood was not attainable by learning. Thus the way to sagehood was lost (Cited by Chang, 1957, p. 227)." Wang Yangming (1916, p. 111) went on to state that it is the function of education that leads one to the stage of rationality, which is a component of sagehood:-

"The function of education is to get from the individual the fullest extent what one's natural endowment can give. To quote: people become sages when they reach the stage of being purely rational. Gold becomes pure when the ingredients have been thoroughly taken out. The natural ability of the sages is different, as some have greater ability than the others. This may be likened to a quantity of gold which is different in different ores, some containing more gold than the others.... The natural ability of the sages is different. But they are the same as far as their rationality is concerned. When people are rational, they are all sages, irrespective of their ability. When gold is pure, it is pure irrespective of its quantity.... Gold is called pure gold because of its purity, rather than its quantity. People are called sages because of their rationality, not their natural ability."

As indicated in the above discussion, reaching the stage of sagehood refers to developing one's potentiality to the fullest extent, which is manifested in one's rationality, and is to be achieved through education. The fact that there are differences in ability does not matter, what is significant is developing potentiality to the fullest extent, as when the gold is purified, it is purified despite the amount of gold in the ore. This echoes what Confucius said:-

"If another man succeeds by one effort, he will use a hundred efforts. If another man succeeds by ten efforts, he will use a thousand. Let a man proceed in this way, and, though dull, he will surely become intelligent; though weak, he will surely become strong (*The Mean*, XX.20-21)."

To the Confucianist, education and learning are always associated with effort. Elaborating the traditional emphasis on effort in the process of education, Lin (1938, pp. 243-5) says:-

"That is the meaning of the passage in the *Ancient Records*, which says, 'The ants are busy all the time' (*the importance of continuous study*).... This is the meaning of the passage in the *Advice of Fu Yueh*, which says, 'Respectfully keep at your studies constantly, and then you will have results.'"

Xunzi has a specific chapter entitled "An Encouragement to Study" in his collected works, in which the significance of effort in the process of learning is profoundly expressed:-

"Sincerely put forth your efforts, and finally you will progress. Study until death and do not stop before. For the art of study occupies the whole of life; to arrive at its purpose, you cannot stop for an instant. To do that is to be a man; to stop is to be a bird or a beast (Hsun Tse, 1928, p. 36)."

It is clear that, for Xunzi, effort constituted the art of study, and paying effort manifested the quality of the human.

Referring to attaining sagehood, Wang remarks that he himself has to suffer "a hundred deaths and a thousand hardships" before he is confident that he can approach sagehood (Tu, 1979). This actually echoes what Mencius said, when he suggested that experiencing hardship may be a blessing in disguise:-

"When Heaven is about to confer a great responsibility on a man, it will exercise his mind [determination] with suffering, subject his sinews and bones to hard work, expose his body to hunger, put him to poverty, place obstacles in the path of his deeds, so as to stimulate his mind, harden his nature, and improve wherever he is incompetent (*Mencius*, VIB.15)."

Self-determination or will power is the driving force of efforts. Will power is sometimes expressed as "steadfastness of purpose" in *Mencius*. Steadfastness of purpose is the direct and immediate result of a person's will power and is, therefore, available to all members of the human community without reference to any differentiating factors. A severely handicapped person may exert a great deal of effort to coordinate his/her physical movements, but his/her willpower is absolutely independent, autonomous, and self-sufficient (Tu, 1979). The only key is whether a person is determined to do so, as "seek and you will get it; let go and you will lose it" (*Mencius*, VIIA.3). Self-determination or will power is also sometimes expressed as *li zhi* (to establish the will). Etymologically, *zhi* refers to the faculty of knowing, and can be translated as will or mind, whereas *li* signifies ordering principle or guiding principle. *Li zhi* is therefore both emotive and rational. It signifies an emotive driving force of effort, but contains an element of rationality, referring to guiding principle, and the human faculty of knowing (Tu, 1979).

It is clear from the above discussion that human perfectibility, learning, rationality, effort, and will power are discussed in the Confucian tradition in close relations. They are so closely interrelated that they are sometimes inseparable. This discloses how Eastern learners view education, and explains why effort is seen to be so important in the process of human perfectibility.

Intrinsic Motivation of Learning: Learning for Self-realization

The notion of human perfectibility has significant implications for the orientation of education - education is meaningful only when it leads to perfection of the self. While much of the discussion on Eastern culture points to collectivism, there is a neglect of 'individualism' or individuality in the Eastern tradition. In fact, in the Chinese tradition, 'self' constitutes a significant reference point in a person's value system. Human relationships actually extend from the self, and are centred around the self (Fei, 1947). However, the self in the Chinese tradition is usually undermined, subject to 'the cult of restraint' within the family, using the term of Lifton (1967). Such a restraint notwithstanding, when a person is free from relational restraint, self will then be emancipated too. This explains why individualism can be quite distinctive among the Chinese who have left their relational circles, when migrating to cities (as a result of industrialization and urbanization) or overseas (Eberhard, 1971; King, 1992). Moreover, throughout Chinese history intellectuals have sought to express their personal autonomy in whatever ways they could, depending on the situation (although enjoying only situational autonomy).

De Bary (1983) argues that the Neo-Confucian tradition is rich in individualism. Analyzing the vocabulary of Neo-Confucian individualism, he points out that central to the meaning of liberalism (*zi you*) in Chinese is the self (*zi*). In classical Chinese usage, *zi* also has the connotation "from, in, or of itself", much like the English prefix 'auto'. This sense of self-originated or self-motivated gains emphasis when used in combination with *you*, which means 'from' or 'out of'. Thus *zi* readily forms compounds corresponding to the prefix 'self-'. For example, the term *zi ren*, meaning 'taking it upon oneself' or 'bearing the responsibility oneself', is in accord with voluntarism in the moral life and of action that is in keeping with 'learning for the sake of one's self'. Another example is *zi de,* literally meaning 'getting it by or for oneself'. This expression was used in two important senses. One, relatively low-key, is that of learning or experiencing some truth for oneself and deriving inner satisfaction therefrom; here *zi de* has the meaning of 'learning to one's satisfaction', 'self-contented', 'self-possessed'. The other sense of the term carries a deeper meaning: 'getting or finding the Way in oneself'.

Returning to education, the notion of 'learning for the sake of one's self' best signifies the individualistic orientation in education. According to this notion, learning is for the sake of the self, which is an end in itself rather than a means to an end (Tu, 1985). It originates from Confucius' dictum in the *Analects* (XIV.25), which was expanded to criticize the attitude of learning for the sake of pleasing others or showing off to others. This notion was seized upon by the Neo-Confucianists who attacked bureaucratic scholarship and the vogue of learning for sitting civil examinations in the Song dynasty (960 - 1279) in China and the Yi dynasty (1392 - 1910) in Korea. Zhu Xi's thought was particularly influenced by this notion, as he placed much emphasis on 'being true to oneself', 'rectifying the mind and making the will sincere', and 'taking self-cultivation as the starting point for reaching out to others' in his teaching, which is actually an elaboration of the meaning of 'learning for the sake of oneself' (de Bary, 1983, pp. 22-24). A major task of the Neo-Confucianists in the Song dynasty was to revitalize the significance of the intrinsic value of education. This was a prime motivation for them to establish *Shuyuan* (academies) in order to counter-balance the public schools which prepared students for extrinsic rewards - success in civil examinations. Su Shi, a literati in the Song dynasty, made a distinctive criticism of the examination-oriented learning in his time. For him, such learning was done at the expense of individuality and creativity. This type of learning, according to Su, should not be regarded as true learning, as true learning encourages relative judgement and creative response (Bol, 1989).

Tu (1985, pp. 55-57) further elaborates 'learning for the sake of the self' to mean self-cultivation. The purpose of learning is therefore to cultivate oneself as an intelligent, creative, independent, autonomous, and what is more, an authentic being, who is becoming more fully human in the process of learning. The process of learning is therefore an inner-directed process. An ideal of learning like this is similar to Maslow's (1968) concept of the peak experience of learning, ultimately oriented towards self-realization. Indeed, as Tu (1979, p. 144) remarks, self-cultivation remains the locus of Confucian learning, and the basic precepts of Wang Yangming's teaching are all centred around the issue of self-realization.

The Deep Approach to Learning: Promoting Reflection and Enquiry

Biggs' (1991, p. 30) observation of the Confucian tradition of learning and teaching is correct and acute:-

> "Confucius himself saw learning as deep: 'Seeing knowledge without thinking is labour lost; thinking without seeking knowledge is perilous' [*Analects* II.15]; his methods were individual and socratic, not expository; his aim was to shape social and familial values in order to conserve a particular political structure. These do not appear particularly conducive to surface learning. However, Confucius did inspire several themes and variations...."

As education in the Confucian tradition is considered important for its intrinsic value, it is by nature inclined towards the deep approach rather than the surface approach to learning. In fact, any attempt to reduce learning to a surface approach is subject to criticism.

There is no lack of stress on the significance of reflective thinking in the process of learning in the Confucian tradition. Apart from suggesting that seeking knowledge (learning) and thinking are two sides of the coin, Confucius's conception of learning was indeed a process of "studying extensively, enquiring carefully, pondering thoroughly, sifting clearly, and practising earnestly .... (*The Mean*, XX.19)." Confucius took this so seriously that he suggested one should not stop unless one has gone through each of these steps successfully:-

> "While there is anything he has not studied, or while in what he has studied there is anything he cannot understand, he will not intermit his labour. While there is anything he has not enquired about, or anything in what he has enquired about which he does not know, he will not intermit his labour. While there is anything which he has not reflected on, or anything in what he has reflected on which he does not apprehend, he will not intermit his labour. While there is anything which he has not discriminated, or his discrimination is not clear, he will not intermit his labour. If there be anything which he has not practised, or his practice fails in earnestness, he will not intermit his labour (*The Mean*, XX.20)."

This principle of learning is so important to Confucianists that Zhu Xi has included it in the "Articles of the White Deer Hollow Academy" as a guideline for study. In his *Reading Method*, Zhu further elaborated that the pursuit of learning is actually a graded sequence and gradual progress in study and intensive reading of text and commentary, to be accompanied by 'refined reflection', reading with an open mind and without reading one's own preconceptions into the text, taking what one reads to heart and making it part of one's own experience, and exerting an all-out effort in all these (Chu, 1990, pp. 46-48; de Bary, 1989). Cheng Yi also pointed out that thinking is essential in the pursuit of sagehood, as "thinking gives insight; insight leads to sagehood (cited by Chang, 1957, p. 226)."

The emphasis on reflective thinking in learning requires a spirit of enquiry and open-mindedness. This is particularly advocated by Zhu in his exhortation on learning: we should not take for granted that what one reads is correct. We should suspend our judgement for the time being, then read more in order to gain a new view. For Zhu, this was important because if we hold fast to one particular view, our mind will be coloured by that particular view (Chu, 1990; Chiang, 1924). In another context Zhu said:-

> "Generally speaking, in reading, we must first become intimately familiar with the text so that its words seem to come from our own mouths. We should then continue to reflect on it so that its ideas seem to come from our own minds. Only then can there be real understanding. Still, once our

intimate reading of it and careful reflection on it have led to a clear understanding of it, we must continue to question. Then there might be additional progress. If we cease questioning, in the end there'll be no additional progress (Chu, 1990, p. 135)."

As the quotation indicates, memorizing (becoming familiar with the text), understanding, reflecting and questioning are the basic components of learning. They are inter-related, integrated and should be repeated for further and deeper learning. It is worth mentioning here that memorization is seen as a significant part of learning in the Confucian tradition, but it should by no means be equated with rote learning. Memorization precedes understanding, and is for deeper understanding. It has never been regarded as an end in itself. As Wang Yangming said, "If you simply want to memorize, you will not be able understand; and if you simply want to understand, you will not be able to know the sources [of truth] in yourself (cited by Chiang, 1924, p. 87)." For Wang, there were three significant aspects of learning. The first is memory, the second is understanding what is in books, and the last is incorporating what one gets from books into one's own experience. To regard memory as an end itself is to be discouraged. To understand what is in books without reference to personal needs or experience is of secondary importance. The most important point is to digest thoroughly what one gets from books so that it becomes an integral part of one's own experience (ibid.). For Zhu, reciting, thinking and understanding actually reinforced one another in the process of learning:-

"Learning is reciting. If we recite it then think it over, think it over then recite it, naturally it'll become meaningful to us. If we recite it but don't think over, we still won't appreciate its meaning. If we think it over but don't recite it, even though we might understand it, our understanding will be precarious (Chu, 1990, p. 138)."

Likewise, when Su Shi was advocating his true learning, he criticized customary learning, i.e. rote learning, as it "debilitates a man's talents and blocks a man's eyes and ears". In contrast, true learning should be illuminating, and should be associated with thinking and comprehension (see Bol, 1989, p. 174).

With emphasis on reflective thinking and enquiry in the process of learning, an ideal teacher in this context should be the one who guides students but does not pull them along, urges students to go forward and does not suppress them, opens the way for students, but does not take them to the place. As Lin (1938, p. 247) said:-

"Guiding without pulling makes the process of learning gentle; urging without suppressing makes the process of learning easy; and opening the way without leading the students to the place makes them think for themselves. Now if the process of learning is made gentle and easy and the students are encouraged to think for themselves, we may call the man a good teacher."

Achievement Motivation in Learning

In the main, the above discussion points to the intrinsic significance of education in the Confucian tradition, where the fundamental value of education lies in ultimate human perfection. However, this is only one side of the coin. The other side places emphasis on the dimension of external manifestation and utility of education, as there is always a correlation between a person's internal establishment and external performance. It is said in *The Great Learning* that a person should "cultivate himself, then regulate the family, then govern the state, and finally lead the world into peace (*The Great Learning*, IV)." This can be interpreted in two ways: if a person wants to govern the state, he should first cultivate himself; on the other hand, if there is a person who has cultivated himself sufficiently well, he should seek to influence the outside world. Hence for Confucius, a scholar should ultimately seek the opportunity to obtain a government office, in order to extend his good influence. This is what is proposed by Mencius too:-

"When you obtain your desire for office, to practise your principles for the good of the people; and when that desire is disappointed, to practise your principles alone (*Mencius*, VIIA)."

The fact that a person should seek perfection (pursue sagehood) within and a government office without has thereby become an ideal type of the Confucian tradition, which is typified in the notion of "sage within and king without" (*neisheng waiwang*) (Chang, 1976, p. 293). The process of building sagehood within has much to do with education, as mentioned above. Likewise, to be able to obtain a government office (i.e. to become 'king' without) is also seen as the product of education. Education is in this sense seen as an important means of leading to a government office. Of course, a government office can also be an extrinsic reward associated with fame, wealth, a beautiful wife, and upward social mobility, which have nothing to do with internal sagehood. This is reflected in the following idioms: "Although studying anonymously for ten years, once you are successful, you will become well-known in the world" and "There are golden houses in books and there are beautiful girls in books." Paradoxically, the aspiration for extrinsic rewards coexists with the ideal of external manifestation of a person's internal establishment in the Confucian tradition. However, whether it is for extrinsic reward or external manifestation, they have provided for another form of achievement motivation for the Asian learners.

It is worth noting that obtaining a higher social status through education was not only a matter of perception but it was realizable in traditional China. For example, early in the Spring and Autumn (722 B.C.-464 B.C.) and Warring States (463 B.C.-221 B.C.) periods, opportunities for social mobility were quite distinctive, due to frequent social restructuring with a constant change of power, with the resulting need for selecting the most competent members for public service. In consequence, the number of persons who rose from obscurity greatly increased. According to Hsu's statistics, the percentage of persons of obscure origin being mentioned in historical records rose from 6% in 722-693 B.C. to 44% in 512-483 B.C. during the Spring and Autumn period, and from 57% in 463-434 B.C. to 74% in 283-254 B.C. during the Warring States period (Hsu, 1965). Concerning the possibility of social mobility in the later periods, according to Ho (1962), the Tang period (612 - 911AD) was an important transition during which the monopoly of political power by the early-medieval hereditary aristocracy was gradually broken under the impact of the competitive examination system. In the Song period, 46.1% of officials with biographical entries in the *History of the Song Dynasty* may be regarded as coming from humble backgrounds, whereas similar biographical entries in the two *Histories of the Tang Dynasty* constituted a mere 13.8% in the late Tang period (Lee, 1985). The trend of increasing mobility continued after the founding of the Ming dynasty (1368 - 1644), when the examination and academic degree system became more elaborate and the school system truly nationwide. One may argue the scope of mobility was so small that it was not at all significant to the general public. However, despite its scope, the belief in the possibility of upward social mobility through educational success was important, and became a significant driving force for many ordinary people to study hard for a better future.

The aspiration for upward social mobility through educational success seems to coexist with the ideal for intrinsic personal growth in the process of education, although they look contradictory to each other. They not only co-exist but can somehow be integrated, as expressed in Huang Jinxing's analysis of achievement motivation in the Confucian ethic:-

"The egalitarian concept of 'everyone can become Yao and Shun' has taught people not to be self-humiliated, but to strive hard for further advancement. The family ethics of 'developing your fame and glorifying your family' has created a strong motivation of pursuing excellence. Moreover, the civil examination system in traditional China is a practical manifestation of the Confucian ideal of selecting the most competent person for public service (Huang, 1987, cited by Cheung, 1991, p. 65)."

Conclusion

The above analysis explains how education is conceived as important from both internal and external perspectives. Internally, education is important for personal development, and associated with it is the notion of human perfectibility, which is believed to be achievable by everyone. Externally, education is important for social mobility, and is also believed to be achievable by whosoever aims to do so. Hence, whether education is viewed important from either internal or external perspectives, it is strongly coloured by a sense of egalitarianism - you can achieve it if you want to. Because of this, there is an extraordinary emphasis on effort, willpower or concentration of the mind in the Confucian tradition. Because there is a strong belief in attainability by all, there is also a strong belief that one's failure is not due to one's internal make-up or ability, but one's effort and willpower. A weak-willed person making no effort is doomed to failure. In contrast, despite your level of intelligence, if one tries and keeps trying, one will certainly 'get there' sooner or later. This tradition seems to have influenced many modern Asian learners with a Confucian tradition. LeVine and White's (1986, pp. 110-111) outline of the characteristics of educational mobilization in Japan is perhaps the best summary for the above discussion. These characteristics include:-

1) A high degree of parental involvement in and commitment to the education of children;
2) A basic eagerness to learn and positive attitude toward school on the part of children;
3) High status for teachers and a strong commitment on their part to teaching and to involvement in their students' overall development;
4) The premise of egalitarian access to the rewards of successful learning;
5) The assumption that it is effort rather than innate ability which yields rewards in schooling;
6) The occupational system values education as appropriate preparation for work.

REFERENCES

Bae, C.K. (1991). Education: top reason behind rapid growth. Schooling for economic takeoff. *Koreana*, *5*(2), 56-68.

Biggs, J.B. (1991). Approaches to learning in secondary and tertiary students in Hong Kong: some comparative studies. *Education Research Journal*, *6*, 27-39.

Bol, P.K. (1989). Chu Hsi's redefinition of literati learning. In de Bary, W.T.

& John W. (eds.), *Neo-Confucian education: the formative stage*. Berkeley, Calif.: University of California Press.

Chai, C. ed. & tr. (1965). *The humanist way in ancient China: essential works of Confucianism*. New York: Bantam Books.

Chang, C. (1957). *The development of Neo-Confucian thought*. New York: Bookman Associates.

Chang, H. (1976). New Confucianism and the intellectual crisis of contemporary China. In Furth, C. (ed.), *The limits of change: essays on conservative alternatives in Republican China*, 276-302. Cambridge, Mass.: Harvard University Press.

Cheung, T.S. (1991). The Confucian ethics and achievement motivation: reality or myth? In Wong, S.L. (ed.), *Chinese religious ethics and modernization*, 62-76. Hong Kong: The Commercial Press. [In Chinese]

Chiang, M. (1924). *A study in Chinese principles of education*. Shanghai: The Commercial Press.

Chu, H. (1990). *Learning to be a sage: selections from the conversations of Master Chu, arranged topically*, tr. D.K. Gardner. Berkeley, Calif.: University of California Press.

Cleverley, J. (1991). *The schooling of China*. Second edition. Sydney: Allen & Unwin.

Confucius (1979). *The Analects*, tr. D.C. Lao. Harmondsworth: Penguin Books.

Confucius (1979). *Confucian Analects, the great learning & the doctrine of mean*, tr. J. Legge. New York: Dover Publications.

de Bary, W.T. (1983). *The liberal tradition in China*. Hong Kong: The Chinese University of Hong Kong Press.

de Bary, W.T. (1989). Chu Hsi's aims as an educator. In de Bary, W.T. & J.W. Chaffee, J.W. (eds.), *Neo-Confucian education: the formative stage*, 186-218. Berkeley, Calif.: University of California Press.

Eberhard, W. (1971). *Moral and social values of the Chinese: collected essays*. Taipei: Cheng Wen Publishing Company.

Fei, X. (1947). *The rural China [Xiangtu Zhongguo]*. Shanghai: Shanghai Observation Press. [In Chinese]

Giles, H.A. (1972). *San Tzu Ching: elementary Chinese*. Taipei: Cheng Wen Publishing Company.

Ho, D.Y.F. (1986). Chinese patterns of socialization: a critical review. In Bond, M.H. (ed.), *The psychology of the Chinese people*, 1-37. Hong Kong: Oxford University Press.

Ho, P.T. (1962). *The ladder of success in imperial China: aspects of social mobility*, 1368-1911. New York: Columbia University Press.

Hsu, C.Y. (1965). *Ancient China in transition: an analysis of social mobility*, 722-222. B.C. California: Standford University Press.

Hsun, T. (1928). *The works of Hsun Tse*, tr. H.H. Dubs. London: Arthur Probsthain.

Huang, J. (1987). The Confucian ethics and economic development: myth or reality? *Chinese Times [Zhongguo Shibao], 19*(December). [In Chinese]

Kim, K.D. (1988). The distinctive features of South Korea's development. In Berger, P.L. & Hsiao, H.H.M. (eds.), *Search of an East Asian development model*, 197-219. New Brunswick, N.J.: Transaction Publishers.

King, A.Y.C. (1992). *Chinese society and culture [Zhongguo Shehui yu Wenhua]*. Hong Kong: Oxford University Press. [In Chinese]

Lee, T.H.C. (1985). *Government education and examinations in Sung China*. Hong Kong: The Chinese University Press.

LeVine, R.A. & White, M.I. (1986). *Human conditions: the cultural basis of educational developments*. New York: Routledge & Kegan Paul.

Lifton, R.J. (1967). *Thought reform and the psychology of totalism*. Middlesex: Penguin Books.

Lin, Y. (1938). *The wisdom of Confucius*. New York: Random House.

Maslow, A.H. (1968). *Towards a psychology of being*. 2nd edition. Princeton, N.J.: Van Nostrand.

Mencius (1970). *Mencius*, tr. D.C. Lao. Harmondsworth: Penguin Books.

Leestma, R. et al. (1987). *Japanese education today*. A Report from the U.S. Study of Education in Japan. Washington, D.C.: Office of Educational and Research Improvement, U.S. Department of Education.

Tu, W.M. (1979). *Humanity and self-cultivation: essays in Confucian thought*. Berkeley, Calif.: Asian Humanities Press.

Tu, W.M. (1985). *Confucius thought: selfhood as creative transformation*. New York: State University of New York.

Wang, Y.M. (1916). *The philosophy of Wang Yang-ming*. 2nd edition. Trans. Frederick Goodrich Henke. New York: Paragon Book Reprint Corp.

Wu, P.Y. (1989). Education of children in the Sung. In de Bary, W.T. & Chaffee, J.W., (eds.), *Neo-Confucian education: the formative stage*, 307-324. Berkeley, Calif.: University of California Press.

Yang, K.S. (1986). Chinese personality and its change. In Bond, M.H. (ed.), *The psychology of the Chinese people*, 106-170. Hong Kong: Oxford University Press.

Zhu, W. (1992). Confucius and traditional Chinese education: an assessment. In Hayhoe, R. (ed.), *Education and modernization: the Chinese experience*, 3-22. Oxford: Pergamon Press.

PERSPECTIVES ON
THE PARADOX OF
THE CHINESE LEARNER

3

Western Misperceptions of the Confucian-Heritage Learning Culture

John Biggs

Environments for Good Learning?

Educational research conducted in Western countries has established what is now conventional wisdom about the conditions for good learning. Good learning involves the use of deep approaches to learning (Chapter 1), by which students engage in appropriate tasks; they use abstract frameworks for conceptualizing the task and for illuminating the data, they are metacognitive in planning ahead and in monitoring their own progress, they achieve well-structured and integrated outcomes, and they actually enjoy the learning process. But let us not get too carried away; correct answers, and scoring well in attainment tests, are to most people (educational researchers included) the bottom line of good learning. High attainment and deep approaches are however complementary bedfellows; one of the reliable outcomes of a deep approach is a correct answer.

Good learning is more likely to take place in teaching environments that possess the following characteristics, as indicated by a number of studies (summarized in Biggs and Moore, 1993):-

1) Teaching methods are varied, emphasizing student activity, self-regulation and student-centredness, with much cooperative and other group work;
2) Content is presented in a meaningful context;
3) Small classes;
4) Warm classroom climate;

5) High cognitive level outcomes are expected and addressed in assessment; and

6) Assessment is classroom-based and conducted in a nonthreatening atmosphere.

Observers remark that such conditions are rare in classrooms in East and Southeast Asia, specifically those Ho (1991) refers to as "Confucian-heritage" cultures: China, Taiwan, Singapore, Hong Kong, Japan, and Korea. The abbreviation 'CHC' is used here to refer to these countries or educational systems, with the main focus being on Chinese CHC students.

Typically, CHC classes are large, in excess of 40 and over, and appear to Western observers as highly authoritarian: teaching methods are mostly expository, sharply focused on preparation for external examinations (see Chapter 9). Examinations themselves address low-level cognitive goals, are highly competitive, and exert excessive pressure on teachers and exam stress on students (Biggs, 1991; Ho, 1991; Morris, 1985). Even in affluent CHC countries such as Hong Kong and Singapore, per capita expenditure on education is much less than that in the West, and resources and support services, such as counselling, are correspondingly lower.

Such an educational environment is the antithesis of what has been identified as a 'good' environment in Western research, as these characteristics have been associated empirically in the Western context with low cognitive level learning strategies and with poor learning outcomes (Biggs, 1979, 1987; Bourke, 1986; Crooks, 1988; Ramsden, 1985).

CHC learning: low quality?

Now let us look at the evidence on the quality of learning in CHC classrooms. Western observers frequently complain that Asian students are prone to use rote-based, low-level, cognitive strategies, both in their own culture (Hong Kong; Murphy, 1987), and overseas in Australian tertiary institutions (Ballard and Clanchy, 1984; Bradley and Bradley, 1984; Samuelowicz, 1987). The following observations by Australian tertiary teachers of overseas students are typical:-

"In my discipline they all want to rote learn material rather than think." (Animal Science and Production)

"Students from Malaysia, Singapore, Hong Kong appear to be much more inclined to rote learning. Such an approach does not help problem solving." (Dentistry)

(quoted in Samuelowicz, 1987; p. 123)

These perceptions are reinforced by classroom behaviour, which is seen as passive and compliant. Overseas Asian students typically take a low profile, rarely asking questions or volunteering answers, let alone making public observations or criticisms of course content, as these quotations illustrate:

"(Asian students) tend to look on lecturers as close to gods. Often they are very reluctant to question statements or textbooks." (Parasitology)

"...it can be difficult to cope, in small (graduate) classes, with overseas students who are reluctant to discuss, criticize reading and express an opinion." (Commerce)

"In my country, we don't have much group discussion or tutorials. We are not supposed to make an argument in class." (Thailand, Ph.D., Science)

(quoted in Samuelowicz, 1987; p. 124-5)

Such behaviour is not, however, the understandable reaction of culture shocked, second language (L2) speakers. Ginsberg (1992), after a visit to China and Japan, reports:-

"In China, knowledge is not open to challenge and extension (by students arguing with their instructors) .... The teacher decides which knowledge is to be taught, and the students accept and learn that knowledge. The lecturer is the authority, the repository of knowledge, leading the student forward into this knowledge, a respected elder transmitting to a subordinate junior." (Ginsberg, 1992; p. 6)

And even in Hong Kong:-

"Hong Kong students display almost unquestioning acceptance of the knowledge of the teacher or lecturer. This may be explained in terms of an extension or transfer of the Confucian ethic of filial piety. Coupled with this is an emphasis on strictness of discipline and proper behaviour, rather than an expression of opinion, independence, self-mastery, creativity and all-round personal development." (Murphy, 1987; p. 43)

The perception of the student-as-tape-recorder could not be clearer.

Or high quality?

Yet CHC students achieve at considerably higher levels than their Western counterparts. This disparity is possibly most dramatic when we look at overseas CHC students, who in many American higher educational institutions are subject to quotas, and who in general perform at levels much higher than would be predictable from their IQ (Flynn, 1992; Sue and Okazaki, 1990). But more to the present point, CHC students in their own countries, obediently receptive in their own fierce and crowded classrooms, have over the years consistently outperformed Westerners. The best large-scale data we have are those obtained in the various International Association for the Evaluation of Educational Achievement (IEA) studies in mathematics and science (Baker, 1993; Garden, 1987; IEA, 1988; Medrich and Griffith, 1992), which regularly show Korea, Japan, and Singapore amongst the highest scoring countries, including Hong Kong, towards the end of schooling, and nearly always higher than the US. This outcome is not necessarily at the expense of other attainment, as an ongoing IEA study indicates: Hong Kong students are above international norms on both mother tongue and L2 competence (Johnson and Cheung, 1991).

More fine-grained data come from the careful comparative studies of Stevenson and his team in China, Taiwan, Japan, and the US (Stevenson and Stigler, 1992). They found that while US students read better than Chinese, Taiwanese, and Japanese in grade 1, by grade 5 the means were similar, but the variance much greater in US students. In mathematics, US students were significantly worse than CHC students in grade 1, a differential that grew progressively larger through to grade 11. For example, in a computation test at grade 5, only 1.4% of Beijing students scored as low as the *mean* of corresponding American students.

Such outcomes could not be achieved through rote learning, and the evidence is indeed that they are not. The superior performance of Chinese children in elementary mathematics, for example, can be traced to the fact that Chinese students are more sophisticated in the strategies they use. Chinese grade 1 students behave more like American grade 5 students in their preference for a decomposition strategy rather than counting, a strategy requiring a "solid conceptual understanding of addition and number sets" (Geary, Liu, and Bow-Thomas, 1992; p. 183). One reason for this may be that the sounding of Chinese numbers takes much less 'space' in working memory than do Western number names, thus leaving more space for higher level strategies (Hoosain, 1991). Be that as it may, the fact is that Chinese students do use these strategies, whatever the reason.

Preference for higher-level conceptual strategies is not confined to elementary arithmetic. Several studies, involving thousands of students, have compared the approaches to learning of CHC secondary and tertiary students with those of comparable groups of Western students, on the basis of self-report questionnaires. In almost every case, CHC students report a stronger preference for high-level, meaning-based, learning strategies, and avoidance of rote learning, than that of Western students, both in their own culture (Hong Kong and Singapore; Biggs, 1990; 1991; Watkins, Regmi, and Astilla, 1991), and overseas in Australian institutions (Biggs, 1987). The only major exception to this pattern was in a medical sample, where the Westerners were lower on rote, and higher on meaningful, learning approaches. However, the Western students were in that most learner-friendly of environments, problem-based learning, while the CHC students were in a highly traditional medical school in which rote learning of technical terms was emphasized (Biggs, 1991).

As this last finding supports the conventional association between environment and approach to learning, it gives the other comparisons some validity. This leaves the majority of comparative studies associating a low propensity for rote learning and a strong meaning orientation with the general run of CHC classrooms, throughout the primary, secondary, and tertiary sectors.

A challenge to Western research

Evidence for each of the following can now be adduced:-

1) CHC classrooms should be conducive to low quality outcomes: rote learning and low achievement;
2) CHC students are perceived as using low-level, rote-based strategies;
3) CHC students have significantly higher levels of achievement than those of Western students; and
4) CHC students report a preference for high-level, meaning-based learning strategies.

One is consistent with (2), and (3) is consistent with (4), but (1) flatly contradicts (3) and (4), and (2) flatly contradicts (3) and (4). We thus have some explaining to do, otherwise some well-supported propositions about the nature of teaching and learning are at risk. And what of the political implications (not to mention the face lost by researchers), if large classes, outdated teaching methods, poor equipment, inadequate public expenditure per student, and relentless low-level examining can produce students who see themselves as engaging in high-level processing, and who outperform Western students in many subject areas!

Possibly people in CHC countries are more highly evolved than Caucasians (Lynn, 1987; Rushton, 1989). In support of this intriguing hypothesis, Lynn proposed that Asians were trapped by the Ice Age between the Himalayas and the Arctic in a bitterly cold environment, which selected physically foreshortened limbs and rounded features to minimize heat loss, and the epicanthic fold under the eyes to protect against glare, and mentally for higher intelligence of a particular kind, with a laterilization of the brain that enhanced visual-spatial ability at the expense of verbal ability. Rushton further pointed out that the Sino-Japanese brain- to body-mass ratio is higher than that in Caucasians, and that civilization appeared in China long before it did in the West; he also advanced more speculative observations involving the distribution of Sino-Japanese body hair and patterns of Sino-Japanese violence.

Genetic arguments are currently politically incorrect, and in any event there are problems with both Lynn's and Rushton's particular proposals that are extensively discussed by Flynn (1992); in particular, the verbal-nonverbal disparity, and generational differences within subpopulations, are more unstable than is genetically likely. It would be foolish to deny the possibility of genetic differences, but it would be poor science to use that argument to preempt further investigation.

To pile paradox on paradox, perhaps we are seeing that when schooling is poor, good students are forced to generate their own self-regulated strategies for deep learning precisely in order to survive bad teaching. That hypothesis at least suggests interesting further research, but at a first glance it seems inconsistent with the low variances reported by Stevenson and Stigler (1992); low variances indicate that *all* students, not just the metacognitively inclined, are benefiting from bad teaching! That hypothesis comes with a very high price tag.

Let us first try the lower cost assumption that our knowledge of teaching is not all wrong. The clue is that assertions (1) and (2) (p.49) are based on Western observations and interpretations. Maybe those observations and interpretations are simply wrong. A first hypothesis, then, is that what some Western observers are seeing is not what they think it is.

The central paradox is that highly adaptive modes of learning emerge from CHC classrooms. This does need explaining. The germs of a resolution are in the cross-cultural literature, and in fact almost each of the Chapters to follow in this book address something of this issue. But first, we need a theoretical framework.

A Systems Model of Teaching and Learning

Research into student learning has for some time been interested in establishing relationships between the teaching context, student learning processes, and learning outcomes. Such relationships are formalized in the so-called presage-process-product, or 3P, model (Biggs, 1993a; see Figure 3.1).

Figure 3.1
The 3P model of teaching and learning

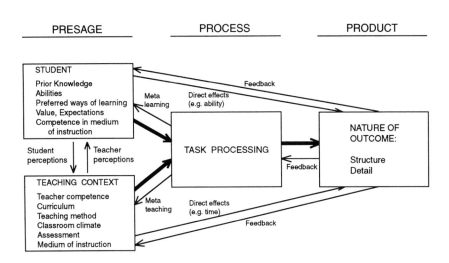

Figure 3.1: The 3P Model of Teaching and Learning

As well as describing a linear progression from presage to process to product, each component interacts with all other components, forming a system in equilibrium. The systems aspect generates predictions that are highly relevant to the present problem.

'Student presage' factors are relatively stable, learning-related characteristics of the student, which would include: prior knowledge and experience relevant to the task, abilities, values and expectations concerning achievement, and approaches to learning as predispositions to engage in academic activities according to prevailing motives and strategies, and competence in the language of instruction.

'Teaching presage' factors refer to the context and superstructure set by the teacher and the institution. Factors personal to the teacher would include teaching competency and teaching style, conceptions of teaching and learning, and classroom climate established. Institutional factors would include the course structure, curriculum content, methods of teaching and assessment, and in some CHC countries, language policy.

The 'process' domain refers to the way students actually handle the task, which is determined by their perceptions of the teaching context, their motives and predispositions, and their decisions for immediate action, all of which comprise their approach to the learning task. Their approach may be of high or low cognitive level. Low-level, or 'surface', approaches result in correspondingly low level outcomes; whereas high-level, or deep, approaches result in high-level outcomes, as discussed in Chapter 1.

The 'product' of learning may correspondingly be of high- or low-cognitive level. Low-level outcomes emphasize quantitative recall, while high-level outcomes emphasize, in addition to being 'correct', well-structured support, abstract conceptualizing, relevance, and even elegance.

A major property of this model arises from the fact that all components interact with each other and reach an equilibrium, thereby taking on the properties of a system (von Bertalanffy, 1968). In the ecology of a system, a change to any one component will, depending on the state of equilibrium already achieved, either effect change throughout, creating a new equilibrium and hence a new system, or the changed component will be absorbed and the system reverts to the *status quo*.

The systems property is crucial in the present discussion, because it is responsible for the paradoxes. Because all parts in a continuing system interact to form an equilibrium, the way students go about their learning, both with regard to particular tasks, and their schoolwork in general, will derive from the teaching/learning environment in which they are placed. Where the classroom or learning context is conducive to deep approaches, the students will tend to approach their learning deeply, with appropriately complex learning outcomes. Where the context is more restrictive, and students perceive that surface approaches will suffice, they tend likewise to adapt and outcomes are poorly·

structured. In both cases, the 3P system is in equilibrium.

In CHC classrooms, however, it appears that presage, process, and product are out of kilter. If poor contexts generate low level processes, then whence the high-level outcomes? But if high level processes are in fact generating the high-level outcomes, how are those processes generated from the poor contexts? The facts that CHC classrooms produce outcomes that compare as well with or better than those coming from the West, and that they are stable, suggests that a working equilibrium has indeed been struck.

Three areas warrant further examination in this context: approaches to learning; the nature of the teaching context in CHC classrooms; and their inter-relationship.

Surface and deep approaches to learning in context

The term 'approach' has been used in two senses: in the sense of describing how a particular task is engaged, as originally meant by Marton and Saljo (1976); and in the sense of describing how a student has come to terms with the teaching environment and is typically reacting to it. Assessment of that reaction is a useful index for the deep- or surface-inducing nature of the teaching environment in question (Biggs, 1993b). According to the systems model, then, an approach represents the students' way of adapting to an environment; it is this use of approach that has been used in comparing CHC with Western students.

Yet large classes, exam pressure, expository teaching, and the rest (not to mention teaching in an exotic language), do not sound like good news in any system. But these features exist, and have achieved a degree of stability, in a system that produces high-level outcomes by any reasonable standard. Are they perhaps not quite what they seem to be to outside observers? Are there other factors that might cast quite a different slant on how a Westerner would interpret them? Again, we need to examine them in terms of the system within which they exist, not in terms of a system within which they could take quite a different meaning.

'Deep' and 'surface' are generic terms; what they specifically mean in any instance depends on the context, the task, and the individual's encoding of both. The surface approach, being based on an intention that is extrinsic to the real purpose of the task, aims to satisfice, not satisfy, task demands by investing minimal time and effort consistent with appearing to meet requirements. A decision to satisfice could well implicate rote learning, in which case material would be reproduced without understanding. But a decision to ensure accurate recall of already understood information, say for a high-stress situation such as an examination, may also implicate learning by repetition. The first is a surface approach, the second is not; indeed, the latter could, depending on context, be part of a deep or an achieving approach as it certainly appears to be in 'deep-memorizing' (Chapter 9).

A useful distinction to introduce at this stage is the difference between 'rote' learning, which as the Macquarie Dictionary says is learning in "a mechanical way *without thought of meaning*" (italics supplied), and 'repetitive' learning, which uses repetition as a means of ensuring accurate recall. Both rely on a rehearsal strategy (Biggs and Moore, 1993), and it could well be that rehearsing precludes conscious thought of meaning in both cases. The difference lies in the learner's 'intentions' with respect to meaning. In rote learning meaning has no place in the learner's intentions, in repetitive learning it has, at some point in the deployment of the learned material. Ausubel (1968) contrasts meaningful and rote learning curiously in terms of the product; rote learned content being verbatim, meaningful being capable of transformation. That method of distinguishing the two forms of learning is not helpful in the present context, where as we have seen, deep approaches lead to more right answers than surface. It is the process that is crucial here.

Further, if to be deep is to relate to the task relevantly, then what is 'relevant' could depend on how it is culturally defined. As is argued in Chapter 4, if the point of learning is to understand (deep), and repetition is seen as a way of coming to understand, then repetition becomes a deep strategy. Thus, while Westerners may correctly see Asian students indulging in a high degree of repetitive work, they could be quite incorrect in seeing that activity as 'rote' learning and therefore as a surface strategy. In that case, summary point (2) (p.49) becomes irrelevant, as Westerners would be mistaking repetitive for rote learning.

This illustrates the central thrust of the systems theory; we should interpret a piece of the action in terms of the system of which it is part, not in terms of an exotic system. In the Western system, repetition could well be part of a task-dodging surface approach; in a CHC system it probably is not. This is not even a cross-cultural argument; SAL theory itself (Chapter 1) insists that learning should be seen in context. Thus, a subject in an experiment who chooses to use repetition in order to handle a serial word-learning task, rather than an elaborative strategy such as imaging, is not using a surface approach to learning, as Christensen, Massey, and Isaacs (1991) argue, but is making a strategic choice appropriate to the laboratory context that is simply irrelevant to the choice that person might make in an academic context.

A student who chooses a repetitive strategy to learn examination material after understanding it in order to optimize retrieval in the examination context (Thomas and Bain, 1984; see also Chapter 9) is likewise not using a surface approach but making a strategic choice. It is, however, possible that the choice to use repetitive learning strategically is more common in CHCs because of traditional beliefs about learning (Chapter 2), or because of the assessment systems in use and the life-choices hanging on the results (Chapter 9).

Good CHC Learning Environments

Gardner (1989) describes how he visited China several times to study art and music teaching. He was struck by the incredible skill that very young Chinese children displayed in their drawing, far in advance of that of American children of a similar age. On the other hand, they appeared to only draw from a few set models. This led him early in his visits to revive the distinction between 'mimetic' and 'transformational' teaching, the former highly directive and imitative, the latter student-directed and creative. Chinese teaching was, he concluded, mimetic.

However, he began to see that matters were not that simple; for example, Chinese children were able to draw novel subjects, which they had not previously copied, extremely competently. The differences between Chinese and American teaching, then, were not simply that the former only stressed imitation. Rather, he saw that the differences lay in beliefs about the appropriate order of various learning-related activities. In the West, we believe in exploring first, then in the development of skill; the Chinese believe in skill development first, which typically involves repetitive, as opposed to rote learning, after which there is something to be creative with. Chinese educators also believe that art should be both beautiful and morally good; the idea of one right way pervades teaching. Thus, skill is developed first, in pursuit of the 'right way'; teaching is 'by holding the hand', not simply to direct, but to create the beautiful. The end is a product, not a process; in China both music and art teaching are performance-oriented. American education is more concerned with the process than with the product; exploring and creating are seen as more important than honing the specific skills needed to achieve a particular artistic product of an acceptable and recognized standard.

Gardner is one Western observer who quickly realized that his first impressions were simplistic, and that things were not as they first appeared to be. He is not the only one to make this point:-

"A common Western stereotype is that the Asian teacher is an authoritarian purveyor of information, one who expects students to listen and memorize correct answers and procedures rather than to construct knowledge themselves. This does not describe the dozens of elementary school teachers that we have observed."   (Stigler and Stevenson, 1991: p.43)

The teachers that Stigler and Stevenson observed, in China, Taiwan, and Japan, saw their task as posing provocative questions, allowing reflection time, and varying techniques to suit individual students: Confucius' 'elicitation' mode in full swing. They use the term 'constructivist' to describe the commonest teaching approach they saw, an ideal espoused by progressive Western educators and in practice realized only by the expert few (Driver and Oldham, 1986; Tobin and Fraser, 1988).

'Constructivist' is also the term used by O'Connor (1991) in his study of PRC teachers. He presented a group of teachers with a series of classroom vignettes (e.g. a case of bullying, a student complains about a mark), and sought their analysis of the situation and their solutions. He found the teachers to be uniformly student-centred, frequently engaging all students collectively in problem-solving, both in the cognitive sense and in determining a course of action for a deviant student, and pushing for high cognitive level thought processes. The teachers were quite Rogerian in their concern for preserving an individual student's face.

This is not to say that these teachers and schools are non-authoritarian. There is after all only one 'right way', and students must tread that path, but it is by 'holding the hand', as Gardner felicitously puts it, not by 'putting in the boot', which is generally the method preferred by authoritarian Westerners in the classroom. Teacher-student relations in modern Chinese universities thus convey a puzzling ambiguity to Western observers. Social relations are as complex as one might expect in a collectivistic culture. Students live on campus in dormitories, and unsurprisingly this environment facilitates a tremendous amount of collective activities, including academic discussions, study groups, and the like (Chan, 1993; see Chapter 10 for the Hong Kong version). The teachers live on campus too, often in the same building as their students, giving rise to much teacher-student interaction outside the classroom, and although teacher-student relations may be strongly hierarchical as compared with these in the West, they are also typically marked by warmth and a sense of responsibility on both sides. This is perhaps another area where Western observers see only part of the picture. Ginsberg's (1992) observations that the lecturer is the authority, "a respected elder transmitting to a subordinate junior" (p. 6), may be true, except that the teaching mode is not one of simple transmission but one based on much interaction, in a complex and not atypically warm social context.

Another example of the apparently curious mixture of authoritarianism and student-centredness is provided by Hess and Azuma (1991) in their comparative study of Japanese and US mothers, children, and teachers. One strategy used by teachers they call "sticky probing", by which a single problem is discussed by students, with their teacher adjudicating, for hours until a consensus acceptable to both the teacher and group is reached. The focus of the probing is typically a maths error made by a particular student, which the teacher believes would be instructive to publicly unpack and reconstruct, with the student the focus of public correction. A Western student would be mortified to be in the corrective spotlight for such a long and public time, whereas Japanese students do not see it as a punishment for making a mistake, but as an opportunity for everyone to learn.

Hess and Azuma also refer to "repetition as a route to understanding" (op. cit.: p.6), which appears as endless going over and over a point. However, this is not rote learning as previously defined; it is a means of gaining, not of side-stepping, understanding. The technique is important in learning to write and to interpret characters. There is obviously a good deal of repetitive learning involved in acquiring the thousands of characters in common usage, and traditionally the sequence is to learn to shape them first before learning what they mean, so in that sense and at that stage such learning is 'rote', but not surface. Characters are traditionally learned by the Two Principles. The First Principle is to use the Five Organs (eyes to see the shape, ears to hear the sound, hand to write, mouth to speak the sound, mind to think about the meaning); the Second Principle is to form each character into a word, and each word into a sentence. Repetitive certainly, rigid maybe, but embedded in meaning always (at least that is the intention), with much use of learner activity and involvement, a key ingredient in quality learning (Biggs and Moore, 1993).

The limited number of characters means that new meanings are created according to which characters are juxtaposed with each other. Text thus becomes multi-layered, with shifts and shades of meaning being revealed on repeated readings. Thus repetition has an important role at both the text level and the word level. The multi-layered aspect of written Chinese makes codification imprecise, hence the metaphoric nature of much Chinese communication, which is skillfully used in negotiation. A metaphor can be thrown on the table meaning what the initiator wants it to mean at any given point in the negotiations; a technique much in evidence in the current Sino-British negotiations over Hong Kong.

Thus, in this complex situation repetition plays a key clarifying role, in the sequence remarked by Gardner: repetitive skill development comes first, followed by meaning and interpretation, with repetition being used as the tool for creating meaning.

If we now review CHC classrooms, we get quite a different picture from that originally presented. Checking against the characteristics of good teaching environments, we find, including informal as well as formal learning situations:-

1) An emphasis on student activity, with much cooperative and their group work;
2) Warm classroom/other learning climate, interpreting 'warm' as appropriate to the culture;
3) High cognitive level outcomes are expected.

Not quite the full list, maybe, but certainly the picture is significantly different from that presented originally. This list is derived from Western research. The present review has thrown up specifically non-Western, deep-oriented, teaching techniques such as sticky probing, and the use of repetition. When we throw in the cultural 'milieu', the picture changes even more in the direction of a positive learning environment.

Dispositions to learn

Hess and Azuma (1991) claim that in contrast to Japanese children, Western children are generally raised to be assertive, independent, curious, and to explore on their own terms. These are not, however, qualities that are rewarded in most schools, Western or Japanese, which require obedience, conformity to group norms, persistence in the absence of feedback at essentially boring tasks the point of which is not evident (Hess and Azuma, 1991). The difference is, it seems, that in Japanese schools the latter qualities are also built into the pre- and extra-school social environment, and that Japanese socialization procedures produce 'internalized dispositions' that ease children into the world of school, by making them more docile, or literally 'teachable'.

An important educational consequence of this process is that teachers do not have to spend the time and energy Westerns teachers do on 'motivating' their students. Docility dispositions create:-

> "A sense of diligence and receptiveness (which) fit uncomfortably into the more familiar American concepts of intrinsic and extrinsic motivation." (ibid., 1991: p.7)

In other words, Japanese children have less need to be motivated to learn because they are already predisposed to do those things that are required of them by their teachers. In the Western system, on the other hand, there is more of a mismatch, with children being socialized one way out of school, another way in school. Their previous socialization does not particularly predispose them to do what they perceive to be pointless and boring tasks; if they are to engage them, they need to be 'motivated' to do so. Classroom activities need to be made attractive, and elaborate systems of positive and negative reinforcement need to be employed. Western classrooms are therefore highly externally controlled, compared with their Japanese counterparts (ibid., 1991).

This question of control colours the interaction between teachers and students. Despite classes of 50 students, or even more, Chinese and Japanese teachers find time to interact one-to-one in their classroom rounds more frequently than Western teachers with smaller classes, spending rather more time with each student. Western teachers see interaction more in whole class terms, with 'quick and snappy' public questioning (ibid., 1991), which does little in terms of higher order cognitive engagement (Tobin, 1987). While it is true that at tertiary level, a Westerner teaching a class of Chinese students is likely to be disappointed at the apparent lack of interaction or responsiveness to public questioning (Biggs, 1990; Murphy, 1987), the number of students seeking one-to-one interaction with the teacher as soon as class is over, and with each other, is almost certainly higher than is the case with Western students. Japanese and especially Chinese teachers have much lighter teaching loads, precisely to enable them to prepare their work more carefully, and to interact with students out of class hours (Stevenson and Stigler, 1992).

Thus, what goes on prior to formal schooling is as important in determining learning as what goes on inside classrooms. Child rearing practices require students to be willing to persist in the face of boredom and lack of immediate feedback, to use a high degree of metacognition or awareness of their own cognitive processes, and to accept rules governing group participation (Hess and Azuma, 1991). Japanese socializing practices thus encourage characteristics that - coincidentally? - are required in institutionalized learning anywhere, not only in Japan.

There are several other culturally-based factors that distinguish Confucian-heritage from Western learners in ways that would encourage more favourable learning outcomes in CHC classrooms.

Attributions for success and failure

Numerous studies have drawn attention to the fact that Asian cultures attribute success to effort, and failure to lack of effort, whereas Westerners tend to attribute success and failure to ability and lack of ability, respectively (ibid., 1991; Holloway, 1988). Effort attributions in the event of failure are obviously more adaptive than ability attributions, which simply lead to resignation and disengagement. Even more effective than effort *per se* is directed effort, that is putting in the kind of effort that is related to skill, strategy, and know-how (Clifford, 1986). It is thus particularly encouraging to see that Hong Kong secondary students attribute success to, in order: effort, interest in study, study skill, mood, and only fifth, ability (Hau and Salili, 1991; see also Chapter 5). The first four are more or less controllable; the fifth, which Western students see as most important for success, is not.

Thus, the attributions acquired by CHC students normally tend to help them see ways in which they can improve their performance; for example, that they cannot only put in more effort, but they can learn how to study more appropriately, and try to create the right mood. In attributing past performance, successful or not, to ability, Western students are relinquishing control over their learning, and failure becomes a self-fulfilling prophecy.

Nevertheless, there is a CHC downside. Effort attributions that dictate persistence when the task is in fact beyond the abilities of the student may be devastating. There is little doubt that at least some of the recent suicides by Hong Kong students have been the result of the enormous stress that effort-attributing teachers and parents can create, as the following essay illustrates. It was written by a 10 year-old shortly before he jumped from his 19th floor bedroom, rather than tell his parents he could not do his maths homework:-

"Nevertheless, there is hardship in studying as well. Every day, there are many homeworks. They are not only in large quantity, but also difficult to do ...

Though after 12 o'clock in every night, I still have to revise my homeworks. I can't go to bed until one o'clock odd. At 6.50 hours, in the next morning, I have to get up. (I) am so hard.

I do wish no studying.

Lau Ka-chun, ten years." (Reported in *South China Morning Post*, May 11, 1991)

There are two other consequences of effort attributions:-

(a) *Time on task*. For the same period of formal time, Asian teachers and students are more task-oriented, with more student time actually spent on task (Stevenson and Stigler, 1992). Students also spend more time on task than Westerners outside the classroom, either on homework, or in voluntary studying. Teachers, for their part, are allowed much more out-of-class time than Western teachers for lesson preparation, conferencing with other teachers, and extra-curricular contact with students. Where teachers and students are domiciled together, as is frequently the case in China, then this process is greatly enhanced.

(b) *Cue seeking*. Attributions to effort and strategy would have quite a specific effect of encouraging cue-seeking in students (Miller and Parlett, 1974). Miller and Parlett's concept was derived in the West, but it certainly is a behaviour to which CHC students seem particularly prone, and which their teachers encourage, as Morris's (1985) study of teachers' exam preparation strategies documents. Cue-seeking is especially tuned to assessment preparation strategies, which is an area where Hong Kong students are particularly adept (Tang, 1991; Chapter 9).

Spontaneous collaboration

One reaction to the lack of perceived cues is for students to work collaboratively, to seek each others' cue-perceptions and views on how in particular, to handle an unfamiliar situation (Tang, 1991). Such spontaneous collaboration, explained at length in Chapter 10, seems a specifically CHC way of reacting in a system that is strongly expository and competitive. In Hong Kong, the cultural supports for learning appear to overtake the classroom structures. Spontaneous collaboration is also a pronounced feature of mainland Chinese study behaviour (Chan, 1993).

These and other learning-related factors are initiated in the culture and transmitted through socialization. They all appear to be highly adaptive for learning. Thus, there is greater harmony between student expectations and metacognitions, and teacher expectations and procedures, in the East than in the West. This makes direct comparison between similar classroom behaviour in different cultural contexts difficult to make, as the same behaviour, for example teacher criticism, takes on quite a different role. In the West criticism is frequently meant, and taken, punitively; in Japan criticism is part and parcel of the teaching process of 'sticky probing', which is meant, and taken, as cognitive feedback.

Redefining the Classroom System

Clearly the original classroom-based 3P model needs extending to take in the cultural context of which both the classroom and school are a part. Such an extension is of course implicit in a systems model from the beginning, but Western research being conducted from within a monoculture makes it like the fish: the last to discover water. The model can thus be redrawn (Figure 3.2).

Teacher and student are specifically shown here as sharing learning-related beliefs and values that arise in the general social *milieu*. In CHC countries it seems likely that these beliefs, values, and practices lead children to internalize dispositions that enhance teachability or docility. Such docility dispositions might include:-

1) Attributions that encourage further involvement and self-management after failure, including: effort, strategy, interest in the task, and skill of the teacher;
2) Metacognitive skills such as scanning to seek cues that help the direction of effort, and that give assent to the direction of effort towards repetitive and boring tasks, knowing that meaning and purpose will be found ultimately; and
3) Recognition of group problem solving and the ability to accept the rules governing social behaviour in groups.

Figure 3.2
The 3P Model, culturally modified

-- Figure 3.2 goes here --

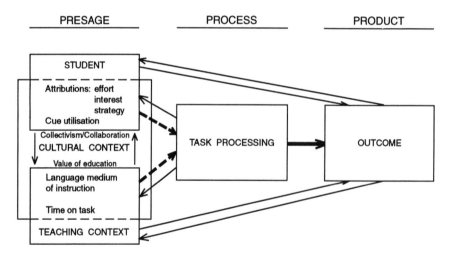

Figure 3.2: The 3P Model, culturally modified

These characteristics are ones that are highly adaptive in institutional settings for teaching and learning, and they favour CHC students over Westerners.

To return to our original 'contradictions', we see that these exist only by taking too narrow and systemic a view of the components in classroom learning:-

(a) *The CHC teaching/learning environment.* Despite large classes, external examinations, seemingly (to Westerners) cold-learning climates, and expository teaching, there are things going on in the fine-grain that are clearly adaptive: predispositions to put in effort and to seek meaning; to persist in the event of boredom or failure; and to foster the kind of interaction between teacher and student, and student and student, that engages higher rather than lower cognitive processes. Thus, gross characteristics, such as class size or even heavy external examinations, take on a different meaning in the CHC context to those in the Western context. The components that foster good learning, in other words, are defined as salient or significant from within the system of which they are a part, rather than from another system. This might be obvious enough to cross-cultural psychologists, but it clearly is not obvious to Westerners teaching CHC students overseas, or, less forgivably, to expatriate Westerners teaching CHC students in their own culture.

(b) *CHC students are rote learners.* This is a Western misperception arising a mistaken interpretation of repetitive effort. CHC students may be repetitive learners but there is no evidence that they rote learn any more than their Western counterparts.

(c) *CHC students perform at high cognitive levels in academic tasks.* The evidence for this is clear, both from large-scale international comparisons of attainment, and from detailed qualitative studies of strategy use.

(d) *CHC students see themselves as deep learners.* If deep learning is defined as handling the task meaningfully, CHC students see themselves as more deep-prone, as opposed to simple rote learning, than Western students.

The last point might raise questions about how far the concept of 'deep approach' translates across cultures. It seems clear that the specifics may not, but a generic deep approach would focus on understanding and performing the task 'appropriately'. Cultural differences may exist on how one might interpret what is appropriate or not, or even on what the task is, but the notion of appropriate engagement, whatever that might mean specifically, is generically deep. Preparedness to invest time, to learn appropriate strategies, to cue-seek, and to discuss with others are likely precursors to a deep approach, however this is defined.

These four statements are now no longer in deep conflict, however much they need to be explored further and developed in detail. One paradox still remains from all this, which is, that whatever cultural factors operate, CHC students are subjected to fierce assessment demands in a highly competitive environment, eliciting obviously 'surface' motives and strategies, yet typically CHC students operate with less surface, and more deep, approaches than Westerners. This particular paradox is elaborated and explored in Chapter 9.

More detailed definition and operationalization of the 'docility syndrome', and its linking with indigenous teaching contexts, could be important in enhancing teaching and learning anywhere. There are obvious lessons here for Western schooling, where the 'fit' between in-school and out-of-school learning environments seems to be so bad (Resnick, 1987). The suggestion is not, however, that the CHC model of schooling should be used in the West; to a large extent it already is, the design and function of schools being in many respects the same everywhere. The suggestion is rather that Western schools need to become more aligned to the ethos of which they are now a part (see also Resnick, 1987), rather than to use the teaching methods common in Chinese or Japanese schools, and which work precisely because they are part of that Confucian-heritage ethos.

Finally, a systems approach to cross-cultural work seems valuable. Accepting our original contradictions at their face value would have led to erroneous conclusions about the nature of Asian schooling, and the quality of learning for Asian students: errors based on Western misperceptions about what is going on in reality.

REFERENCES

Ausubel, D.P. (1968). *Educational psychology: a cognitive view*. New York: Holt, Rinehart & Winston.

Baker, D.P. (1993). Compared to Japan, the U.S. is a low achiever ... really: new evidence and comment on Westbury. *Educational Researcher, 22*(3), 18-20.

Ballard, B. & Clanchy, J. (1984). *Study abroad: a manual for Asian students*. Kuala Lumpur: Longmans.

Biggs, J.B. (1979). Individual differences in study processes and the quality of learning outcomes. *Higher Education, 8*, 381-394.

Biggs J.B. (1987). *Student approaches to learning and studying*. Hawthorn, Vic.: Australian Council for Educational Research.

Biggs, J. (1990). Asian students' approaches to learning: implications for teaching overseas students. In M. Kratzing (Ed.), *Eighth Australasian Learning and Language Conference* (pp. 1-51). Queensland University of Technology Counselling Services.

Biggs, J. (1991). Approaches to learning in secondary and tertiary students in Hong Kong: some comparative studies. *Educational Research Journal, 6*,

27-39.

Biggs, J.B. (1993a). From theory to practice: a cognitive systems approach. *Higher Education Research and Development, 12*, 73-86.

Biggs, J.B. (1993b). What do inventories of students' learning processes really measure? A theoretical review and clarification. *British Journal of Educational Psychology, 63*, 1-17.

Biggs, J.B. & Moore, P.J. (1993). *The process of learning.* Sydney: Prentice Hall of Australia.

Bourke, S. (1986). How smaller is better: some relationships between class size, teaching practices, and student achievement. *American Educational Research Journal, 23*, 558-571.

Bradley, D. & Bradley, M. (1984). *Problems of Asian students in Australia: language, culture and education.* Canberra: Australian Government Printing Service.

Chan, S.L. (1993). Approaches to learning of medical and economics-low students in a Guangzhou university. University of Hong Kong: M.Ed. Dissertation.

Christensen, C.A., Massey, D. & Isaacs, P. (1991). Cognitive strategies and study habits: an analysis of the measurement of tertiary students' learning. *British Journal of Educational Psychology, 61*, 290-299.

Clifford, M.M. (1986). The comparative effects of strategy and effort attributions. *British Journal of Educational Psychology, 56*, 75-83.

Crooks, T.J. (1988). The impact of classroom evaluation practices on students. *Review of Educational Research, 58*, 438-481.

Driver, R. & Oldham, V. (1986). A constructionist approach to curriculum development in science. *Studies in Science Education, 13*, 105-122.

Flynn, J.F. (1992). *Asian Americans: achievement beyond IQ.* Hillsdale, NJ: Erlbaum.

Garden, R. (1987). The second IEA mathematics study. *Comparative Education Review, 31*, 47-68.

Gardner, H. (1989). *To open minds.* New York: Basic Books.

Geary, D., Liu, F. & Bow-Thomas, C. (1992). Numerical cognition: loci of ability differences comparing children from China and the United States. *Psychological Science, 3*, 180-185.

Ginsberg, E. (1992). Not just a matter of English. *HERDSA News, 14*(1), 6-8.

Hau, K.T. & Salili, F. (1991). Structure and semantic differential placement of specific causes: academic causal attributions by Chinese students in Hong Kong. *International Journal of Psychology, 26*, 175-193.

Hess, R.D. & Azuma, M. (1991). Cultural support for schooling: contrasts between Japan and the United States. *Educational Researcher, 20* (9), 2-8.

Ho, D.Y.F. (1991). Cognitive socialization in Confucian heritage cultures. Paper presented to Workshop on Continuities and Discontinuities in the Cognitive Socialization of Minority Children. US Dept. of Health and

Human Services, Washington, DC, June 29-July 2.

Holloway, S.D. (1988). Concepts of ability and effort in Japan and the US. *Review of Educational Research, 58,* 327-345.

Hoosain, R. (1991). *Psycholinguistic implications for linguistic relativity: a case study of Chinese.* Hillsdale, NJ: Erlbaum.

International Association for the Evaluation of Educational Achievement (IEA) (1988). *Science achievement in seventeen countries: a preliminary report.* Oxford: Pergamon Press.

Johnson, R.K. & Cheung, Y.S. (1991). Reading literacy in Hong Kong in Chinese and English: a preliminary report on the IEA study. Paper read to Annual Conference, Institute of Language in Education, December 15-17, Hong Kong.

Lynn, R. (1987). The intelligence of the Mongoloids: a psychoactive, evolutionary and neurological theory. *Personality and Individual Differences, 8,* 813-844.

Marton, F. & Saljo, R. (1976). On Qualitative Differences in Learning -- I: Outcome and Process, *British Journal of Educational Psychology, 46,* 4-11.

Medrich, E. & Griffith, J. (1992). *International mathematics and science assessments: what have we learned?* US Department of Education, Washington, DC: National Center for Education Statistics.

Miller, C.M.L. & Parlett, M. (1974). *Up to the mark: a study of the examination game.* London: Society for Research into Higher Education.

Morris, P. (1985). Teachers' perceptions of the barriers to the implementation of a pedagogic innovation: a South East Asian case study. *International Review of Education, 31,* 3-18.

Murphy, D. (1987). Offshore education: a Hong Kong perspective. *Australian Universities Review, 30*(2), 43-44.

O'Connor, J.E. (1991). A descriptive analysis of Chinese teachers' thought processes. Paper presented at the Conference on Chinese Education for the 21st Century, Honululu, November 21.

Ramsden, P. (1985). Student learning research: retrospect and prospect. *Higher Education Research and Development, 5*(1), 51-70.

Resnick, L.B. (1987). Learning in school and out. *Educational Researcher, 16*(9), 13-20.

Rushton, J.P. (1989). Evolutionary biology and heritable traits: with reference to Oriental-White-Black differences. Paper presented at the Annual Meeting of the American Association for the Advancement of Science. San Francisco.

Samuelowicz, K. (1987). Learning problems of overseas students: two sides of a story. *Higher Education Research & Development, 6,* 121-134.

Stevenson, H.W. & Stigler, J. (1992). *The learning gap: why our schools are failing and what we can learn from Japanese and Chinese education.* New

York: Summit Books.

Stigler, J. & Stevenson, H.W. (1991). How Asian teachers polish each other to perfection. *American Educator, 15*(1), 12-21 & 43-47.

Sue, S. & Okazaki, S. (1990). Asian-American educational achievements: a phenomenon in search of an explanation. *American Psychologist, 44,* 349-359.

Tang, K.C.C. (1991). *Effects of different assessment procedures on tertiary students' approaches to learning.* university of Hong Kong: Ph.D. Dissertation.

Thomas, P. & Bain, J. (1984). Contextual dependence of learning approaches: the effects of assessment. *Human Learning, 3,* 227-240.

Tobin, K. (1987). The role of wait time. *Review of Educational Research, 57,* 69-95.

Tobin, K. & Fraser, B.J. (1988). Investigations of exemplary practice in high school science and mathematics. *Australian Journal of Education, 32,* 75-94.

Von Bertalanffy, L. (1968). *General systems theory.* New York: Braziller.

Watkins, D.A., Regmi, M. & Astilla, E. (1991). The-Asian-learner-as-rote-learner stereotype: myth or reality? *Educational Psychology, 11,* 21-34.

4

Memorizing and Understanding:
The Keys to the Paradox?

Ference Marton, Gloria Dall'Alba and Tse Lai Kun

In an investigation of student learning in Sweden, Marton and Säljö (1976, 1984) identified two approaches that the students adopted to learning tasks, namely, 'deep and surface approaches'. A deep approach to learning is characterized by a focus on the meaning or message underlying the learning material, on 'what is signified' by the material. In contrast, a surface approach is characterized by a focus on the learning material itself, that is, on 'the sign'. This distinction highlighted a major difference in the ways in which the students carried out the learning task. The approach that the students adopted was shown to be related to what they learned. These two approaches to learning were subsequently identified among students in Australia (Dall'Alba, 1986), Britain (Laurillard, 1978; Ramsden, 1981) and Holland (van Rossum and Schenk, 1984) and were shown to be applicable to a range of types of learning tasks, including reading a passage of text (as in the original study by Marton and Säljö), problem solving, summarizing a text, and carrying out scientific experiments (see also Chapter 1).

Features of learning that are typically associated with deep and surface approaches were used by Biggs (1987a,b) in developing questionnaires to identify how students generally approach their study at both secondary school level (the Learning Process Questionnaire, LPQ) and tertiary level (the Study Process Questionnaire, SPQ). These questionnaires have been used primarily in Australia and Southeast Asia.

Research results obtained with the use of the LPQ and SPQ suggest that students in Hong Kong and a range of other Asian countries at both levels are more orientated to deep and less orientated to surface learning than Australian students at corresponding levels (see Chapters 1 and 3). However, in the interpretation of these results, frequently a surface approach is treated as being characterized by rote learning, while a deep approach is equated with understanding. This interpretation is an oversimplification of Marton and Säljö's original definition. While a surface approach may be associated with rote learning in some contexts, it is not characterized by this form of learning. Rather, a surface approach is characterized by a focus on the learning material or task in itself and not on the meaning or purpose underlying it, as would be the case for the deep approach. In oversimplifying the deep/surface distinction, the results outlined above may not therefore indicate the extent to which rote learning is emphasized by the two groups of students.

The paradox of the Asian learner remains, however. The reason that Asian learners are believed by Westerners to be orientated towards rote learning is due to the notion that the teaching philosophy and practice in Asia (and particularly in Chinese cultures) is directed towards memorization. In Western countries it is believed that memorization does not enhance understanding but, rather, the two are generally considered to be mutually exclusive. Furthermore, studies have shown a positive relationship between a deep approach to learning materials and tasks (or a focus on understanding the underlying meaning) and achievement, but a negative relationship with a surface approach. If it is the case that educational systems in Asian (and particularly Chinese) countries are directed to memorization, how is it possible that Asian students demonstrate such high achievement?

Earlier research has identified conceptions of students' learning in Western countries (Säljö, 1979; Marton, Dall'Alba, and Beaty, 1993). Learning was seen as:

A. Increasing one's knowledge;
B. Memorizing and reproducing;
C. Applying;
D. Understanding;
E. Seeing something in a different way; and
F. Changing as a person.   (Marton, Dall'Alba AND Beaty, 1993, p.283)

Conceptions D to F are concerned with the constitution of meaning, while A to C lack this emphasis. Such an emphasis can be seen to be closely related to a directedness to understanding. Furthermore, conception B is limited to a memorization view of learning. If it is the case that Chinese education is directed to memorization, one might expect a high incidence of this conception among Chinese teachers and students.

This chapter will explore the ways in which learning is understood by a group of Chinese teacher-educators and the extent to which memorization features in these conceptions. It will also examine how this group conceives understanding, memorizing and meaning, with a view to a more adequate solution of the paradox of the Chinese learner.

Method

The present study is part of a large investigation into learning within various cultural contexts. Twenty teacher-educators from all over mainland China travelled to Hong Kong to participate in a course for English language teachers. These teacher-educators agreed to participate in the present study. They were interviewed in Mandarin, their native language, about learning, understanding, memorizing and the teaching-learning relationship, as seen from their perspectives. The interviews were audio-taped and typically took between 50 to 110 minutes. Due to technical faults, two of the interviews and the latter part of a third interview could not be included in the data. Hence 18 teacher-educators made up the final group of subjects, with incomplete data for one of these. Four women and 14 men aged between 32 and 56 years comprised the group.

In order to explore their understanding of the phenomenon of learning, the teacher-educators were asked to give examples of something they had learned and to describe how the learning had taken place. If the examples they offered related to learning in school, they were asked to give further examples related to out-of-school learning, and vice versa. They also described what learning meant for them and how they learned. They compared learning in and out of school. In a similar way, they were asked to give examples of something they had understood in both school and out-of-school contexts. Following this, they discussed memorizing and remembering, then related these ideas to understanding. They then commented upon the extent to which meaning is important in learning and how it relates to knowledge. The teaching-learning relationship was discussed.

The interview questions of particular relevance to this paper were:-

1) Can you tell me about something you have learned?
2) Now, what would you say learning means in general?
3) Can you tell me about something you have understood?
4) What would you say understanding means in general?
5) How do learning and understanding compare?
6) How do we remember things?
7) What about memorizing, how does that compare with understanding?
8) Is it possible to memorize and understand something at the same time?

In the remainder of the interview, the teacher educators read a passage of text that reported the six conceptions of learning that were identified in an earlier study (Marton, Dall'Alba and Beaty, 1993). They described what they understood the passage to be about and how they had read it. They then discussed each of the conceptions of learning (referring to the passage where necessary) and the extent to which their own experience of learning related to the conceptions expressed in the passage.

After the interviews, each teacher educator was invited to transcribe his/her own interview verbatim and translate it into English. All 18 agreed to participate further in this way and received payment for their work. Following the verbatim transcription and translation of the interviews, they were analyzed following the phenomenographic approach. Phenomenography is a research approach that seeks to identify the ways in which phenomena, or aspects of phenomena, are understood or appear to people (Marton, 1986; see also Chapter 1). This approach is based upon the principle of intentionality (described by Husserl, 1970/1901), namely, that experiences such as understanding or perceiving are directed towards something understood or perceived. Accordingly, understanding or perceiving cannot be separated from what is understood or perceived. In phenomenographic studies, phenomena are described as they appear to people, that is, the descriptions are based on what is understood by the phenomena and how they are seen to occur.

The present study is regarded as a broadening of phenomenographic research in the sense that it not only identifies a range of ways in which particular phenomena are understood but it also focuses on aspects of those conceptions in order to address an issue raised from earlier research results. However, this study maintains the phenomenographic tradition as it describes the ways in which selected phenomena are conceived or understood, while addressing the paradox of the Chinese learner.

Results

The results obtained in the present study shed light on the paradox of the Chinese learner. Two principal results that contribute to the solution of this paradox were: (a) Chinese are similar to Europeans in that there is variation in their ways of understanding the phenomena investigated in this study; and (b) Chinese differ from Europeans (at least some of them do) in their ways of understanding these phenomena.

Before describing these results, relationships between learning, memorizing and understanding from an earlier study of conceptions of learning among Western students (Marton, Dall'Alba and Beaty, 1993) will be explored. These relationships will be compared with those identified in the present study. The results will be used in reexamining the paradox of the Chinese learner.

Learning, memorizing and understanding

The relationships between learning, memorizing and understanding that were identified in the earlier study provide a background to the present study. In the earlier study of conceptions of learning (as outlined on p.70), conceptions A, B and C were regarded as being more similar to each other than were conceptions D, E, F on the basis that the latter group focused on the constitution of meaning, while the former group did not. In accordance with conceptions A to C, all the pieces of knowledge that are remembered or memorized make up understanding. In other words, understanding is seen as the sum total of all that is remembered or memorized. Hence, memorizing and understanding are seen not to differ in nature. This view was also expressed by some of the teacher-educators in the present study, as exemplified in the extract below. (Numbers in parentheses indicate transcript and page numbers, while 'I' refers to interviewer and 'T' to teacher-educator.)

I   How do you memorize things?

T   I can still remember when I was in primary school ...(and) our class teacher suddenly fell ill. His facial [expression] was [really] terrible, we were alarmed and scared ... I can't forget it because the impression is so deep ... it is said that memorizing things makes a deep groove in the brain. That accident may have left a deep groove, so I could not forget it forever. Whenever I recalled this in my mind, as I closed my eyes the teacher's ugly face which was crooked and shapeless might appear clearly, because at that time I was given a very deep impression ... But if we read an article, a newspaper, it would not likely give us (a) very deep impression because we are not so upset so we could not remember [it] so well ... (Thus) when the teacher asks us to memorize something which will be tested, we'll have to give ourselves some pressure, try to bear in mind, recite it repeatedly...

I   Do you think that memorizing by force and understanding can take place at the same time?

T   ... if you understand something, really understand it, you will have (a) very strong impression and can memorize it without much effort. (12:11-2)

A view of memorizing and understanding as being essentially the same is not in accordance with conceptions D to F in which memorizing and understanding are seen as being separate, even to the extent that they could occur separately in time. This view of the relationship between memorizing and understanding is illustrated in the following extract, taken from the present study:-

I   Can memorization and understanding occur at the same time?

T   ... it may be like the speed of light. When we turn on the switch, the light is on, there is always some time between. Here I think, if you say understanding and memorization occur simultaneously, I will say either will be earlier. Understanding may come ahead of memorization. It is simple. I understand something, then put the result into memory ... The other case is memorization occurs ahead. That's simple too. That is, something in the past suddenly occurs to you and acts on understanding. (20:10)

The conceptions of learning identified in the earlier study and their relationships to memorizing and understanding are represented in Figure 4.1.

Figure 4.1
Relationship of conceptions of learning, understanding and memorization

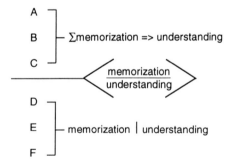

Figure 4.1: Relationship of conceptions of learning, understanding and memorization

While the relationships between learning, memorizing and understanding that were outlined above were also found among some of the teacher-educators in the present study, a new way of considering this relationship was also identified that was not evident in the earlier study. This new relationship was based on a view of understanding and memorizing as being intertwined, that is, of contributing to each other in a developmental sense (See Figure 4.1). The extract below illustrates this view:-

I   How do you generally learn something by heart?

T   The simplest way is repeating over and over again, making ourself remember. I often use this ancient method. Repeating again and again is something like the old saying 'Practice makes perfect' or 'Reading one hundred times the meaning appears'. For example, if I fail to find out (the) general idea or meaning of the paragraph I would read, read for one hundred times ... If you read a poem then the tune will be clearly shown. You have the feeling that you would understand and remember it in the process of enjoyment of beauty and poem. (2:13)

In the phenomenographic spirit, the ways in which memorization and understanding were understood by the Chinese teacher-educators in this study were explored. While some aspects are not dealt with in this chapter (for example, other forms of memorizing), those aspects that contribute to the solution of the paradox of the Asian learner will be described. (The results reported below are based on 17 of the interviews as the relevant section of the eighteenth interview was lost due to a technical fault.)

Memorization

In the previous study of conceptions of learning (Marton, Dall'Alba, and Beaty, 1993), a distinction was made by some of the participants *between* memorization and understanding. While this distinction was also found in the present study, a more prevalent distinction was made *within* memorization. In this study, 10/17 teacher-educators spontaneously distinguished mechanical memorization from memorization with understanding (see Figure 4.2). An additional three made this distinction when questioned by the interviewer about different types of memorizing. These two forms of memorizing are described in the following extract:-

I   What are the relations between them (different kinds of memories)?

T   Mechanical memory means something is memorized through (a) mechanical process, not much thinking or understanding involved. And understanding memory involves thinking in your mind. You try to make clear the relationship between things then remember them. (6:7)

Figure 4.2
Distinguishing forms of memorization

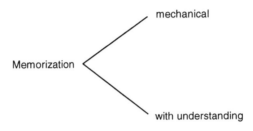

Figure 4.2: Distinguishing forms of memorization

A further distinction was identified within one of these forms of memorization, *viz.*, memorization with understanding (see Figure 4.3). The first form of memorization with understanding involved the notion that we more readily memorize or remember what we understand. This view was expressed in the extract on page 74 from transcript 20. Sixteen of the 17 teacher-educators expressed such a notion. Less common was the second form of memorization with understanding, expressed by seven of the teacher-educators. This form concerned the idea that understanding could be developed through memorization, that is, when we memorize we can deepen our understanding. The extract on page 75 from transcript 2 illustrates this form of memorization with understanding.

Figure 4.3
Distinguishing forms of memorization with understanding

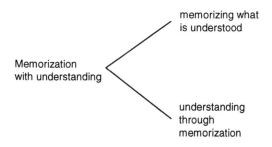

Figure 4.3: Distinguishing forms of memorization with understanding

Understanding

In this study there were two senses in which understanding was described (see Figure 4.4). These are relevant to the paradox of the Chinese learner. The first sense of understanding may be referred to as the S-O form, that is, a subject (S) understands an object (O). This sense of understanding was most frequently expressed by Swedish children and adults in a study of conceptions of understanding (Helmstad and Marton, 1991). The following extract illustrates this sense of understanding:-

I   I'd like you to give (an) example of something you have understood.

T   ... I had the experience in my studying, when I came across the question of the composition and decomposition of force, there was something I couldn't understand in the former texts, I insisted on continuing to read the latter texts. Though the content and some definitions hadn't been taught by the teacher I tried to read through ... When I persevered in finishing reading the whole textbook to the end, all of a sudden, I got it. (14:5)

Figure 4.4
Alternative senses of understanding: Subject-object and temporal

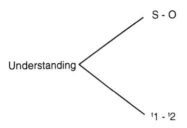

Figure 4.4: Alternative senses of understanding: Subject-object and temporal

The second sense of understanding differed from the first in its strong temporal nature. Understanding was seen to develop from one point in time, t_1, to the next, t_2, and so on. The development of understanding was described as a gradual process, not a distinct or abrupt change at a particular moment in time. This second sense of understanding is illustrated below:-

I   Can you give me one more example ... of understanding?

T   For example, when we had just arrived here, we had some modules like 'Instructional Cycle' and 'Management of Classroom' in the course of methodology. We came across some terms we didn't understand. For example, we didn't know what the term 'application' meant. We usually got confused with such terms. After class we often talked about our problems. We usually couldn't find appropriate definitions of some terms in the dictionary. Through continuous study, having lessons and doing exercises, we gradually came to understand the implications of these terms. (5:6)

Relationships between understanding and memorization with understanding

In Figure 4.3 two forms of memorization with understanding are represented, namely, memorizing what is understood and understanding through memorization. Figure 4.4 shows two senses of understanding, namely, the subject-object (S-O) and the temporal (t_1 - t_2) forms. In Figure 4.5, these two earlier figures are brought together to represent the relationships between understanding and memorization with understanding that this study demonstrated. Where memorization with understanding took the form of memorizing what is understood it parallels the S-O sense of understanding. On the other hand, the notion of developing understanding through memorization implies a temporal sense of understanding.

Figure 4.5
Relationship between understanding and memorization with understanding

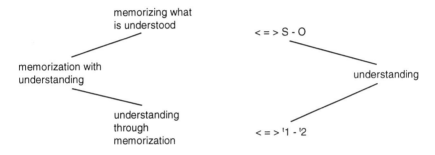

Figure 4.5: Relationship between understanding and memorization with understanding

Relationships between memorization and understanding

In this study different forms of memorization and understanding were identified that relate to the paradox of the Chinese learner. Figure 4.1 shows the general ways in which memorization and understanding relate to conceptions of learning identified previously. In addition, Figure 4.1 includes a new way of considering the relationship between memorization and understanding as being intertwined. In Figure 4.2 mechanical memorization and memorization with understanding are represented as two forms of memorization. The relationship between the senses of understanding and forms of memorization with understanding are represented in Figure 4.5. In Figure 4.6 these various relationships are brought together to illustrate the relationships between understanding and memorization that emerged in the present study. These relationships will be shown to contribute to the solution of the paradox of the Chinese learner.

Figure 4.6

Relationships between forms of memorization and understanding

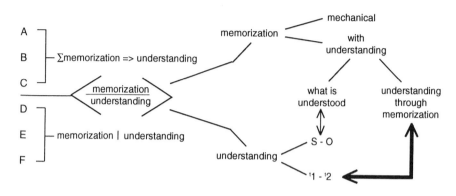

Figure 4.6: Relationships between forms of memorization and understanding

Developing understanding through memorization and repetition

In this paper several forms of memorization and understanding have been outlined and, in so doing, a new way of regarding memorization and understanding as intertwined and enhancing each other has been identified. The extract below indicates how understanding deepens memory:-

I   Is it possible for memory and comprehension to appear at the same time? ...

T   It is possible that the two happen simultaneously. They are closely related. I'll still take the word 'study' for an example. At the beginning I just remember the meaning of the word study through mechanical memory. Then I comprehend the word from the context through reading. I know its different parts of speech, different uses and so on. This helps deepen my memory. So memory and comprehension relate to and promote each other. (5:8)

The question remains, however, about how memorization can facilitate understanding. The data from the present study shed light on this question. In the process of memorizing, the text being memorized is repeated several times which may be suggestive of rote learning. However, seven of the teacher-educators explained that this process of repetition contributes to understanding and can be distinguished from the mechanical memorization that characterizes rote learning. Three of the teacher educators explained how repetition can enhance understanding. The following extract provides such a description:-

I   Do you realize that this is mechanical repetition when you repeat again and again?

T   Mechanical, in fact it is not completely, not exactly. I had no advanced equipments which could help me to remember, or use video-audio, I had to use this method-repeating. During the repetition I felt I could also understand. Yes right. Take an article, I wanted to learn it by heart so I repeated again and again, but I often stopped at a certain place, I had to read it more. Maybe I had some problem, maybe there was something wrong with the (structure) of the article, you would feel as if there was a gap between two sentences. If I had this feeling, so did others, or two or three had the same feeling, that showed it was a difficult point. Maybe the topic changed suddenly, or the connection of the sentences. You should pay more attention to the place. I think the best method is repeating. In the process of repetition, it is not a simple repetition. Because each time I repeat, I would have some new idea of understanding, that is to say I can understand better. (2:14)

It is apparent from the extract above, and similar descriptions in the data from the present study, that when a text is memorized, it can be repeated in a way that deepens understanding; different aspects of the text are focused on with each repetition. The notion of deepening understanding through repetition is not new. In earlier studies (for example, Gruber, 1976; Marton and Wenestam, 1987; Marton et al., 1992) repeated readings of a passage of text were described by some of the participants as bringing about improved understanding. Furthermore, some participants indicated that each time they read the passage, they did so in a different way, focusing on different aspects or reading from a different perspective.

In the process of repeating and memorizing in this way, the meaning of a text is grasped more fully: "In the process of repetition, it is not a simple repetition. Because each time I repeat, I would have some new idea of understanding, that is to say I can understand better." It is upon this use of memorization to deepen understanding that the solution of the paradox of the Chinese learner rests.

Solving the Paradox of the Chinese Learner

In the introduction to this paper the paradox of the Chinese learner was described as arising from previous research. The paradox was presented, as follows: how is it possible that students directed to memorization demonstrate high achievement? Something of a solution to the paradox emerges from the results of the present study.

In Western countries memorization and rote learning are generally equated and it is commonly believed that they do not lead to understanding. A new way of seeing the relationship between memorization and understanding as being intertwined was identified in this study. In addition, a distinction was found 'within' memorization, rather than 'between' memorization and understanding. These results enable us to see that the traditional Asian practice of repetition or memorization can have different purposes. On the one hand, repetition can be associated with mechanical rote learning; on the other hand, memorization can be used to deepen and develop understanding. If memorization is understood in this latter way, the paradox of the Asian learner is solved.

It is noteworthy that researchers from Western cultures have previously assumed an interpretation of memorization that was equated with mechanical rote learning, even when studying learning in Asian cultures. While rote learning is regarded as being characterized by mechanical memorization in the West, such a notion was found not to describe learning practices associated with repetition in the Chinese culture adequately. This study provides the evidence that it is necessary to exercise caution when making assumptions about students' learning methods from other cultures. It is the authors' hope that the results of the present study will help educators to understand more clearly the learning practices of Chinese students. They encourage educators to set aside previous assumptions made about student learning and to explore understandings developed and learning practices with an open mind.

REFERENCES

Biggs, J.B. (1987a). *The learning process questionnaire (LPQ): manual.* Hawthorn: Australian Council for Educational Research.
Biggs, J.B. (1987b). *The study process questionnaire (SPQ): manual.* Hawthorn: Australian Council for Educational Research.
Dall'Alba, G. (1986). Learning strategies and the learner's approach to a problem solving task. *Research in Science Education, 16,* 11-20.
Gruber, H.E. (1976). Creativity and the constructive function of repetition. *Bulletine de Psychologie de la Sorbonne.*
Helmstad, G. & Marton, F. (1991). Conceptions of understanding. Paper

presented at the fourth meeting of the European Association for Research on Learning and Instruction, Turku, Finland.

Husserl, E. (1970/1901). *Logical Investigations Vol.2.* London: Routledge and Kegan Paul. (Translated by J.N. Findlay from the original German version, *Logische Untersuchugen*).

Laurillard, D. (1978). A study of the relationship between some of the cognitive and contextual factors in student learning. Unpublished Ph.D. thesis, University of Surrey.

Marton, F. (1986). Phenomenography - a research approach to investigating different understandings of reality. *Journal of Thought, 21,* 28-49.

Marton, F., Asplund Carlsson, M. & Halász, L. (1992). Differences in understanding and the use of reflective variation in reading. *British Journal of Educational Psychology, 62,* 1-16.

Marton, F., Dall'Alba, G. & Beaty, E. 1993. Conceptions of learning. *International Journal of Educational Research, 19,* 277-300.

Marton, F. & Säljö, R. (1976). On qualitative differences in learning I - outcome and process. *British Journal of Educational Psychology, 46,* 4-11.

Marton, F. & Säljö, R. (1984). Approaches to learning. In Marton, F., Hounsell, D. & Entwistle, N. (eds.), *The experience of learning,* 36-55. Edinburgh: Scottish Academic Press.

Marton, F. & Wenestam, C. (1987). Qualitative differences in retention when a text is read several times. Paper presented at the Second International Conference on Practical Aspects of Memory, University College of Swansea, Swansea, U.K.

Ramsden, P. (1981). A study of the relationship between student learning and its academic context. Unpublished Ph.D. thesis, University of Lancaster, U.K.

Säljö, R. (1979). Learning in the learner's perspective I, Some common-sense conceptions. Reports from the Department of Education, University of Göteborg, No.76.

Van Rossum, E.J. & Schenk, S.M. (1984). The relationship between learning conception, study strategy and learning outcome. *British Journal of Educational Psychology, 54,* 73-83.

5

Accepting Personal Responsibility
for Learning

Farideh Salili

It is now an established finding that students of Asian origin out-perform Westerners academically whether at home or abroad (see also Chapter 3). More Asian students complete secondary school and pursue higher education, as compared with white Americans (Bureau of Census, 1983, 1984). Typically, they perform significantly better than Americans on Scholastic Aptitude Test mathematics (SAT-M) subscores and in science subjects (Sue and Okazaki, 1990). They are also among the top high-performers in cross national studies in both reading and maths (Stevenson and Lee, 1990; Stigler, Lee, Lucker, and Stevenson, 1982).

Various explanations have been proposed for this extraordinary achievement. These include hereditary differences in intelligence (Lynn, 1977; Sowell, 1978) and differences in cultural values (Mordkowitz and Ginsburg, 1987; Stevenson, Lee, and Stigler, 1986). More recently, based on reliable research (i.e. Flynn, 1982; Stevenson et al., 1986), Sue and Okazaki (1990) have presented a convincing argument against an hereditary explanation of Asian achievement and have also downplayed the role of culture. They have proposed, instead, 'relative functionalism' as the likely reason behind the achievement of Asian students in the US. It is argued that education as an important tool for upward mobility assumes an increasingly significant role far and beyond the contribution of culture in situations where there is severe racial discrimination. The minority status of Asians would place them in such a situation in the US. Relative functionalism does not, however, explain why other minority groups, such as African and Mexican Americans, do not benefit from the same phenomenon; nor does it explain the high level of achievement of Asians compared with Westerners in their home countries where they enjoy a majority status.

The present author believes that the cultural values that mediate the achievement orientation of Asian students are of far greater importance than relative functionalism. Students from different cultures are socialized according to different beliefs, values, expectations, and norms. This disparity in socialization practices will lead to different concerns and expectations about achievement, and different success criteria (De Vos, 1973). Students from different cultural backgrounds develop disparate beliefs about causes of success and failure and use different approaches to learning and achievement (Ho, Salili, Biggs and Hau, 1995). These mediators of achievement are important determinants of success and failure. The influence of cultural values, however, should be viewed against other situational and contextual factors that affect achievement. Indeed, the author believes that the phenomenon of relative functionalism is itself influenced by both cultural values and situational factors.

The purpose of this chapter is to examine the achievement orientation and learning characteristics of Chinese students in relation to their sociocultural and educational contexts within the framework of attribution theory. Individual differences (i.e. high versus low achievers) in achievement orientation among Hong Kong students are also explored. An examination of intra-cultural variability would be illuminating since the social contexts of Asian students in Western countries differ drastically from those of their home countries, especially in relation to majority-minority status and in social and cultural values and practices (Sue and Okazaki, 1990).

In the following sections the relevant literature on determinants of achievement among the Chinese, with a special focus on Hong Kong, will be reviewed.

Collectivism in the Chinese Culture

Chinese culture is marked by collectivism, and is centered on obedience and loyalty towards the family. In collectivistic cultures extended families or groups protect their members in exchange for their loyalty. The individual derives his or her identity from the social group rather than his or her own attributes (Hui, 1988). In such cultures, achievement through cooperation and mutual dependence is encouraged (Hofstede, 1980). Increased interdependence among individuals in the group, results in increased mutual obligation among members. They work hard not only to satisfy their own goals but also to meet the goals set by their families or the group to which they belong (Stevenson and Lee, 1990).

A number of studies have revealed this collectivistic characteristic among the Chinese. Domino and Hanah (1987) conducted a content analysis of stories written by Chinese and American students. The Chinese stories revealed a greater orientation to the social world, more concern with ethical and moral rectitude, and other traditional values than their American counterparts.

Feldman and Rosenthal (1991) in a study comparing Hong Kong Chinese, Australian, and American youths on the age at which they expected to achieve autonomy, found that Chinese youths in Hong Kong expected later autonomy than their Western counterparts. They also valued individual success and competence less, and prosocial activities more than Australian and American youths.

In another study aimed at examining cooperative and competitive behaviour of Chinese children in Taiwan and Hong Kong, Li, Cheung, and Kau (1979) asked children to participate in the Madsen Cooperative Board experiment (Madsen, 1971). Unlike American children in the US (Madsen, 1971), older Chinese children were found to be more cooperative under both competitive and cooperative reward conditions (see also Bond and Leung 1982; and Leung and Bond, 1984).

The strong social orientation of the Chinese has far-reaching consequences for their achievement: in the West achievement is defined in terms of individual accomplishment... "to do things as rapidly and/or as well as possible... To master, manipulate and organize physical obstacles and attain a high standard... To excel one's self. To rival and surpass others" (Murray, 1938, p.164). There is evidence to suggest that the conception of success for the Chinese is radically different from that above. Salili and Mak (1988) using the antecedent consequent method (Triandis, 1972), as well as the Cantonese Semantic Differential Scales (Osgood, Miron, and May, 1975), explored the subjective meaning of achievement among secondary school children in Hong Kong. They found that the concept of success was clustered with happy family, academic achievement, career success, and having many friends.

In another large-scale study using British and Chinese secondary school students, Salili (1993) explored cross-cultural differences in the meaning and dimensions of achievement. Subjects had to rate the importance attached to a number of achievement situations. Regardless of culture, four categories of success situations were found, including two affiliative and two individualistic achievement categories. However, for the Chinese, individualistic and affiliative achievement goals were highly and positively correlated, whereas, for the British, the correlation was either negative or approaching zero. That is, for the Chinese, succeeding in academic work, career and other individualistic achievement goals related very closely to succeeding in family and social life, and vice versa, whereas, for the British these two areas of achievement were unrelated.

Similarly, other studies (Blumenthal, 1977; Wilson and Pusey, 1982) have provided evidence that the Chinese place greater importance on family and group goals than on individual goals in achievement and they are concerned about loss or gain of their collective face in their pursuit of achievement. Wilson and Pusey (1982), for example, found that Chinese people with a strong sense of collectivism and face consciousness tend to be more achievement motivated. Yang (1988, cited in Stevenson and Lee, 1990) has described characteristics of Chinese achievement motivation. Firstly, in Chinese culture achievement goals are often described as being for the benefit of the group (e.g. family or state) rather than the individual. Secondly, the standard of achievement is often defined by other people rather than the individual.

The collectivistic culture of the Chinese results in students expending more effort and performing better in cooperative learning contexts (Yu, 1980). This is quite obvious to teachers of Chinese students who witness such learning among their students, particularly at examination time. Empirical studies, have also supported this claim. Gabrenya, Wang, and Latane (1985) explored 'social loafing' among the Chinese. The social loafing phenomena suggests that people usually expend more effort when they work alone, than when they work in a group, where individual performance is obscured. Subjects were Grade 6 to Grade 9 American students in the US and similar aged subjects in Taiwan. It was reported that American subjects showed social loafing, whereas, Chinese exhibited social striving. Chinese students performed better in pairs than alone.

In another study, Yu (1980) compared performance of Chinese students under individual and collective failure situations. It was reported that the individual failure condition did not arouse the need for achievement. The Chinese students responded most favourably under collective situations. It was concluded by Yu (1980), that striving to achieve solely for individualistic purposes was meaningless in the Chinese context.

Socialization for Achievement

Under the influence of Confucian philosophy, Chinese culture emphasizes effort, hard work, and endurance (Yang, 1986). Chinese parents tend to restrict and control the behaviour of their children from the outset, often using harsh disciplinary methods to ensure compliance (Ho, 1981). Children are taught from an early age to work hard, even when the chances of success are low (Hau, 1992). This inherent characteristic is reflected not just in their educational achievement but also in other domains of achievement. Great emphasis is also placed on learning and education, not only as a social ladder but more importantly for building ones' character (Ho, 1981). Hence, Chinese children are socialized to value hard work and excellence in education (Yang, 1986).

Chen (1989) compared Grade 1 to Grade 5 students in the US and China. He found that regardless of grade, Chinese children in general were more concerned about their school work and education than American children. Chinese children liked school more and had more education-related wishes (e.g. books), while American children had more materialistic wishes (e.g. money).

In line with collectivistic values, academic success of the children is "an important source of pride for the entire family and academic failure is a stigma to the family" (Stigler and Smith, 1985, p.1260). Hence, to a certain extent, Chinese students consider school work as a duty towards their parents. Chinese parents on the other hand, are very demanding, hold high achievement expectations of their children (Morkowitz and Ginsburg, 1987; Stevenson and Lee, 1990) and seldom give a positive appraisal of their performance (Hau, 1992).

Salili and Ho (1992) asked a sample of 80 Grade 7 students and their parents to rate their perceived attainment and satisfaction with their own performance in a recent test on Chinese Language as well as their causal attributions of their academic performance. The results revealed that two-thirds of the students had low expectations of their own performance, while their mothers generally had high expectations of their children's achievement. Both students and their mothers were generally dissatisfied with the results of the examination. These findings are also in line with Hess, Chang, and McDevitt's (1987) findings that Chinese mothers usually showed negative feelings about their children's performance because of their high expectations.

In a recent study of secondary school students who had just completed their certificate examination, Salili and Ching (1992) asked subjects to rate the importance of various factors as reasons for working hard. It was found that both high and low achievers rated pleasing parents as the most important reason, followed by career advancement, academic success, and improving oneself, in that order.

Driven by a sense of duty towards their parents, and influenced by cultural values which emphasize hard work and endurance, Chinese students take more personal responsibility for their success and failure. They spend much more time doing homework and drill than their Western counterparts, yet the majority still believe that they can work harder and are not satisfied with their own achievement.

Educational Context

The context of learning is an important determinant of motivation and learning. Studies in the West have revealed a positive relationship between under achievement and poor school conditions (see for example, Coleman, et al. 1966). Similar claims are made about the educational context in Hong Kong.

The Hong Kong school system can be characterized by a high level of discipline, strict teachers and much homework. Besides being important for building one's character, education has a utilitarian function. In Hong Kong, as in other Chinese societies, education is considered a highly important means to a good job and economic prosperity (Llewllyn, *et al.* 1982). Hence, academic success is strongly emphasized, often at the cost of personal development and fulfillment (Hau, 1992). As a result, the authority status of the school is strengthened and schools and educational establishments enjoy a more superior status in Hong Kong than in Western societies which are suffering from a 'bankrupt' curriculum (Lewis and Lovegrove, 1987) as a consequence of high unemployment among school leavers.

Studies conducted have revealed that there is a greater emphasis on academic performance in Hong Kong than in the UK (Morris, 1983; Winter, 1990). Cheung and Lau (1985) in a study of secondary school classroom environment in Hong Kong found that students perceived too much emphasis was placed on completing the classroom task and that their teachers maintained a strict control over the class. The students also reported that their parents paid more attention to achievement-oriented activities and school work than their social and cultural activities. The limited places in higher education have led to competitive examinations and pressure on the students to achieve good results. Students "may have to go through as many as eight sets of competitive examinations in their school years... In addition most schools have examinations at least twice a year, and formal and informal tests at regular intervals (monthly or even weekly)" (Hau, 1992, p.79). In the process many less able students are screened out. Llewellyn and colleagues (1982) pointed out that the 1971 figures showed that of every 1,000 students enrolled in Grade 1, only 55 survived to Grade 13. The situation has greatly improved in recent years, yet the projected figure for 1980 was 130 in Grade 13 out of 1,000 enrolled in Grade 1. In the 1980s only 3% of the secondary school population was able to enter local universities.

The content of the curriculum in Hong Kong is at an unreasonably high standard, particularly that of Grade 12 and Grade 13 level, so that it is often difficult for the average child to survive without help in the form of individual or group tuition. Thus, there is great pressure on children from parents and teachers to do drill work and homework, often at the expense of their social life. The situation has improved in recent years with the expansion of tertiary institution places, but it is still far from those in Western cultures.

An added burden to the students is that the majority at secondary school level have to switch the medium of instruction from Chinese to English, their second language. Hence, there is a danger that students who have insufficient knowledge of the English language, may resort to superficial memorization of important topics in order to cope with the demand of learning in a second language.

According to Wong (1992) the most common way of helping pupils who fall behind in their studies is by making them repeat grades. The Hong Kong Education Department (1990) reported that one-fifth of all students in Form 1 (Grade 7) and one-third in Form 3 (Grade 9) were over-aged.

In this harsh learning environment, many students, especially the less able, are eventually forced to drop out of the school system after repeated failures. Thus, high level of motivation is needed to keep up with such demands. Indeed, Chinese students in Hong Kong, particularly those who survive the education system, tend to be more motivated to achieve academically than their Western counterparts as will be seen in the following section. This is because of the importance attached to education as well as other cultural values (i.e. filial piety and collectivism) and practices as discussed above. Hence, despite pressure to achieve, and the lack of positive reinforcement, Chinese students in general, hold a more positive attitude towards school than their Western counterparts (see Stevenson and Lee, 1990).

Chinese Achievement Orientation

The personality approach to achievement motivation

As discussed earlier, Chinese achievement motivation is more socially based. Achievement only for oneself is considered a sign of immoral and excessive egoism (De Vos, 1973). Thus, families and groups are vicarious partners in the success and failure of the individual. These collectivistic values and practices may well enhance individual achievement striving as was reported by Wilson and Pusey (1982).

Early studies of Asian achievement motivation were based on McClelland and colleagues' (McClelland et al., 1953) Western individualistic conception of achievement, using Western instruments and criteria of success. The results of these early studies, which used content analysis of children's books, and Thematic Apperception Tests (TAT), often labelled Chinese as low in achievement motivation (see for example, McClelland, 1963). Blumenthal (1977), however, reported an increase in achievement-oriented activities among the Chinese in mainland China. Blumenthal, in analyzing the content of children's stories published after the Cultural Revolution, reported:-

"Achievement appeared as a central behaviour in half of the stories. The most frequent behaviour was altruism, and the third was social and personal responsibility. Since achievement was always for the group, rather than personal goals, the three behaviours together indicate a strong emphasis on actions which further the interest of the society as a whole." (p.6357A).

In a more recent study of the Chinese people, Yang (1986), using a self-report inventory, also found a high level of achievement motivation, but that their achievement was more socially based.

In another study, Salili (1993) compared achievement motivation of British and Chinese secondary school students in Hong Kong. Subjects were administered an adapted version of the TAT. Chinese students were found to have a significantly higher level of achievement motivation than their British counterparts. However, similar to the findings by Yang (1986), Chinese achievement motivation was more affiliatively based than those of the British subjects.

The differences between findings of the earlier studies and those of the more recent ones concerning the level of achievement motivation among the Chinese reflect their methodological differences. However, despite their different methods and findings, all these studies have reported that the Chinese achievement motive is collectivistic and socially oriented (see, for example, McClelland, 1963).

Causal attribution for achievement among the Chinese

Studies based on attribution theory, have focused on thoughts, and perceptions of causes of achievement. Judgments made about the causes of achievement are considered to be important mediators of learning and achievement behaviour. Weiner (1979), for example, found that people who scored high on personality measures of achievement were more likely to attribute success to their own ability and effort and were more inclined to attribute their failure to external factors (see Weiner, 1986 for a detailed coverage of attribution theory).

There is now overwhelming evidence from cross-cultural studies to show that cultural factors mediate causal attributions for achievement. In the West, there is a tendency to equate human value with ability to achieve. Hence self-perception of competence becomes the dominant manifestation of self-worth in the classroom context (Covington, cited in Ames and Ames, 1984). Studies in the US have revealed that pupils of all ages, particularly the older students, value ability (Nicholls, 1976) and prefer to achieve by means of ability rather than by effort (Covington and Omelich, 1979). On the other hand, in the face of failure, American students frequently make effort attribution to avoid the threat to their self-worth. At the same time, ability, in American society, is considered to be a given and rather stable attribute (Weiner, 1986).

The Chinese attribute their performance more to internal and controllable factors such as effort and study skills than to ability (Hau and Salili, 1989; Salili, Hwang and Choi, 1989). This reflects the importance of effort and endurance in Chinese culture. Achievement through hard work is more highly valued than achievement through high ability, and attempting tasks beyond one's ability is considered a virtue (Yang, 1986). Ability is considered relatively less important and an attribute that can be acquired or modified through effort (Hau and Salili, 1991). In a study conducted among secondary school children in Hong Kong, Hau and Salili (1990) found that for these children ability was not rated as important as effort, interest in study, study skill or mood as a cause of achievement.

Hess, Chang and McDevitt (1987), comparing families' belief about their children's achievement in China and in America, report a gradual change in attributional pattern among Chinese living in China, Chinese living in America and American Caucasians. Chinese mothers in China attributed their children's failure mainly to a lack of effort, whereas, Chinese mothers in America viewed effort as important, but assigned considerable responsibility to other sources as well. American Caucasians rarely attributed their children's failure to effort.

Similar findings have been replicated in many recent studies among the Chinese in Hong Kong (see Hau, 1992). Emphasis on effort rather than ability is more adaptive as it protects one's self-esteem and minimizes learned helplessness in the face of failure. Hence, Chinese students work harder and spend more time studying than their Western counterparts even in the face of failure.

The above findings on ability and effort attributions should, however, be interpreted with caution. While causal attribution to effort is congruent with the Chinese belief that effort is virtuous, attribution to high ability is in conflict with the Chinese cultural value of modesty. Hence, when subjects attribute success more to effort than ability, they may be engaged in a self-effacing attribution which is a desirable Chinese cultural value. Bond, Leung and Wan (1982) in a study among the Chinese reported that contrary to the findings in the US, where competent people are liked more, Chinese students, making self-effacing attributions were better liked despite their perceived low ability. This is because, self-effacing attribution is in line with Chinese social values as it promotes interpersonal relationship and harmony. Hence, although the findings of the above studies concerning the Chinese attribution style are consistent with informal observations, more rigorous field research using systematic observations is needed to resolve this issue.

Teachers' evaluation of students' performance

Attributional style and cultural practices may have a detrimental effect on students' perception of teachers' evaluative feedback. In the West, praise for effort, which is frequently used to motivate students, is found to have a negative implication for the ability perception of older students (i.e. implying low ability; Meyer, Folks and Weiner, 1976). This is because in the West effort is the primary determinant of reward and punishment. Furthermore, ability and effort, are perceived to have a compensatory (i.e. negative) relationship (see Kelley, 1972; Kukla, 1972). For example, little effort is required of a high-ability person to succeed at an easy task, but with decreasing ability, more effort is needed to succeed at the same task. Thus, successful outcome is rewarded more when the ability is low (implying high-effort expenditure) than when it is high, and failure is punished more when the person involved is perceived to have high ability (Covington and Omelich, 1979; Weiner, et al. 1972).

Chinese teachers, however, seldom use praise and consider it harmful to a child's character if it is given without an outstanding cause. On the other hand, severe discipline is often considered necessary and used in the education of children. Ho (1981) reported that "physical punishment in school such as hitting the pupil's hand is still practiced... Ridicule or shaming of the child, such as making him stand out before his classmates remains a common technique of control" (Ho, 1981, p. 89).

Wong (1992) in a survey of secondary school teachers and students in Hong Kong reported that "banning of corporal punishment (since 1991) remained an isolated attempt to improve the pastoral system. Sanction strategies still operate at the level of 'what fits the crime'. As for incentives, it is usually only service to the school (e.g. monitors, prefects, chairman of clubs and societies) and outstanding achievement (e.g. first in the grade, champions in competitions) that can qualify. They come in the form of merits, certificates and book coupons." (p. 36).

Hence, students seldom receive positive verbal feedback about their performance. In such classroom contexts, students learn from an early age to work hard without any expectation of external reward or praise.

In an attempt to explore Chinese student's perceptions of their teachers' evaluative feedback following success or failure, Salili, Hwang and Choi (1989) replicated Meyer, Folks and Weiner's (1976) German studies in Hong Kong. Subjects were students from tertiary institutions. Following Meyer and colleague's method, subjects were asked to "imagine themselves in a mathematics class solving problems" (p. 119). They were then presented with hypothetical situations in which task difficulty, task outcome and teacher evaluation (neutral for success and failure or praise for success and criticism for failure) were manipulated and asked to rate the teachers' perception of the students' ability and effort. The results supported their findings for effort but not ability. Generally, praise indicated both high ability and high effort, and blame was perceived as an indication of low ability and low effort.

A similar result was found in another study conducted by Salili and Hau (1992) using both scenarios and an actual classroom situation. Subjects were students at different educational levels. The results revealed a developmental trend which showed that effort was an increasingly more important determinant of reward or punishment with age. However, contrary to findings from Western studies, the results revealed that ability and effort were positively correlated. This suggests that, for the Chinese, ability is more controllable and can be increased through high effort (Salili and Hau, 1992).

The above studies suggest that in the adult-oriented and authoritarian education context of Hong Kong, students are less dependent on praise or external reward. Praise, which is given infrequently, may be interpreted differently (i.e. indicating high ability, high effort as well as other virtues) and may have a more motivating effect than in the West, where praise is given frequently, but inconsistently, and often for trivial reasons (Brophy, 1981).

Chinese achievement goals

In recent years, a number of studies (Dweck, 1986; Elliott and Dweck, 1988) in the US have pointed out the importance of achievement goals and reward structures in determining motivation and achievement. Two types of achievement goals have been the focus of research. In one, the learning goal, emphasis is placed on increasing one's competence and mastery of new tasks. In the other, the performance goal, the individual strives to maintain a positive self-judgment by trying to prove his or her competence and superiority. Western studies have revealed that an individual's approach to learning is influenced by his or her achievement goals. Those with learning goals believe in intrinsic value of the task and in learning it through deep understanding. Hence effort and effective strategies are perceived to be important in achieving the goal (Maehr, 1993).

Individuals with performance goals, on the other hand, will focus on competing and outperforming their peers and proving their superior ability (Ames and Archer, 1988). A learning goal results in willingness to work hard and meaningful learning, while a performance goal promotes rote and superficial learning (Dweck and Leggett, 1988).

Achievement goal orientations vary as a function of situational demands and educational context (Ames, 1984). Ames and Archer (1988) found that students who perceived mastery emphasis in the classroom, used more effective strategies in learning, had more positive attitudes towards learning and stressed effort as the cause of their success. Studies have found that cooperative reward structures in the classroom and emphasis on self-improvement rather than social comparison promote learning goals, whereas, competitive settings encourage performance goals (Ames, 1984).

It has been suggested that Chinese students are more concerned with self-improvement and tend to have learning goals (Hess et. al., 1987). However, the competitive and examination oriented educational setting in Hong Kong encourages performance goals. Hau (1992) in three different studies explored learning/performance goal distinctions and causal attributions of Chinese students in Hong Kong across different educational settings. He found that learning goals were highest among elementary and tertiary students and lowest among the secondary school students. This is probably due to the high emphasis which is placed on competitive examinations in secondary schools. The study, also revealed that at all educational levels, effort and study skills were consistently the most important attributions for academic performance, regardless of the level of achievement, thus confirming the previous research findings among the Chinese.

Learning strategies of Chinese students

A closely related and similar line of research has focused on students' approaches to learning, which link students' motives in learning a particular task to the strategies they use. Three approaches to learning: 'deep', 'surface' and 'achieving' approaches, each based on its corresponding motives and strategies have been identified (see Chapter 1).

In Chinese culture, which stresses hard work, effort, and perseverance, one would expect students to adopt a predominantly deep / achieving approach to learning. On the other hand, Hong Kong's competitive and examination oriented education system and expository teaching methods, encourage a surface approach to learning (see Chapter 9). Furthermore, learning in a second language may lead to surface learning as students have to focus only on well-defined but important topics (Kember and Gow, 1989), although Biggs (1989) in comparing Chinese students, who used their second language (English) in learning, with native English speakers, found that the Chinese students scored higher on deep and achieving approaches. In another study of Biggs (1990), Chinese students attending English speaking expatriate schools were compared with students attending Anglo-Chinese schools. The results revealed that secondary students in both types of school scored higher on deep approach measures than the elementary students. In addition, students with experience in the second language were more motivated academically and scored higher in deep and achieving approaches to learning. Biggs (1990) also found that Chinese students in Hong Kong scored higher on deep approach and lower on surface approach measures to learning than Australian students. In this paradoxical situation the relative influence of cultural values and educational context is of interest to researchers.

Kember and Gow (1989) found that tertiary students in Hong Kong used an approach which combined aspects of both deep and surface learning. Apparently students first tried to understand the task and then memorized it. They tended to use tasks that were clearly defined by the teacher. Kember and Gow explained this as a survival strategy: to learn with understanding, but highly focused and selectively, in order to be able to cope with instruction in a second language and cultural values which emphasized respect for authority and teacher.

All these findings underscore the importance of cultural values and situational factors in shaping students' approaches to learning. The findings cast further doubt on the validity of observations made by some educators, portraying Chinese students as rote-learners (see for example, Liu, 1984) who use 'low level cognitive strategies' in learning (also see Chapter 3). Memorizing with prior understanding of a well-defined topic may be the only way to cope with the excessive demands made on Chinese students, in Hong Kong, but may not necessarily lead to surface learning (also see Chapter 9).

In an effort to explore the relationship between causal attributions for achievement, learning strategies, and actual performance, Ho, Salili, Biggs and Hau (1995) conducted a study among high- and low-achieving Chinese secondary students in Hong Kong. It was expected that while the more able students would have the advantage and flexibility to choose between deep and surface approaches, the situation would be quite different for the less able and low achieving students. It was predicted that these students may have no other choice but to engage in surface learning in order to survive in the highly competitive education system of Hong Kong.

The results of this study again confirmed earlier findings that Chinese students in Hong Kong attribute success and failure more to internal than external causes. Following the Western pattern (Weiner, 1986), however, the ratings for internal factors were higher for the success situation. The pattern of attributions were quite similar for success and failure conditions except for a tendency to give more credit to study skills in success and to blame course difficulty more in failure situations (see Table 5.1). In line with previous findings in Hong Kong, effort was perceived as a major determinant of both success and failure, while ability was considered to be relatively unimportant. This suggests that although low achievers see course difficulty as a major obstacle, they are not necessarily affected by a sense of helplessness as they would be if they saw a stable and uncontrollable factor such as ability to be responsible for their failure. Attributing failure to lack of effort and interest in study, lessens the debilitating effects of failure on one's self-esteem. Hence, Hong Kong students have quite adaptive attributional patterns, since effort and study skills, are under one's control. Teacher's help was also rated as relatively important in both success and failure situations, revealing the importance attached to teachers in the Chinese culture.

Table 5.1
Means for causal attributions in ranked order (standard deviations in brackets)

Rank	Success		Failure	
Cause	Cause	Mean	Cause	Mean
1 Effort		5.46 (0.92)	Course difficulty	4.42 (1.30)
2 Teacher's help		4.65 (1.45)	Effort	4.43 (1.34)
3 Study skills		4.56 (1.24)	Interest	4.23 (1.42)
4 Interest		4.36 (1.55)	Teacher's help	4.12 (1.42)
5 Course difficulty		4.06 (1.35)	English instruction	4.09 (1.31)
6 Ability		3.88 (1.47)	Study skills	3.87 (1.30)
7 English instruction		3.29 (1.42)	Ability	3.64 (1.12)
8 Family's help		3.27 (1.63)	Family's help	3.58 (1.52)
9 Luck		2.71 (1.07)	Luck	2.54 (1.13)
Internal cause		18.74 (2.65)		16.85 (3.50)
External causes		14.23 (3.28)		14.00 (3.25)

Source: Ho, Salili, Biggs, and Hau (1995)

With regard to motives and strategies, the results also revealed that the two groups did not differ much in the use of deep motives and strategies. However, high achievers were higher on achieving motive and strategies than low achievers. Low achievers, on the other hand, were higher on surface motives and strategies. This may reflect their respective history of success and failure. The fact that the two groups did not differ on deep strategies but differed on surface and achieving strategies reveals an adaptation to the examination-oriented system (Biggs, 1990), since those students who have a high expectation of success, achieving rather than deep-learning strategy enables them to systematically plan and organize their learning activities to ensure coverage of exam materials. While for those with a low expectation of success, getting a pass is the main goal, hence, the surface strategy is the natural choice.

As expected, the results of this study also showed that internal attributions were more related to deep and achieving approaches, while external attributions were related to a surface approach to learning.

The most interesting finding of this study was concerned with the degree of influence of various factors on the level of actual achievement outcome. Path analysis revealed that the achieving motive was the variable that had the strongest direct relationship, and was mainly responsible for high level achievement. Hence, these results provide support for the hypothesis that success in the competitive education context of Hong Kong depends on a high level of achievement motivation. This implies that ability to organize and plan learning activities is crucial for academic success and should be promoted in any intervention programme.

Conclusion

While the education system in Hong Kong and other Chinese societies is fraught with problems, one cannot ignore the fact that Chinese students in general, perform at a higher level than their Western counterparts. As noted by Stevenson and Stigler (1992), even those Chinese students who failed in their own country, performed at an average level compared with American students in mathematics achievement tests. Similar observations are made in Hong Kong, when underachieving Chinese students are transferred from a Chinese school to an expatriate school or have continued their studies in Western universities because they failed to gain entry into one of Hong Kong's tertiary institutions.[1]

An analysis of Chinese achievement orientation in its sociocultural context would enable us to identify factors that may contribute to the differences between achievement of Asian students and their Western counterparts. These factors are highlighted in the following comparisons:-

"In the Chinese cultural context, achievement orientation is based firmly on collectivistic values rather than individualistic ones. This can have a highly motivating effect on Chinese students because success and failure in a collectivistic culture, affect not just oneself (as in Western cultures) but the whole family or group.

There is a strong belief in hardwork and effort. Effort has a different significance and different interpretation for a Chinese to that of a Westerner. Effort in the service of one's filial duty and for building one's character has moral value and is important in itself. In the Western world, on the other hand, effort is no longer for serving or glorifying God, as the Protestant work ethic once advocated, and often has no other value but to

---

1   The author has lived and worked in Hong Kong for many years. Comments such as this are based on formal and informal evidence gathered in the course of her work. The author would also like to thank Dr G. Blowers for his valuable comments on this chapter.

serve one's egoistic and narrow interests. Hence, even though hardwork and effort are praised, being a 'success' or a 'winner' is more important. In the individualistic and competitive Western climate there is a risk that effort may not serve to increase one's knowledge but may be used in deviant ways in order to outperform others and to achieve success (Spence, 1985)."

In collectivistic cultures individual differences in ability are deemphasized. Ability is perceived as more controllable and can be increased through hard work. Hence, there is less risk to one's self-esteem and of apathy in the face of failure. It is common knowledge in Hong Kong, for example, that students repeat the classes or exams many times when they fail even when they may lack ability. The individualistic competitive conception of achievement in the West, on the other hand, emphasizes the importance of ability which is considered less controllable. Hence, failure that is attributed to low ability in the West, may result in a loss of self-esteem and learned helplessness.

In Chinese societies education is typically both higher in value and in standard (by Western criteria) than in the West. Teachers and parents in the West often make unrealistically positive appraisals of their students' and children's performance and set lower expectations for their achievement. Students, particularly at the elementary level, often pass from one grade to the next regardless of their academic performance (Stevenson and Stigler, 1992). This unrealistically positive evaluation of students' achievement could have negative implication for their ability and undermine their motivation to achieve. Chinese teachers and parents, on the other hand, are too harsh and punitive towards students. They set high standards of achievement and seldom praise them for their accomplishments. While this may enhance their motivation to achieve, it can affect their social and emotional development and mental health as well.

In conclusion, while the West can learn a lot from Chinese cultural values in education, these cultural values as well as the education system are not without their problems. It has long been claimed, for example, that the authoritarian education system among the Chinese, and the pressure for conformity may not be conducive to the development of creative and analytical thinking (Spence, 1985). Hence, even though Chinese students do better than Western students in mathematics and sciences, they are not known for their creativity and original thinking.

REFERENCES

Ames, C. (1984). Achievement attributions and self-instructions in competitive and individualistic goal structures. *Journal of Educational Psychology, 76*, 478-487.

Ames, C. & Ames, R. (1984). Systems of student and teacher motivation. Toward a quantitative definition. *Journal of Educational Psychology, 76*(4), 535-556.

Ames, C. & Archer, J. (1988). Achievement goals in the classroom: students' learning strategies and motivation processes. *Journal of Educational Psychology, 80*(3), 260-267.

Biggs, J.B. (1989). Student's approaches to learning in Anglo-Chinese Schools. *Educational Research Journal* (Hong Kong), *4*, 8-17.

Biggs, J.B. (1990). Effects of language medium of instruction on approaches to learning. *Educational Research Journal* (Hong Kong), *5*, 18-28.

Biggs, J.B. (1992). Learning and schooling in ethnic Chinese: an Asian solution to a Western problem. In S. Lau (Ed.), *Youth and child development in Chinese societies.* Under review.

Blumenthal, E.P. (1977). Models in Chinese moral education: perspective from children's books. *Dissertation Abstracts International, 37*, 6357A-6358A.

Bond, M.H., Leung, K. & Wan, K-C. (1982). How does cultural collectivism operate? The impact of task and maintenance contributions on reward allocation. *Journal of Cross-Cultural Psychology, 13*, 186-200.

Brophy, J. (1981). Teacher praise: a functional analysis. *Review of Educational Research, 51*, 5-32.

Bureau of Census. (1983). *Asian and Pacific Islander population by state: 1980 census of population* (Supplementary report PC80-1-C). Washington, DC: U.S. Department of Commerce.

Bureau of Census. (1984). *Detailed population characteristics: 1980 census of population* (PC80-1-D1-A). Washington, DC: U.S. Department of Commerce.

Chen, C. (1989). A study of Chinese and American children's attitudes towards schooling. *Eric Document.* No. ED. 305 165.

Cheung, P.C. & Lau, S. (1985). Self-esteem: its relationship to the family and school social environments among Chinese adolescents. *Youth and Society, 16*(4), 438-456.

Coleman, J.S., Campbell, E., Hobson, C., McPartland, J., Mood, A., Weinfield, F. & York, R. (1966). *Equality of educational opportunity.* Washington, DC: U.S. Government Printing Office.

Covington, M.V. (1984). The motives for self-worth. In R. Ames & C. Ames (Eds.), *Research on motivation in education: Student motivation* (pp. 77-113). New York Academic Press.

Covington, M.V. & Omelich, C.L. (1979b). Effort: the double-edged sword in school achievement. *Journal of Educational Psychology, 71*,(2), 169-182.

De Vos, G.A. (1973). *Socialization for achievement: essays on the cultural psychology of the Japanese.* Berkeley: University of California Press.

Domino, G. & Hanah, M.T. (1987). A comparative analysis of social values of Chinese and American children. *Journal of Cross-cultural Psychology, 18* (1), 58-77.

Dweck, C.S. (1986). Motivational processes affecting learning. *American Psychologist, 41*(10), 1040-1048.

Dweck, C. & Leggett, E.L. (1988). A social-cognitive approach to motivation and personality. *Psychological Review, 95,* 256-273.

Education Department (1990). *Annual Report 1989-1990.* Hong Kong: Government Printing.

Elliott, E.S. & Dweck, C.S. (1980). Goals: an approach to motivation and achievement. *Journal of Personality and Social Psychology, 37*(4), 621-634.

Feldman, S.S. & Rosenthal, D.A. (1991). Age expectations of behavioural autonomy in Hong Kong, Australian and American youth: the influence of family variables and adolescents' values. *International Journal of Psychology, 26*(1), 1-23.

Flynn, J.R. (1982). Lynn, the Japanese, and environmentalism. *Bulletin of the British Psychological Society, 35,* 409-413.

Gabrenya, W.K. Jr., Wang, Y.E. & Latane, B. (1985). Social loafing on an optimizing task: cross-cultural differences among Chinese and Americans, *Journal of Cross-Cultural Psychology, 16*(2), 223-242.

Hau, K.T. (1992). *Achievement orientation and causal attribution of Chinese students in Hong Kong.* Unpublished Doctoral Dissertation, The University of Hong Kong.

Hau, K.T. & Salili, F. (1989). Attribution of examination results: Chinese primary students in Hong Kong. *Psychologia, 32,* 163-171.

Hau, K.T. & Salili, F. (1990). Examination results attribution, expectancy and achievement goals among Chinese students in Hong Kong. *Educational Studies, 16*(1), 17-31.

Hau, K,T. & Salili, F. (1991). Structure and semantic differential placement of specific causes: academic causal attributions by Chinese students in Hong Kong. *International Journal of Psychology, 26*(2), 175-193.

Hess, R.D., Chang, C.M. & McDevitt, T.M. (1987). Cultural variations in family beliefs about children's performance in mathematics: comparisons among Caucasian-American families. *Journal of Educational Psychology, 79*(2), 179-188.

Ho, D.Y.F. (1981). Traditional pattern of socialization in Chinese society. *Acta Psychologica Taiwanica, 23*(2), 81-95.

Ho, D.Y.F. & Kang, T.K. (1984). Intergenerational comparisons of child-rearing attitudes and practices in Hong Kong. *Developmental Psychology,*

20(6), 1004-1016.

Ho, T.F., Salili, F., Biggs, J.B. & Hau, K.T. (1995). The relationship between causal attributions, learning strategies, and level of achievement: a Hong Kong Chinese study. Unpublished manuscript, The University of Hong Kong.

Hofstede, G. (1980). *Culture's consequences: international differences in work-related values*. Beverly Hills, CA: Sage.

Hui, C.H. (1988). Measurement of individualism-collectivism. *Journal of Research in Personality, 22*, 17-36.

Kelly, H.H. (1972). Causal schemata and the attribution process. In E.E. Jones, D.E. Kanouse, H.H. Kelley, R.E. Nisbett, S. Valins & B. Weiner (Eds.), *Attribution: perceiving the causes of behaviour*. Morristown, NJ: General Learning Press.

Kember, D. & Gow, L. (1989). Cultural specificity of approaches to study. Paper presented at the 6th annual conference of the Hong Kong Educational Research Association.

Kukla, A. (1972). Foundations of an attributional theory of performance. *Psychological Review, 79*, 454-470.

Leung, K. & Bond, M.H. (1984). The impact of cultural collectivism on reward allocation. *Journal of Personality and Social Psychology, 47*(4), 793-804.

Lewis, R. & Lovegrove, M. (1987). What students think of teachers' classroom control techniques: results from four studies. In N. Hastings & J. Schwieso (Eds.), *New directions in educational psychology: 2 behaviour and motivation in the classroom*. New York: The Falmer Press.

Li, M.C., Cheung, S.F. & Kau, S.M. (1979). Competitive and cooperative behavior of Chinese children in Taiwan and Hong Kong. *Acta Psychologica Taiwanica, 21*, 27-33.

Liu, I.M. (1984). *A survey of memorization requirement in Taipei primary and secondary schools*. Unpublished manuscript, National Taiwan University, Taipei.

Llewellyn, J., Hancock, G., Kirst, M. & Roeloffs, K. (1982). *A perspective on education in Hong Kong: report by visiting panel*. Hong Kong Government Printer.

Lynn, R. (1977). The intelligence of the Japanese. *Bulletin of the British Psychological Society, 30*, 69-72.

Madsen, M.C. (1971). Developmental and cross-cultural differences in the cooperative and competitive behavior of young children. *Journal of Cross-Cultural Psychology, 2*, 365-371.

Maehr, M.L. (1993). *Enhancing human development: an emerging theoretical perspective*. Unpublished manuscript, University of Michigan.

Marton, F. & Säljö, R. (1984). Approaches to learning. In Marton et al. (Eds.), *The experience of learning*. Edinburgh: Scottish Academic press.

McClelland, D.C. (1963). Motivational pattern in Southeast Asia with special reference to the Chinese case. *Journal of Social Issues, 19*(1), 6-19.

McClelland, D.C., Atkinson, J., Clark, R. & Lowell, E. (1953). *The achievement motivation*. Glenview, Il: Scott, Foresman.

Meyer, W.U., Folks, V.S. & Weiner, B. (1976). The perceived informational value and affective consequences of choice behavior and intermediate difficulty task selection. *Journal of Research in Personality, 10*, 410-423.

Mordkowitz, E.R. & Ginsburg, H.P. (1987). Early academic socialization of successful Asian-American college students. *Quarterly Newsletter of the Laboratory of Comparative Human Cognition, 9*, 85-91.

Morris, P. (1983). Teachers' perceptions of their pupils: a Hong Kong case study. *Research in Education, 29*, 81-86.

Murphy, D. (1987). Offshore education: a Hong Kong perspective. *Australian University Review, 30*(2), 43-44.

Murray, H.A. (1938). *Explorations in personality*. New York: Oxford University Press.

Nicholls, J.G. (1976). Effort is virtuous, but it's better to have ability: evaluative responses to perceptions of effort and ability. *Journal of Research in Personality, 10*, 306-315.

Osgood, C.E., Miron, M. & May, W.(1975). *Cross-cultural universals of affective meaning*. Urbana: University of Illinois Press.

Salili, F. (1993). *Achievement motivation: a cross-cultural study of British and Chinese motivational pattern*. Unpublished Report. The University of Hong Kong.

Salili, F. (1994). Age, sex, and cultural differences in the meaning and dimensions of achievement. *Personality and Social Psychology Bulletin, 20*(6),648-661.

Salili, F. & Ching, S.L. (1992). Motivation and achievement. Unpublished research report, The University of Hong Kong.

Salili, F. & Hau, K.T. (1992). The effect of teachers' evaluative feedback on Chinese students' perception of ability: a cultural and situational analysis. *Educational Studies, 20*(2), 223-235.

Salili, F. & Ho, W. (1992). Achievement and motivation. Unpublished research report, The University of Hong Kong.

Salili, F., Hwang, C.E. & Choi, N.F. (1989). Teachers' evaluative behavior: the relationship between teachers' comments and perceived ability in Hong Kong. *Journal of Cross-Cultural Psychology, 20*, 115-132.

Salili, F. & Mak, P.H.T. (1988). Subjective meaning of success in high and low achievers. *International Journal of Intercultural Relations, 12*, 125-138.

Sowell, T. (Ed.) (1978). *Essay and data on American ethnic groups*. Washington,, DC: Urban Institute.

Spence, J.T. (1985). Achievement American style: the rewards and costs of individualism. *American Psychologist, 40*(12), 1285-1295.

Stevenson, H.W. & Lee, S. (1990). *Context of achievement*. Monographs of the Society for Research in Child Development, Serial no. 221, Vol. 55, Nos. 1-2.

Stevenson, H.W. & Stigler, J.W. (1992). *The learning gap: why our schools are failing and what we can learn from Japanese and Chinese education*. New York: Summit Books.

Stevenson, H.W., Lee, S. & Stigler, J.W. (1986). Mathematics achievement of Chinese, Japanese, and American children. *Science, 231*, 693-699.

Stigler, J.W., Lee, S.Y., Lucker, G.W. & Stevenson, H.W. (1982). Curriculum and achievement in mathematics: a study of elementary school children in Japan, Taiwan, and United States. *Journal of Educational Psychology, 74*, 315-322.

Stigler, J.W. & Smith, S. (1985). The self-perception of competence by Chinese children. *Child Development, 56*, 1259-1270.

Sue, S. & Okazaki, S. (1990). Asian-American educational achievements: a phenomenon in search of an explanation. *American Psychologist, 45*, 8, 913-920.

Triandis, H.C. (1972). *The analysis of subjective culture*. New York: Wiley.

Weiner, B. (1979). A theory of motivation for some classroom experiences. *Journal of Educational Psychology, 71*(1), 3-25.

Weiner, B. (1986). *An attributional theory of motivation and emotion*. New York: Springler-Verlag.

Weiner, B., Heckhausen, H., Meyer, W. & Cook, R.E. (1972). Causal ascriptions and achievement behavior: the conceptual analysis of effort. *Journal of Personality and Social Psychology, 21*, 239-248.

Wilson, R.W. & Pusey, A.W. (1982). Achievement motivation and small business relationship patterns in Chinese society. In S.L. Greenblatt, R.W. Wilson, & A.A. Wilson (Eds.), *Social interaction in Chinese society*. (pp. 195-208). Praeger.

Winter, S. (1990). Teacher approval and disapproval in Hong Kong secondary school classrooms. *British Journal of Educational Psychology, 60*, 88-92.

Wong, O.H.F. (1992). *Perceived effectiveness of rewards and punishment by secondary school students*. Unpublished Master's dissertation, Psychology Department, The University of Hong Kong.

Yang, K.S. (1986). Chinese personality and its change. In M.H., Bond (Ed.), *The psychology of the Chinese people*. Hong Kong: Oxford University Press.

Yang, K.S. (Ed.) (1988). *Chinese people's Psychology*. Taipei: Gwei Gwan Tu Shu. (In Chinese).

Yu, S.H. (1980). Chinese collective orientation and need for achievement. *The International Journal of Social Psychiatry, 26*(3), 184-189.

6

Hong Kong Secondary School Learners: a Developmental Perspective

David Watkins

Other chapters in this book have highlighted the role of personal factors (such as locus of control, Chapter 5, and conceptions of learning, Chapter 4) and cultural and contextual factors (such as Chinese values, Chapter 2, the language of instruction, Chapter 7, and the assessment system, Chapter 9) on the approaches to learning adopted by Hong Kong students. However, those chapters have looked at these aspects in relative isolation from each other, whereas it is argued in Chapters 1 and 3 that to fully understand how students learn we need to adopt a system's model linking personal, cultural and contextual factors with the strategies utilized and the outcomes achieved on a particular learning task. Such a model is a dynamic, recursive one which to investigate adequately needs a developmental perspective where causal interrelationships can be probed. Once again both quantitative and qualitative approaches to such research are possible. To test the validity of competing, complex causal models computer programmes such as LISREL (Joreskog and Sorbom, 1984) can be utilized (see, for example, Reynolds and Walberg, 1992). Alternatively, (or better, in conjunction) in-depth interviews can be conducted which probe significant components of the system's model and their interrelationships from a developmental perspective. It is this second approach that is utilized here.

In any such study of change it is preferable to analyze longitudinal data where the same subjects are followed up over, say, the duration of their under-graduate studies (e.g. Watkins and Hattie, 1985). However, due to the realities of time and financial resources, it is not uncommon to attempt such analyses with cross-sectional data where the time element is inferred by comparing the responses subjects of different ages. The danger of such research is that inferences about change within subjects may actually be due to differences between subjects (contrary to the basic assumption of this approach, the cohorts may differ from each other at the same age). In this chapter developmental aspects of student learning will be inferred by comparing the views of students in junior (first to third) and senior (fourth to sixth) years of secondary schooling. However, it was possible to trace such development at an individual level (at least as seen in historical perspective by the subjects themselves) by probing how each subject perceived the changes in their approach to learning and its causes as they progressed through primary and secondary schooling. It was hoped that the developmental perspective of this investigation would add a needed dimension to our understanding of the paradoxes surrounding the Chinese learner, in particular the role of memorization.

Method

The present study was conducted in the context of a part-time MEd (Psychology of Student Learning) course unit on qualitative research methods taught by the writer in conjunction with three other contributors to this book at the University of Hong Kong[1]. The participants in this course were all experienced teachers and had a background knowledge of the student learning literature from earlier graduate courses. As part of the course unit students were taught how to conduct the type of interview required, which they then practised through role play and pilot interviews. It was emphasized that while they should ask all of the questions on the interview schedule at some time, the vital part of the interview was the follow-up probing of the answers provided. In particular, the prospective interviewers were instructed to listen carefully to the words used by each interviewee and then to probe further by asking the subjects to reflect once again on the meanings and give examples of the most salient concepts they had voiced.

The full interview schedule is shown in Appendix 1, but the questionnaires' main focus was: to ask the subjects to describe their approach to a recent learning task; to assess whether that approach was typical; to decide what factors might affect their approach; to identify whether (and if so why) their approach had changed from their earlier years of schooling; to describe

---

1   The MEd unit on qualitative research methods was taught by the writer with three lectures on interview technique being presented by Dr Tang and Professor Biggs. The interview assignment which was the focus of the unit was planned by the three of us in collaboration with Professor Marton.

their own, and their teachers conceptions of learning and understanding; and to establish their attributions for their academic successes and failures.

Each member of the MEd class was asked to interview four pupils from Hong Kong Anglo-Chinese secondary schools typical of the public secondary schooling in Hong Kong. It was emphasized that the pupils should if possible be in either junior or senior years of study and that the overall sample should be reasonably balanced for academic ability and gender. The final sample consisted of 20 junior (including one third year) and 24 senior year pupils, of whom 20 were males and 24 females and 21, 12, and 11 were high-, medium-, and low-academic achievers, respectively.

The interview schedule questions were discussed with the prospective interviewers who then formulated a Cantonese version of these questions (with advice from Dr Catherine Tang). The interviews were conducted during the school day, audio-taped, and usually lasted between 25 to 45 minutes. Each interview was transcribed verbatim and translated into English by Dr Tang. Each transcript was analyzed independently in terms of the approach to and conception of learning (see Chapter 6) espoused by the student, Dr Tang and the writer (with an 80% + level of agreement). The transcripts were also analyzed from the phenomenographic perspective with emphasis on the structural components of the conceptions of learning and understanding voiced by the students (see Marton, Watkins, and Tang, 1995). In addition, the transcripts were analyzed by the writer with emphasis on developmental differences and consistencies across the subjects' approach to and conceptions of learning. This latter analysis forms the data reported in this chapter.

Results

There appeared to be three clearcut stages which the students seemed to have reached or to have passed through.

Stage one: the intention is to achieve through reproduction: the strategy is to rote learn everything

Students tended to report this view of learning in primary and/or junior secondary years. A surface-level approach to learning and quantitative conceptions of learning, such as expressed by the following students, predominate. Below and in the remainder of this chapter the code number and the form of the students are shown in parentheses while the interviewer's questions are designated by 'I' and the subjects' responses by 'S':-

I: How has your approach to learning changed since primary school?
S: I feel I have to study earlier .... remember every detail. (Pa2, Form

1 student).

S: I do not think there is any subject that I do not have to rote learn.
I: What do you mean by learning?
S: I have to pay attention in class, study, and do the exercises. (Pa4,
     Form 1 student).

Learning at this level is strongly affected by both the assessment system
and the language of instruction. At primary/junior secondary level the students
perceive the assessment system as rewarding reproduction:-

S: In primary school I just looked at the book and memorized as much
     as I could. In secondary school, I think that I know that only looking
     at the book is not enough and I have to know the explanation. (He2,
     Form 5).
S: Our own answers would not be correct. We still have to copy them
     from the teacher. (To3, Form 1).
S: In primary school understanding was not enough to achieve results.
     I had to rote learn as well. (Be1, Form 1).

This is exacerbated in many cases as the students have difficulty with the
transition from Chinese to English as the language of instruction as indicated
in the following comments:-

S: I came from a Chinese primary school and I could not understand in
     Form 1 as the instruction was in English, so I just rote learned and
     forced everything into the brain and did not care if I understood or
     not. (Am1, Form 5).
S: .... We are taught in English now and I find it easier to understand
     and absorb it if taught in Chinese. (Tw1, Form 4).

The students' conceptions of understanding at this level tended to be very
basic, often at the word level because of difficulties with English language:-

S: Understanding is to know a word that I did not know before either
     from the teacher or from looking at the dictionary, remember it
     always, and be able to use it in a test. (Pa3, Form 1).
S: (Understanding) is to know the meaning. If the teacher says one
     word, we will know the meaning of that word. (Da2, Form 1).
S: (Understanding) means we have to know the things the teachers teach
     us. (Am4, Form 1).

The above three comments are also typical of this stage in that it is the teachers who decide virtually all of what is to be learnt. Attributions at this level are typically to the effort put into memorizing.

Stage two: the intention is to achieve through rote learning important things

Typically, the students interviewed typically soon found that as they progressed through secondary school the pressure to reproduce was still there, but that the memory load was such that they needed to be selective about what they had to memorize. Initially they tended to follow their teachers' advice about what were the most salient points, but later the more able learned to select the things worth remembering themselves:-

> S: Many of the subjects in the lower forms require rote learning in answering the tests, the questions can be exactly the same as those in the exercises or workbooks .... (Now) There is so much to learn .... you must rely on your teacher. (Ed1, Form 6).
>
> S: In primary school I mainly rote learned. The teachers always asked us to do dictations and copying from the books. It was more spoon feeding .... (I) select those which are important for the test. (Now) you cannot rote learn and remember so many things. (Be3, Form 4).
>
> S: I will rote learn the things that I find useful. (Ce1, Form 6).

Rote learning is also utilized at this stage because of problems with the use of English in examinations:

> S: I read the test syllabus once, underlined the special words, and then learned the spelling of those words. (Be4, Form 4).
>
> S: If you do not rote learn the passage then you cannot know how to write the things out, you may not know how to write some of the words. You may know them in Chinese but not in English. (Fl1, Form 2).

Because of this English language production problem these students report utilizing rote learning, or at least memorizing, more for essay rather than multiple choice tests; a reversal of the typical findings in Western countries (see, for example, Watkins, 1984):-

> S: If it is an essay, I will study and rote learn. (Ed4, Form 6).
>
> S: I have to memorize more for essays. (Al4, Form 1).

Stage three: the intention is achievement through reproduction: the strategy is to understand first

Many of these students faced by the increasing memory load realize that their memorizing capacity is enhanced by understanding the material. Of course, it is well known to learning researchers that retention in long-term memory is aided through chunking, use of advanced organizers, etc. (Biggs and Telfer, 1987). As four of the students we interviewed commented:-

> S: I try to understand as much as possible. It is difficult to rote learn if I do not understand. (Ce1, Form 6).
> S: Some of my classmates asked me after the test how I managed to remember as they could not reproduce the things. I told them that one had to understand. I understood so I was able to reproduce the things in the test. (To1, Form 4).
> S: Sometimes you cannot rote learn as there are too many things. I will have to understand and then write out. (Ce4, Form 5).
> S: They (the teachers) always ask us to rote learn at home. But I feel that you do not have to rote learn all the time. It is the same if you understand and then write it out. (Tw1, Form 4).

The above comments were typical of the majority of the more senior secondary school students interviewed. They learned to appreciate the value of understanding but as a tool for reproduction. Their 'understanding' was incidental to their objective of reproducing model answers to achieve good grades.

Whereas in primary and junior secondary classes examination questions tended to be fact-oriented and predictable, encouraging rote learning without understanding, several of the senior students interviewed indicated that a change in the type of questions asked encouraged them to adopt a more flexible approach to learning:-

> S: One cannot rely on rote learning. Because (now) there are many different ways of asking the questions. (Be3, Form 4).
> S: The other thing is the difference in the ways questions are being asked now. They are not so straight forward, they require you to understand before you can answer. (Ed1, Form 6).

But some of the students who were trying to adopt a deeper level approach to adjust to the changing assessment requirement still seemed to want to rote learn:-

S: The questions now are not directly from the books, they require us to understand and explain .... It is my disability that I cannot rote learn. I will rote learn if I can. (Fl3, Form 2).

S: I find that I could not rote memorize as I did in School Certificate. I am lazy. (Ed4, Form 6).

Students at this level were no longer so dependent on the teacher and had accepted responsibility for their own learning:-

S: Learning depends on yourself. If you do not learn yourself you will not know even if people teach you. (Ce3, Form 3).

S: (In Form 1) I only studied those things which the teachers said were very important. As I am older, I start to actively read more books .... I try to look up books myself or ask the teachers to recommend books. (Cel, Form 6).

At earlier levels students perceived little difference in the nature of each subject except for the quantity of memorizing and effort required. But at this level, because they were thinking more independently, they were becoming more aware of the cognitive requirements of various subjects:-

S: In studying for a test in Chinese I will start with the text. You have to understand the content first, why the author wrote such a passage before you can understand the other information in the notes. This approach seems to be opposite to that for Economics which requires understanding in class first. (Ed1, Form 6).

S: Biology is more factual and there are more things to memorize. Maths requires thinking. (Am1, Form 5).

Stage four: the intention is both to understand and achieve and the strategy is to understand or to combine understanding and memorizing

Although a number of the Chinese teachers interviewed by Marton and colleagues (see Chapter 4) who had reached this stage seemed to be combining understanding and memorizing, the writer is not convinced that any of the students interviewed adopted this strategy. Rather the few, perhaps three students, who had passed the Stage Three level and appreciated the value of understanding for its own sake seemed to reject the memorizing (or at least the rote learning) forced upon them by the assessment system and course content:-

S: We are always told that we should not rote learn for History, but we will surely not get good results in the test if we do not rote learn.

This is the problem of the education system .... I still think the most important thing is to understand but you still have to remember some of the things and have to revise again before the tests. Sometimes you will have to memorize the formulae but you still have to understand how these formulae come about.

For Chinese, we are given many School Certificate questions with answers. I will study those questions and rote learn the answers as we know that the teacher will set the same questions, so we have to memorize. I know I should not do that, but I do it in order to get high marks. (Al1, Form 4).

S: I think to rote learn is a disgrace to myself because I am spoon-fed and have been deprived of my right to understand .... In Chemistry there is a set of texts which if you rote learn then you will be all right. They only give you the graph, ask you to memorize it, and then test you on the same thing. They do not tell you how that graph has been derived. I personally do not like that. I think knowing the basic theory can enable me to derive other things and I will be very happy if I could connect the things. (Fl4, Form 6).

S: If I have to study for the sake of tests then I would rather not study .... It is still learning but rote learning rather than really learning something (where "you have to understand"). (Be3, Form 4).

Conclusions

The aim of this chapter is to try to add a developmental perspective to our understanding of the Hong Kong learner. The findings are summarized here in a tentative model, linking the stages of approach to learning which the students appear to pass through, and personal and context variables which seem to be plausibly related to these stages (see Table 6.1).

The Stage One level, as identified in this study, is consistent with the literature on Chinese education practices. According to Liu (1986) two of the guiding behavioural rules for Chinese societies are that the best way to acquire knowledge is to memorize it, and that the best way to acquire a skill is to practice it repeatedly. Thus even at pre-school Chinese, unlike American and Japanese, students focus on academic subjects that emphasize memorization and group recitation (Tobin, Wu, and Davidson, 1989). This emphasis continues at primary and junior secondary school levels. Liu (1986) reported how in Taiwan teachers at these levels required their pupils to memorize every lesson in their Chinese language texts. With all this practice, Chinese students develop skills in memorizing that Western students do not. Such skills are thought to account in part for the superior performance of Chinese pupils even at higher conceptual levels in mathematics (Geary, Fan, and Bow-Thomas, 1992).

Table 6.1
Tentative stage model linking learning intention and strategy with personal
and context variables

Stage	Intention	Strategy	Assessment	Locus	Metacog-nitive level	Workload
1	Achievement through reproduction	Rote memorizing	Rewards reproduction	Teacher dependent	Low	Reasonable
2	Achievement through reproduction	Rote learn important things	Rewards reproduction	a) Teacher dependent b) Self-selections	Low	Too much to rote learn
3	Achievement through reproduction	Understand then memorize	More flexible exam questions	Self	Medium-high	Still increasing
4	Understanding and achievement	Combines understanding and memorizing OR focuses on understanding	More flexible exam questions	Self	High	Still increasing

However, as the Hong Kong students advanced through the early years of secondary school they typically realized that, while reproduction of model answers was still rewarded in examinations, the amount to be learned was becoming excessive. So at the Stage Two level they first relied on their teachers' advice about what were the most important facts to rote learn but later the more able began to choose the points worth remembering themselves. This transition (from teacher- to self-reliance) is probably an important one, as it signifies an early stage of metacognition where the student is starting to become responsible for his or her own learning.

At the Stage Three level, reached by virtually all the senior students in this study, the students were combining memorizing and understanding as reported by Marton and colleagues (see Chapter 4). Thus the writer believes that qualitative research reported in these two studies has satisfactorily solved the apparent contradictions referred to as 'the paradox of the Asian Learner' (at least in the case of Chinese and probably Japanese heritage students). Many Asian students combine the processes of memorizing and understanding in ways not commonly found with Western students.

Indeed, these processes appear to be seen as almost mutually exclusive in the eyes of some Western educators (see, for instance, Iran-Nejad, 1990). Independent qualitative investigations of learners from China, Hong Kong, and the eyes of some Western educators (see, for instance, Iran-Nejad, 1990). Independent qualitative investigations of learners from China, Hong Kong, and Japan found evidence of 'deep-memorizing' (K. Tang, 1991); a narrow-deep approach characterized by the sequence 'understand-memorize-understand-memorize ....' (Kember and Gow, 1990); understanding-through-memorization (see Chapter 4) of an elaborative surface approach (T. Tang, 1991); and that repetition is a route to understanding (Hess and Azuma, 1991).

Combined with the cultural belief that the words of authorities should not be altered and the problems of expressing their answers in English, virtually a foreign language to them, Chinese students reproduce the words in texts and lecture notes. Not surprisingly this appears to their Western teachers as mere mechanical rote learning, but in self-report questionnaires and in-depth interviews the role of understanding comes through. But the writer is unable to assess the extent to which these students' intention is to memorize through understanding or to understand through memorizing. This may not make much difference to the immediate learning outcome, but may have a marked affect in later situations where the quantity of learning is not a problem. Have they really appreciated the value of understanding for its own sake?

As in the 3P Model of Learning (see Chapters 1 and 3) it is emphasized that the model described in Table 6.1 is a complex, multivariate causal system and that changes to just one factor such as the assessment system is likely to be necessary but not sufficient to bring about changes in approach to learning. Of course, there may well be other factors not considered here which play a vital role. In Hong Kong, problems with English as the language of instruction influence many students to rote learn at least at early secondary level. Maturation in terms of cognitive development from concrete to formal operations (Piaget, 1964) is another factor which may affect the approach to learning of which a student is capable at the primary and junior secondary level. Self-esteem is another factor which has been shown to be consistently related to academic achievement (Hansford and Hattie, 1982). It is likely that a minimum level of self-esteem must be attained before the student has the confidence to accept responsibility for his or her own learning. Only some of these factors are clearly in the hands of the teacher to influence. How the classroom teacher can establish a learning environment which will maximize the likelihood of a student adopting a deeper level approach to learning is discussed by Biggs and Watkins (1995; see also Chapter 3).

REFERENCES

Biggs, J.B. & Telfer, R. (1987). *The process of learning.* Sydney: Prentice Hall.
Biggs, J.B. & Watkins, D. (1995). *Classroom learning: educational psychology*

for the Asian teacher. Prentice Hall: Singapore.

Geary, D.C., Fan, L. & Bow-Thomas, C. (1992). Numerical cognition: loci of ability differences comparing children from China and the United States. *Psychological Science, 3,* 180-185.

Hansford, B.C. & Hattie, J.A. (1982). The relationship between self and achievement/performance measures. *Review of Educational Research, 52,* 123-142.

Hess, R.D. & Azuma, M. (1991). Cultural support for schooling: contrasts between Japan and the United States. *Educational Researcher, 20,* 2-8.

Iran-Nejad, A. (1990). Academic and dynamic self-regulation of learning processes. *Review of Educational Research, 60,* 573-602.

Joreskog, K.G. & Sorbom, D. (1984). *LISREL: analysis of linear structural relationships by the method of maximum likelihood.* Chicago, Illinois: SPSS.

Kember, D. & Gow, L. (1990). Cultural specificity of approaches to study. *British Journal of Educational Psychology, 60,* 356-363.

Liu, I.M. (1986). Chinese cognition. In Bond, M.H. (Ed.), *The psychology of the Chinese people.* Hong Kong: Oxford University Press.

Marton, F., Watkins, D. & Tang, C. (1995). Discontinuities and continuities in the experience of learning. Paper presented at the 6th European Conference for Research on Learning and Instruction, Nijmegen, The Netherlands, August.

Piaget, J. (1964). Developmental learning. In Ripple, R.E. & Rockcastle, V.N. (Eds.), *Piaget rediscovered.* Ithaca: Cornell University.

Reynolds, A.J. & Walberg, H.J. (1992). A structural model of science achievement and attitude. *Journal of Educational Psychology, 84,* 371-382.

Tang, K.C.C. (1991). Effects of different assessment methods on tertiary students' approaches to studying. Unpublished PhD thesis, The University of Hong Kong.

Tang, T.Y.H. (1991). Students' perceptions of the learning context and their effects on students' approaches to learning - a phenomenographic study. Unpublished MEd dissertation, The University of Hong Kong.

Tobin, J.J., Wu, D.Y.H. & Davidson, D.H. (1991). *Preschoolers in three cultures: Japan, China, and the United States.* New Haven, CT: Yale University Press.

Watkins, D. (1984). Student perception of factors influencing tertiary learning. *Higher Education Research and Development, 3,* 33-50.

Watkins, D. & Hattie, J. (1985). A longitudinal study of the approaches to learning of Australian tertiary students. *Human Learning, 4,* 127-141.

APPENDIX: INTERVIEW SCHEDULE

Part I: Introduction

1(a)   How are you enjoying your first term at school? For instance, what do you like best about your studies this term?

(b)   And what do you like least?

Part II: Actual Task

(The student was asked to be prepared to talk about a test or essay he/she had done recently for his/her class.)

2.   Can you tell me about the task? (Expand)

3.   How did you go about it exactly? For instance, what did you do first?

4.   What did you do next?

5.   Was any part difficult? Why? How did you tackle the problem(s)?

Part III: General Questions

6.   You have told me how you went about studying one particular task. Would that be typical of the way you study?

7.   What sort of things affect your approach to learning? (Expand)

8.   Would you change your approach:-

(a)   For different subjects?

(b)   If you are taught by a different teacher?

(c)   If you are faced with a different assessment method (e.g. a multiple choice test or an essay)?

(d)   If you are really interested in the topic?

Ask for examples of (a) - (c).

Part IV: Conceptions and Approaches to Learning

9.   What do you mean by the word 'learning'?

10.   What do you think your teachers mean by 'learning'?

11.   What do you mean by the word 'understanding'? Could you give me an example?

12.   Do you think your approach to learning has changed from first year (primary school)? If 'yes', in what way? Why do you think you have changed?

Part V: Language of Instruction

13(a) The test/essay you described earlier. Was the teaching/text book in English?
  (b) What language do you prefer to be taught in? Why?
  (c) What language do you think in when your studying? (Expand).

Part VI: Attributions

14. How satisfied are you with your results in this test? (ask about a recent test result).
15. What factors do you think contributed to this result?
16. Are these the same factors which influenced the grades you have gained for other tests? (Explain).
17. Do you think that you can control these factors? (Explain).

COPING WITH THE CONTEXT
OF LEARNING

7

Coping with Second Language Texts: the Development of Lexically-Based Reading Strategies

Robert Keith Johnson and Agnes Yau So Ngor

Introduction

This chapter presents and discusses the strategies that Hong Kong students use when dealing with English texts. It describes a particular approach to text processing, identified here as 'lexical' processing. It is argued that this approach derives from the language teaching practices adopted in Hong Kong and has negative consequences for the students' overall English language development, as well as for their ability to establish the meaning of texts. While discussion and data are limited to the Hong Kong context, it seems likely that such approaches could be developed in any educational context in which reading in a second language is heavily emphasized within the teaching and learning programme, and where productive skills (speaking and writing) are neglected. This chapter reports research into the reading strategies developed by Hong Kong students, and attempts to link these findings to the general pattern of language acquisition amongst Hong Kong students. In so doing, we enter a major controversy within language acquisition theory regarding the roles and relative importance of input and output in language development.

Second language (L2) acquisition theory throughout the 1980s was dominated by Krashen's 'Input Hypothesis' (Krashen, 1982). In broad terms Krashen takes the intuitively attractive position that language acquisition results from exposure to the target language in contexts where it is being used purposefully and meaningfully. He claims that the optimal input for acquisition is language which is slightly in advance of the level of proficiency already achieved by the learner, i.e. close enough to ensure understanding while offering opportunities for further language development. While the general role and importance of input has not been challenged, specific features of Krashen's theory have been questioned. The criticisms most relevant to this paper concern Krashen's emphasis on input, and neglect of the roles of interaction and output in language acquisition. A number of researchers have argued that interaction is important because of its function in negotiating meaning and thus ensuring the comprehensibility of input (Ellis, 1991; Pica et al, 1989; White, 1987). Swain (1985, 1990) focused explicitly upon output, claiming that active, productive language use by the learner plays an important role in acquisition in its own right, and is essential for the development of grammatical competence.

As Swain notes, Krashen accepted that grammatical competence may not always be utilized in processing input:-

"In many cases we do not utilize syntax in understanding - we often get the message with a combination of vocabulary or lexical information plus extra-linguistic information." (Krashen, 1982, p.66).

If syntax, or more broadly grammar, need not be utilized as part of the process of comprehending input, then it follows that the development of grammatical competence may be retarded if comprehensible input is the major or only form of exposure to the language. Krashen's position is, presumably, that the cases he describes would not occur sufficiently frequently to have any negative effect on the acquisition of grammar. Swain's position is that without the need to generate output, which demands grammatical competence, there may be little incentive for a learner to focus upon grammatical aspects of input. As supporting evidence, Swain refers to studies of French immersion programmes in Canada which show that, after several years of comprehensible input in French, students' comprehension skills approach or are equivalent to those of native speakers, while speaking and writing skills are considerably less advanced.

Rather more than in Canadian immersion programmes, English medium schools in Hong Kong have placed their emphasis upon input and in particular on reading. Large classes and a traditional teacher-centred approach limit the opportunities for students to speak English in the classroom, and there is little or no opportunity or incentive for them to do so outside the classroom. Teachers make considerable use of Cantonese and a mixed code of Cantonese and English terms (Johnson, 1983; Johnson et al, 1991) and students' exposure to spoken English is therefore limited. Writing has also tended to receive limited attention. The public examinations and examinations within the schools place little value on writing skills. Either writing is not required, because multiple-choice or other objective types of testing are used, or, where writing is required, markers look solely for evidence of factual knowledge, ignoring grammatical accuracy and presentation (Johnson, 1994). In Hong Kong, where examiners lead, teachers are quick to follow, but the large classes and the potential burden of marking might be sufficient in themselves to deter teachers from setting more writing tasks and showing a greater concern with students' accuracy. Reading is the one skill area in which no compromise or evasion is possible. The textbooks and examination papers are in English, and students succeed or fail academically primarily through their ability to deal with these texts.

The expression 'dealing with texts' was used rather than 'getting meaning out of texts' or even 'reading' to make a point. When Hong Kong students move from Chinese medium primary to English medium secondary education, there is a gap between the level of proficiency students have and the level they need in order to be able to follow the curriculum through English. As a result, students develop strategies for dealing with texts too advanced for their level of proficiency. Amongst students with low ability or little motivation, these tend to be 'survival' strategies; ways of completing tasks with only a superficial understanding of the text content. At the other extreme, able, well motivated students develop sophisticated problem-solving strategies. In their case it is appropriate to describe this process as 'getting meaning out of texts', since this is their aim, though the meaning obtained may not be the one intended by the writer.

A reader using lexical processing focuses primarily upon the meaning of the content words in a sentence. By guessing or by a process of inductive reasoning and hypothesis testing, the reader establishes what the grammatical relationships could be or must be amongst those words. This reader constructs or invents a proposition containing the content words. A reader whose proficiency matches the text would make use of the grammatical structures and function words to establish those relationships. In the terminology used in reading-strategy research, the reader using lexical processing relies on top-down strategies (knowledge of the world, about texts and about language in general) to compensate for deficiencies in bottom-up processing (text decoding strategies based on knowledge of the particular language of the text).

In the sections that follow, lexical processing is described and illustrated through 'think aloud' protocols from primary and secondary students reading English texts. The students described their understanding of what they read, the problems they encountered, and the strategies they used to overcome those problems. The think aloud was in Cantonese. An English translation is presented here. The number of think aloud protocols collected and analyzed so far is small. Far more research will be required before it can be determined whether these cases are typical. The account given of survival strategies is drawn from observation of students and from discussions with teachers and examiners. Again, it is not possible to estimate what proportion of students might use such strategies occasionally and what proportion might be largely dependent upon them. In what follows, lexical processing is defined operationally; then the negative consequences of lexical processing are described and illustrated, and related to the development of survival strategies and, for some students, increasing reliance on them. Finally, before the discussion and conclusion, examples are given of more positive, problem-solving strategies which the more academically able and linguistically proficient students bring to the task of extracting meanings out of texts.

Lexical Processing

Operational Definition

The first example illustrates lexical processing being used by a beginning reader.

1.)   S: If I don't know most of the words, I look at the picture. Then
                 I look at the words I know.

This L2 reader is adopting a strategy any beginning reader might use. The mother tongue (L1) reader, however, soon learns to recognize the high-frequency function words and to make use of the grammatical knowledge they already control. L2 students, who have not internalized the grammar, are less able to make this transition and may continue to rely on lexical processing.

Example (2) is from a student in primary grade 6. (R stands for researcher):

2.)   R: How do you work out the meaning of the sentence?
      S: By intuition. I use the words that I have learned and by
intuition.
      R: What about unknown words?
      S: I guess. If my guess is wrong, it doesn't matter.

This student is dealing with a narrative text, not a text book, and we should not attach too much importance to "it doesn't matter" in this context. However, the willingness to guess and to rely on 'intuition' is important.

Examples (3) and (4) are taken from the same protocol. (Words in capital letters are quoted from the English text.)

3.) R: Did you pay attention to this word (WITHIN)?
     S: No.
     R: Why?
     S: Because I know it is a preposition. I don't have to care about prepositions.

In lexical processing, long, and sometimes not so long sentences are broken down into sub-sections for decoding. The fact that the meanings of these sub-sections are interdependent within the text is ignored, as in examples (4) and (5).

4.) R: Have you ignored any words in this sentence?
     S: I only look at words such as THE OTHER BOYS, A DAY'S WORK, TWO DAY'S WORK and comma.
     R: Do you usually read in that way?
     S: Sometimes there are sentences I can read that way. I feel I often come across this kind of sentence comparing two things. When I read it, I know what it means.

5.) R: How do you interpret the sentence?
     S: I divide the sentence into parts.
     R: How?
     S: For example: She smiles; then she explains to him, another part; Andy thinks, another part.

The text referred to in (5) reads as follows:

> THAT OLD LADY'S SMILE DOES NOT MEAN THAT HIS HAIR IS WELL CUT, ANDY THINKS.

As can be seen, the meaning of the text bears little resemblance to the reader's interpretation. However this leads to examples which focus more specifically upon the negative effects of this approach to reading rather than to a description of the process itself.

Negative Consequences of Lexical Processing

In the protocol of the primary grade 6 student already quoted, WITHIN HALF AN HOUR is interpreted as 'half an hour', and HAS NOT BEEN ABLE as 'will not'. The process by which the latter interpretation was arrived at is worth quoting in more detail.

6.) Text: ANDY HAS NOT BEEN ABLE TO GET ON A BUS.
     S: HAS NOT means will not. HAS NOT BEEN ABLE is a
             structure that you often use together. It means ANDY usually
             won't take a bus to school.

This particular reader is intelligent and articulate, and all too willing to
rationalize. The complete protocol is too long to present, but two extended
examples will help to illustrate the dangers of this approach. In (7) this reader
makes a wild guess, then builds a story around that guess, which she then
attempts to maintain in spite of her own realization that her interpretation does
not match the text. She eventually corrects her interpretation but only after the
researcher has redirected her attention to the text a number of times. (English
words spelled out and not pronounced are represented as, for example,
H.O.P.E.)

7.) Text: HE IS WALKING DOWN THE ROAD IN A HURRY,
             HOPING TO WALK TO SCHOOL WITHIN HALF AN
             HOUR.
     S: He is hopping and it will take him half an hour.
     R: You said he is hopping. Can you explain this point more
clearly?
     S: The whole sentence?
     R: Yes.
     S: He finds there are too many people. There are two ways I
             think, an upper road and a lower road. When he finds there are
             too many people in the upper road, he walks along the lower
             road. H.O.P.I.N.G.. I think this is the I.N.G.. form of H.O.P.E.
     R: Just now you said he is hopping here and there. Which word
             says he is hopping?
     S: H.O.P.E.
     R: You said H.O.P.E. What does that mean? At first you said he
             hops here and there. What is he doing? What makes you think
             that?
     S: He says he has to be quick; so he walks quickly.
     R: Just now you said it is the I.N.G. form of H.O.P.E. Do you
             really know its meaning?
     S: No
     R: Do you know the meaning of H.O.P.E.?
     S: Yes, hope.
     R: So you were making a guess?
     S: Yes. H.O.P.E. means 'hope', but I think it is not logical. HOPE
             means 'hope' There is no reason it should mean ..... hope to
             get to school. Ah, yes. Hope to get to school in half an hour.

It was unusual for R to press a reader as hard as she did in (7), since from a research perspective this could affect the reader's approach to the text. From the students' point of view however, it is a great pity that more time cannot be spent working with texts in this kind of one to one interaction.

Example (8) shows an even more extreme divergence from the facts of the text. In interpreting this story as a whole, perhaps based upon her own experience, S has decided that Andy's parents are disappointed in his academic performance and feel he does not work hard enough. This interpretation of the first part of the passage, which was not entirely accurate, carried so much conviction for S that she continued to use it to interpret new text even when the topic and setting had changed completely as in the following episode. Andy was standing waiting for traffic lights to change. He notices that an elderly woman is looking at him and smiling.

8.)　Text:　SHE SEEMS TO LIKE ANDY'S HAIRCUT. HIS MOTHER DID IT FOR HIM TWO DAYS AGO.

　　　S:　His mother gave him two days... She wanted to give him two days to let her know how he could do better.

　　　R:　I don't quite understand this part.

　　　S:　His mother gave him a chance. In two days he has to think how he can learn to work better.

　　　R:　How do you work this out?

　　　S:　TWO DAYS AGO means his mother gave him two days.

This is the approach to reading English texts which at least some Hong Kong students develop, and which they take with them when they move from learning English as a subject in primary education to using it as the medium of instruction at secondary level. Kwan (1989) studied the ability of Form 1 students to deal with their History and Integrated Science texts in Form 1.

Examples (9) and (10) are taken from that study.

9.)　Text:　IF HE DID NOT (rule wisely) THE PEOPLE WOULD SOON REBEL AGAINST HIM.

　　　S:　He was not the people.

10.)　Text:　WHILE HE WAS IN EGYPT, A PRIEST TOLD HIM HE WAS A GOD. ALEXANDER BELIEVED HIM AND FELT HE COULD DO ANYTHING.

　　　S:　He was in Europe. He was a god. Alexander lived (in his home) and did not do anything. Because he was a god, he did not do anything.

Kwan studied some of the best and worst students entering her (above average) school. The more able students dealt adequately with the texts, but the ability of the less able students is well illustrated by (9) and (10) above. Kwan asked her students to indicate words they could recognize. In the History text the percentage of words recognized by the lower ability group ranged from 65% to 44%. In the Science text it was from 42% to 18%. Sentences interpreted correctly ranged from 41% to 3% (out of 17 sentences) in the History text and from 28% to 0% in the Science text (out of 25 sentences).

To further illustrate the plight of students entering English medium secondary education, placement tests for two extensive reading schemes introduced in Hong Kong (I.L.E, 1988; Lai, 1991) showed that approximately 15% of students could not manage even the simplest of the simplified readers, and the great majority needed to begin at the lowest level. Comparatively few were placed above the level requiring a vocabulary of 500 words or more.

Lexical processing might be regarded as better than a total inability to deal with texts at all, and no doubt some students are able to progress beyond the constraints it imposes. Others do not. The following examples are from Form 4 (grade 10) students.

11.) Text: SHE ADDRESSED ME BRIGHTLY.
  S: I think she must have put on a special dress. So the author did not recognize her because the previous part says she was at the play, on the stage.

The elements 'DRESS' and 'BRIGHT' are picked out of the text, and an interpretation is constructed around them (special dress). This interpretation is then integrated with information the reader had already drawn from the text. (Two people had met at a play, and the man had almost failed to recognize the woman). In matching the new information with what had already been established, S jumped to the incorrect and unsupported conclusion that the brightly dressed woman must be an actress performing on the stage.

12.) Text: LOCATED IN A NEW ESTATE, THE CENTRE WAS NOT AS CROWDED AS THE STUDY ROOM WE WERE ACCUSTOMED TO IN SHEK KIP MEI ESTATE.
  S: The centre was crowded. If we want to study our books, we have to go to Shek Kip Mei estate.

The key words which seem to have contributed to this interpretation are: centre, crowded, study, we, to and Shek Kip Mei estate. Amongst the key words ignored is 'not'. The interpretation could hardly be more wrong, even though the content words appear to have been understood.

Given the unreliability of students' attempts to elicit meaning out of

English texts, it is not surprising that teachers use strategies which minimize students' need to rely on texts. Some teachers rewrite the material into a more accessible form, usually point by point notes. Others preteach the material (in Cantonese). When the more academically able students turn to their textbooks, they already have the knowledge they need to interpret it correctly. The need for them to progress beyond lexical processing has been greatly reduced, since key words act as prompts for the recall of what these students already know. As a result, students are able to maintain this approach even when texts become more complex grammatically and more abstract conceptually. Students annotate textbook margins as a guide for subsequent lexical processing: e.g. when reviewing the texts before examinations.

Survival Strategies

If teaching and learning strategies of this kind enable the better students to deal relatively successfully with information in texts, weaker students, i.e those less able to use the Cantonese-assisted instruction and the handouts as advance organizers, have to learn to deal with texts in other ways. Where students cannot understand the text they resort to 'survival strategies'. The basic survival strategy is to identify the section of a text relevant to the given task and copy it. In a comprehension test, key words in the question are identified; the text is examined until a section is identified which contains these words; and finally an answer is constructed which maps the relevant section onto the wording of the question. As a crude example of this process at work, consider the following invented nonsense text, question and answer.

13.) Text: BLINKS ARE FORMED WHEN GONKS FLUNGE.
     Q: How are blinks formed?
     A: Blinks are formed when gonks flunge.

If the task is to produce a summary, certain sentences or clauses are identified as more important than others, while all bracketed material and subordinate or embedded clauses are eliminated. The key sentences are then copied down. This may be done more or less skillfully, but generally there is little attempt at sophistication.

Survival strategies are not reading strategies. They are substitutes for them, and their use inhibits the development of valid strategies. Nevertheless, survival strategies are developed and passed on from student to student, and are even taught and their use encouraged by some, perhaps many Hong Kong teachers. The argument for survival strategies is legitimate, so far as it goes. In terms of survival within the education system, weak students who use survival strategies can complete tasks they could not otherwise complete, and this means that students obtain marks in examinations that they would not otherwise obtain. More important, on a day-to-day basis, is the survival of the social and interpersonal relationships between teachers and students in the classroom. Survival strategies enable teachers and students to maintain the appearance of a credible teaching and learning environment. It is acceptable (to teachers, school principals, parents and students) for teachers to set tasks that are difficult, and for students to perform badly, because the potential for improvement is there. It would not be acceptable to acknowledge that no learning is possible, nor is it acceptable for students to do nothing when a task has been set. This would amount to confrontation, and, understandably, teachers and students will go to considerable lengths to avoid that. Survival strategies enable at least the appearance of an effective teaching and learning environment to be maintained.

Memorization can also be a survival strategy and it is not just single statements that are memorized, but complete discourses. Nor is the memorized material meaningless to the students, who may understand the concepts and the Chinese equivalent of the argument presented in the discourse perfectly well, though they may not understand precisely how that argument relates to the text they have memorized. Again teachers defend 'survival' memorization because it enables students to perform successfully in examinations. Again, they are right, and students with what would appear to be an inadequate level of English may obtain high grades through judicious use of memorized material.

Survival strategies aim to complete tasks regardless of the meaning of the texts, and therefore go well beyond the deficiencies of lexical processing. However, the writers would argue that the roots of survival strategies, i.e. the need for them, lie precisely in the gap between proficiency levels and texts which first promotes lexical processing. Once that approach has been established, the negative consequences follow for the development of language proficiency itself as much as for reading skills. The conditions are then established under which teachers as well as students may move towards and accept survival strategies as alternatives to learning strategies.

The More Positive Consequences of Lexical Processing

Given the argument presented above, it may seem surprising that any claim could be made for positive effects arising from lexical processing of texts. Certainly, any such claims must take account of the fact that lexical processing is at best an incomplete and inadequate approach to reading, and one which inhibits students' ability to establish the precise meaning of texts. The negative effects described above, and the need to resort to survival strategies, affects most strongly poorly-motivated students who do not care, or have ceased to care how well they understand texts. Amongst well-motivated students who continue to seek a precise meaning in texts, lexical processing can involve the development of complex and sophisticated 'top-down', problem-solving strategies. The examples that follow illustrate a range of ways in which readers have drawn on their knowledge of the world, their knowledge about texts and about language to help them to construct meanings.The understanding of the text that is achieved is sometimes faulty, but the strategies used are very different from survival strategies and from guessing based on intuition.

Examples (14) and (15) show a student analyzing the structures of words to determine their probable meanings.

14.) S: DIS is a negative; so DISBELIEF means do not believe.

15.) S: CONFUSION means unwilling. CONFUSION. It appears to be like REFUSE. REFUSE means not willing REFUSE and CONFUSE. Both words have FUSE. So I think they have similar meanings.

In examples (16) and (17) readers demonstrate their awareness of and willingness to exploit textual redundancy.

16.) S: I don't understand what it is trying to say. I'll read the next sentence first and come back later.

17.) S: GRAVEYARD. What is GRAVEYARD?
     Text: ALL THE DEAD PEOPLE WERE BURIED IN THE GRAVEYARD.
     S: Oh, now I know what GRAVEYARD means.

The readers in (18) and (19) make use of their knowledge of structural relationships to establish meaning.

18.) Text: THEY WERE SLIM AND PLEASANT TO LOOK UPON.

     S: I don't know PLEASANT TO LOOK UPON, but here is the word AND joining SLIM and PLEASANT TO LOOK UPON. They imply the same thing; so their appearance is quite good.

19.) Text: AS USUAL THE PEOPLE MOST LIKELY TO SUFFER ARE THOSE AT THE POORER END OF SOCIETY AND NOT THE ELITE.
     S: I don't know the word ELITE but I think it must be the opposite of poor because it says AND NOT.

The reader in (20) had formed a false hypothesis about when the characters in the story met, and had carried that hypothesis forward through a large part of the text. But when the reader realized that there had been a mistake, the story is restructured and the reader adds a prediction or advance organizer for the next section of the text.

20.) S: I've misinterpreted the first part. This means that the opening of the story described how they met again at the play. They didn't get to know each other for the first time at the play. They met twenty years ago. Now they have met again, and he (the author) is going to describe what happened twenty years ago.

Some think aloud protocols show a coherence and inductive logic that is impressive, whether the clue is a capital letter (21), knowledge of the world (23) or a more complex interaction of strategies is at work (22).

21.) S: FOYOTS. Capital letter. I think he was going to invite her for lunch in a restaurant. It has a capital letter, so it is the name of a restaurant.

(22) and (23) come from the same reader and the same piece of text.

    Text: I CAUGHT SIGHT OF HER AT THE PLAY AND IN ANSWER TO HER BECKONING I WENT OVER DURING THE INTERVAL AND SAT DOWN BESIDE HER.

22.) S: I don't know this word B.E.C.K.O.N.I.N.G. .....IN ANSWER means reply..... ANSWER...... There must be someone who gives a signal so that you can make a reply. The girl saw the author. The author noticed her. In reply he walked to her and sat beside her.

23.) S: I guess INTERVAL means a break because I remember when people are watching a play, they are not allowed to move around while the actors are on stage.

Relating Theory and Practice

These data appear to support the view that a strongly input-based programme of learning leads to a grammatically limited, and limiting, competence in the language. Where that input is primarily derived from texts which are too difficult for the level of proficiency achieved by the reader, learners may develop a range of strategies to compensate for their lack of proficiency. Precisely because lexical processing strategies are developed, readers can ignore grammatical information in the text and in doing so deprive themselves of the opportunity to acquire that information.

Further evidence of the effects of input-biased programmes and of lexical processing is provided by the two studies evaluating extensive reading schemes already mentioned (Institute of Language in Education, ILE, 1988; Lai, 1991). Both studies revealed a similar pattern of results. Students in the extensive reading programmes showed gains over control groups on tests of word knowledge, reading speed and listening comprehension. They showed no gains or fell behind the control groups on tests of reading comprehension, grammatical competence, and writing performance, though the latter was only tested incidentally in the ILE study. These findings seem consistent with the argument presented here: i.e. lexical processing leads to gains in vocabulary, speed and reading for the gist of the information in a text, but it does not develop grammatical control or the ability to understand the precise meaning of a text.

Up to this point in the argument, the case of Hong Kong students is no different from that of language learners in any input-oriented and in particular, text-oriented language programme. The Hong Kong situation is different in that, for most students at secondary level, the texts they have to deal with are no longer within the zone of proximity to their English language competence that Krashen argues is ideal for acquisition. The texts are too difficult for them. They have to rely heavily upon their bilingual dictionaries, thus reinforcing the lexical processing approach to reading that they already seem to have developed by primary 6. The best students add sophisticated problem-solving strategies to their repertoire of reading strategies. The weak students tend to give up and resort to survival strategies. This division into 'good' and 'weak' students is nevertheless simplistic and potentially misleading. The degree of excellence of the student is relative, a function of the match between the reader and the text or task (Kletzien, 1991). The best students might resort to survival tactics if the text is largely unintelligible to them. On the other hand, relatively weak students will not need to use survival strategies on a text that matches their level of proficiency or their content knowledge.

These outcomes address two substantive and controversial theoretical issues: the role of L2 proficiency in the development of L2 reading strategies, and the extent to which reading strategies, regardless of whether they involve L1 or L2, are universal. Alderson (1984) and Carrell (1991) raise the question whether reading in a foreign language is best regarded as a reading or as a language problem. It might be assumed that the two are complementary with, following Krashen, more L2 reading promoting more L2 acquisition and higher levels of proficiency in turn facilitating more reading. In terms of the universal reading hypothesis (Goodman, 1971; Sarig, 1987), Cummins' theory of linguistic interdependence (Cummins, 1991; Koda, 1987) and a common underlying language proficiency (Cummins and Swain, 1986), higher proficiency should in turn reduce the need for compensatory reading strategies, if indeed these theories allow for their existence, and facilitate the deployment of strategies already developed from L1 reading to L2 texts. What is not predicted by these theories is the possibility that in some contexts compensatory strategies are far from being temporary expedients. They take over, creating a strategic competence for L2 reading which is increasingly divergent from that of the L1. It follows also from the existence of L2 specific strategies that there is unlikely to be a single developmental continuum for biliteracy, but rather a range of continua (Hornberger, 1989) depending upon the environment in which the L2 develops.

Swain argues that the need to produce language output reveals to L2 learners the inadequacy of their grammatical competence. Through this awareness, and in order to acquire the grammatical competence they lack, the learners focus upon the ways in which grammatical relationships are expressed in speech and in texts. She argues further a positive role for the teacher in encouraging students to reprocess their own output and in providing feedback on the outcomes of reprocessing (Swain, 1993). It remains a matter for empirical investigation whether, to what extent and under what circumstances 'forced' output from learners promotes the development of grammatical competence.

A great deal more work needs to be done before a full understanding can be achieved, even in general terms of how reading skills develop in a second language, the extent to which L1 reading strategies are transferrable, the conditions under which they can and cannot be transferred, and the extent to which learning to read a second language may be a different process from learning to read in a first language. The data presented above suggest that the processes may indeed be different if the L2 language learning programme results in a low level of grammatical competence and in a lexical approach to reading, since lexically-based strategies would be unlikely to be used by a native speaker beyond the early beginner stage of reading.

Summary and Conclusion

This chapter has reviewed, broadly, theories of language acquisition and of the development of reading strategies. It has been argued that input-based learning programmes lead to a type of L2 proficiency that is unbalanced: biased towards lexis and away from the grammar of the target language. Hong Kong students' reading strategies show a heavy reliance upon content words, and a tendency to ignore function words and grammatical relationships, i.e. the approach to reading described here as lexical processing. Data from two studies of extensive reading in Hong Kong suggest that more reading, even when the texts are matched to the readers' levels of proficiency, does not necessarily improve the situation and may make it worse.

The data in the protocols are readily explained, up to a point, in terms of generally accepted models of reading (Barr et al., 1991; Carrell et al., 1988; Grabe, 1991; Levine and Reves, 1994; Rumelhart, 1977). Reading is an interactive process in which textual clues are tested against the reader's knowledge until an understanding of the text is arrived at that is acceptable to the reader. Stankovich (1980) predicted that where readers are weak in one area of competence, they rely more heavily upon their relative strengths. Hong Kong students, who tend to lack grammatical competence, compensate by over-reliance on lexis and on top-down processing. The weaker students guess at meanings or adopt survival strategies which can operate almost independently from the meanings of texts. Stronger students develop a wide range of problem-solving strategies which they can apply to texts. Whether the type of development and the strategies described here apply to some extent to all L2 learners, or only to L2 learners who have followed a particular type of learning programme is not clear.

What does seem to be clear, however, is that reading an L2 text can involve completely different strategies from those needed for reading an L1 text. This is not just a matter of low L2 proficiency inhibiting the deployment of universal reading strategies, i.e. strategies appropriate to the reading of any language. L2 proficiency that is inadequate for the task in hand forces the reader to develop strategies which are not developed in L1 reading. L1 readers may use survival or problem-solving strategies in compensating for, for example, lack of relevant background information, but L1 readers do not require strategies which compensate for lack of grammatical knowledge. The argument presented and illustrated in this paper is that such compensatory strategies are developed by L2 readers. Once developed, these strategies actively inhibit the development of grammatical competence, since these strategies make advances in grammatical competence redundant, at least so long as dealing with texts is the major or the only L2 requirement.

From a practical perspective, it seems clear that Hong Kong schools need to place far more emphasis upon the acquisition of grammatical competence. If Swain's output hypothesis is correct, this can be achieved by building into the teaching and learning programme the requirement that students speak and write English more often and at greater length and that teachers actively encourage and facilitate students' 'focus on form'. In relation to reading itself, far more attention needs to be given to 'bottom-up' processing; that is to the meaning of what is in the text and to the ways in which the forms of language in the text signal that meaning.

Finally, the writers would like to emphasize that the argument and the conclusions presented here are speculative at this stage. A great deal more research is required before the development of second languages, and of reading strategies, and of the relationships between the two are adequately understood. If this chapter stimulates teachers and others in language education to engage in that research, it will have achieved its primary objective.

REFERENCES

Alderson, J.C. (1984). Reading in a foreign language: a reading problem or a language problem? In: Alderson, J.C. & Urquhart, A.H. (Eds.), *Reading in a foreign language.* London: Longman.

Barr, R., Kamil, M., Mosenthal, P. & Pearson, P. (Eds.) (1991). *Handbook of reading research, Volume II.* New York, N.Y.: Longman.

Carrell, P.L. (1991). Second language reading: reading ability or language proficiency? *Applied Linguistics, 12*(2), 159-179.

Carrell, P.L., Devine, J. & Eskey, D.E. (Eds.) (1988). *Interactive approaches to second language reading.* New York: Cambridge University Press.

Cummins, J. (1991). Interdependence of first- and second-language proficiency in bilingual children. In Bialystok, E. (Ed.), *Language processing in bilingual children.* Cambridge: Cambridge University Press.

Cummins, J. & Swain, M. (1986). *Bilingualism in education.* New York: Longman.

Ellis, R. (1991). The interaction hypothesis: a critical evaluation. In Sadtono, E. (Ed.), *Language acquisition and the second/foreign language classroom.* Singapore: SEAMEO Regional Language Centre, 179-211.

Goodman, K.S. (1971). Psycholinguistic model universals in the reading process. In Pimsleur, P. & Quinn, T. (Eds.), *The psychology of second language learning.* Cambridge: Cambridge University Press, 135-142

Grabe, W. (1991). Current developments in second language reading research. *TESOL Quarterly, 25*(3), 375-406.

Hornberger, N.H. (1989). Continua of biliteracy. *Review of Educational Research, 59*(3), 271-296.

Institute of Language in Education, (1988). *Evaluation of an extensive reading scheme.* Hong Kong: Institute of Language in Education.

Johnson, R.K. (1983). Bilingual switching strategies: a study of the modes of teacher-talk in bilingual secondary school classrooms in Hong Kong. *Language Learning and Communication, 2*(3), 267-285.

Johnson, R.K. (1994). Assessment, examination and the medium of instruction. In Boyle, J. & Falvey, P. (Eds.), *English language testing in Hong Kong.* Hong Kong: The Chinese University Press, 125-144.

Johnson, R.K., Shek, C. & Law, E. (1991). Implementing Hong Kong's proposed language policy for secondary schools: research and its implications. In Crawford, N. & Hui, E. (Eds.), *The curriculum and behaviour problems in schools*. Education Papers 11: 95-109. (Faculty of Education, The University of Hong Kong).

Kirby, J.C. (1988). Style, strategy and skill in reading. In R.R. Schmeck (Ed.), *Learning strategies and learning styles*. New York: Plenum.

Kletzien, S.B. (1991). Strategy use by good and poor comprehenders reading expository texts of differing levels. *Reading Research Quarterly*, xxvi (1), 67-85.

Koda, K. (1987). Cognitive strategy transfer in second language reading. In Devine, J., Carrell, P. & Eskey, D. (Eds.), *Research in reading in English as a second language*. Washington, DC: TESOL, 127-144

Krashen, S. (1982). *Principles and practice in second language acquisition*. Oxford: Pergamon Press.

Kwan, K. (1989). An evaluation of students' language difficulties in using History and Integrated Science materials in form 1 in an Anglo-Chinese secondary school. M.Ed. Dissertation. Faculty of Education, The University of Hong Kong.

Lai, E.F.K. (1991). *Extensive reading as input for second language acquisition*. Hong Kong: The University of Hong Kong. Unpublished PhD thesis.

Levine, A. & Reves, T. (1994). The four dimensional model: interaction of schemata in the process of FL reading comprehension. *TESL Canada Journal*, *11*, 71-84.

Long, M. (1990). The comprehensible output hypothesis and self-directed learning: a learner's perspective. *TESL Canada Journal*, *6*, 9-26.

Pica, T., Holliday, L., Lewis, N. & Morgenthaler, L. (1989). Comprehensible input as an outcome of linguistic demands on the learner. *Studies in Second Language Acquisition*, *11*, 63-90.

Rumelhart, D. (1977). Towards an interactive model of reading. In Dornic, S. (Ed.), *Attention and performance VI*. Hillsdale, N.J.: Erlbaum.

Sarig, G. (1987). High-level reading in the first and in the foreign language: some comparative process data. In Devine, J., Carrell, P. & Eskey, D. (Eds.), *Research in reading in English as a second language*. Washington, DC: TESOL, 107-120

Stankovich, K. (1980). Towards and interactive-compensatory model of individual differences in the development of reading fluency. *Reading Research Quarterly*, *16*, 32-71.

Swain, M. (1985). Communicative competence: some roles of comprehensible input and comprehensible output in its development. In Gass, S. & Madden, C. (Eds.), *Input and second language acquisition*. Rowley Mass.: Newbury House, 235-253.

Swain, M. (1990). Manipulating and complementing content teaching to maximise second language learning. In Philipson, R. Kellerman, E., Selinker, L., Sharwood-Smith, M. & Swain, M. (Eds.), *Foreign/second language pedagogy research*. Clevedon: Multi-lingual Matters.

Swain, M. (1993). The output hypothesis: just speaking and writing aren't enough. *Canadian Modern Language Review*, *50*(1), 158-164.

White, L. (1987). Against comprehensible input: the input hypothesis and the development of L2 competence. *Applied Linguistics*, *8*, 95-110.

8

Studying in A Second Language: the Experiences of Chinese Students in Canada

John R. Kirby, Rosamund A. Woodhouse and Yamin Ma

It sometimes comes as a surprise to the English-speaking Anglo-Saxon world that many people around the world speak more than one language, and that at least some of these people do so willingly. Bi- and multilingualism have long been common (Mackey, 1967), but have undoubtedly increased in this century with immigration and travel. Another contributor has been the rise of English in particular, as an international language (McCrum, Cran and MacNeil, 1986). It is now common for students from virtually every country in the world to either study in English at home, or to study abroad in an English-speaking country. Asian students are no exception to this, and, with the increasing importance of Asian economies in the global economy, their desire to study in a second language is also likely to increase.

However, Asian students who are studying in a second language (L2) frequently face a triple challenge: not only must they master the content and concepts of their discipline, and do so through the medium of a language which they may not fully command, but frequently they must do this within an educational and cultural context quite different from their own. These cognitive, linguistic and cultural challenges interact to restrict, or at least modify, the nature of learning. We focus here upon the cognitive processes of learning, because these form the more adaptive interface between two less mutable entities, the students' cultural-linguistic background and the academic discipline/context. This chapter reviews:-

1) Ways in which a relative lack of familiarity with L2 may result in interference with comprehension and learning processes;
2) Describes the results of two small studies of students' learning strategies in L2; and
3) Suggests two approaches which may help students compensate for these difficulties and study more effectively.

Sources of Difficulty Encountered in L2 Learning

Students learning in a second language are likely to encounter a number of sources of difficulty, above and beyond those inherent in the material that they are studying. Evidence of such problems is reflected in the comments of those who assess the work produced by these students, and in the experiences reported by, and observations of, these students themselves (e.g. Ballard and Clanchy, 1991; Stevenson and Yee, 1990; see also Chapter 3, and the comments made by students in the studies reported below). These problems may have profound effects on the ways in which L2 students are able to approach learning tasks; a thorough analysis of these problems and their consequences may help illuminate the most effective interventions and strategies that students can use to overcome them.

One potential source of difficulty arises from L2 students' relative lack of familiarity with the specialized culture and conventions of the academic environment within which they are studying. At a cultural level, Asian students may view their academic role and tasks from a different perspective than do Western staff and students, and accordingly tend to adopt particular approaches or strategies to accomplish these tasks. It has been argued (e.g. Ballard and Clanchy, 1991) that Asian cultures and educational systems emphasize a view of knowledge as that which should be conserved and reproduced, in contrast with Western systems, which emphasize a more speculative, questioning approach. As Ballard and Clanchy point out, such a disjunction between the attitudes to knowledge held by Asian students and Western staff can have important consequences for the assessment of Asian students. Furthermore, for at least some groups of Asian students, the individualistic emphasis of the Western academic system may require that students develop a whole new 'identity' to approach tasks in the expected way (e.g. Shen, 1989).

Shen also highlighted the importance of knowledge of cultural conventions for presenting and structuring material (rhetorical structure). A number of authors have argued that cultures differ in the way that textual information is typically organized and that L2 readers may suffer from their lack of familiarity with the rhetorical structures prevalent in the second language. English and Asian written discourse styles have been contrasted by Barnitz (1985), Hinds (1983), Kaplan (1986, cited in Ballard and Clanchy, 1991),

Onaka (1984), Shen (1989) and Tsao (1983), although the status of much contrastive rhetoric research is currently controversial (for example, Hamp-Lyons, 1991). Carrell (1992) and Hague and Olejnik (1990) have shown that L2 subjects who were aware of the organizational or rhetorical structure of an expository text subsequently recalled the text better than did unaware subjects.

In addition to the challenges posed by cultural factors, other difficulties can arise from a student's lack of familiarity with L2. This is especially important for those in an academic environment, because of its specialized use of language. A number of authors have referred to the academic context as a second - and even a third - culture, with language as one of its central features. Academic discourse (whether spoken or written) is primarily information focused (Tannen, 1985). It is often abstract, and information is expressed in isolation from supporting cues in the environment, using complex syntactic structures and specialized vocabulary. Cummins (1985) referred to such language as 'decontextualized', and contrasted it with the concrete language, supported by paralinguistic and prosodic cues, that is typically used in social communication. Cummins argued that decontextualized language usage requires specialized skills, beyond the level required for daily social interactions.

A similar distinction has been drawn by Wells (1987) in the domain of literacy skills, which are essential for academic tasks. He contrasted performative and functional levels of literacy (essentially used to express what is already known by the communicator) with informational and epistemic levels, which require the sophistication to access knowledge and transform it. These are precisely the levels emphasized in the academic environment.

Furthermore, the characteristics of typical academic texts require students to engage high-level processing and literacy skills. Such texts may be inherently hard to comprehend and recall, because of the nature and organization of their content. In contrast to narratives, expository texts often present abstract content, connected by logical relations which do not follow a clearly defined pathway of event sequences (Varnhagen, 1991). Asian and other L2 students may find such structures challenging, in part because they may be unfamiliar (as described above), and also because of their lack of familiarity with the vocabulary used to convey structural links in exposition. Both L2 university students and under-prepared L1 university students may have difficulty in understanding terms such as 'therefore' and 'however' that express these relations (Cohen, et al., 1979; Johns, 1985). Indeed, such vocabulary difficulties may even hinder L2 students from becoming aware of the existence of appropriate rhetorical structures and benefitting from them as described above.

More generally, lack of familiarity with vocabulary can cause L2 students to misidentify or misinterpret words, and thereby give rise to comprehension difficulties. Bernhardt (1991) classified vocabulary-related difficulties as reflections of problems at three possible levels:-

1) Phonemic/graphemic decoding (in which words are misidentified based on their visual or oral similarities with other words);
2) Word recognition (when word meanings are misinterpreted); and
3) Syntactic feature recognition (when relationships between and among words are misinterpreted).

Using a task which required secondary school students to reconstruct a business letter written in L2, Bernhardt showed that both abstract vocabulary and syntax were a frequent source of difficulty in both comprehension and recall of L2 material. Even apparently familiar vocabulary may carry a cost for the L2 reader. L2 students may be mislead by some words that may have quite different meanings or connotations in the two cultures (for example, words such as 'liberalization', 'dragon' and 'park' may have different connotations in Chinese and Canadian cultures (Qi, 1992)).

Lack of vocabulary can also affect the way that students approach studying in L2. Yu and Atkinson (1988) argued that students resort to rote learning in subjects with a high language dependency (such as history), because they do not have the vocabulary or fluency to support self-expression. Similarly, Yee (1989) reported that Asian university students commonly respond to the intense pressure for academic achievement by adopting memorization strategies, and that this may be particularly true for such students in English-language (L2) universities. The tendency for Asian students to adopt such strategies may be increased by background cultural beliefs about knowledge and the appropriate learning processes by which to achieve it. The data reported in the following section show that less fluent L2 students are indeed likely to adopt such strategies in a learning task.

Another reason why L2 students, particularly those who are less fluent, may tend to adopt strategies such as memorization arises from the relative difficulty of working in L2. A number of studies have shown that word-recognition processes are slower for bilingual than monolingual readers (e.g. Soares and Grosjean, 1984). This disadvantage is maintained even in highly skilled bilinguals, and is associated with decreased automaticity of word recognition (Favreau and Segalowitz, 1983). Inefficient L2 word-recognition processes overload the limited-capacity working memory (e.g. Just and Carpenter, 1992) and this impairs readers' capacity to use higher-order strategies for comprehending and learning (Koda, 1990). Evidence consistent with this notion was reported by McLeod and McLaughlin (1986), who found that although advanced L2 readers had the skills and knowledge to process L2 text in a meaningful fashion, they did not always do so in practice.

In contrast to the evidence and opinion presented above, there is some evidence that L2 students, in particular Asian students, have habitually deep approaches to learning, and are remarkably successful when studying in English (Biggs, 1992; Watkins and Regmi, 1990; see also Chapters 1 and 3). Consistent with this, Cantwell and Biggs (1988) found that L2 subjects used a more abstract, 'top-down' approach than did L1 subjects in a task which required them to read a text, and then write an essay about it. Questions remain, however. Are the deep approach scores obtained by Asian students a true reflection of how they go about learning, or rather more a reflection of cultural values about how they think learning *should* take place? This question addresses the cross-cultural validity of the instruments used to obtain the scores (see Chapter 1). A second, more practical question is whether the L2 students can apply their habitual (L1) approaches in a second, weaker, language.

The Studies

These studies were designed to observe the experience of two groups of L2 students in a typical academic learning task, to understand more about the difficulties they meet and the strategies they use when learning from text in L2. The students selected were adult, native-Chinese speakers from mainland China, studying in Canada. To encourage the students to externalize their study processes we asked them to summarize the texts they studied, and to verbalize their strategies. Because of the time-consuming nature of the data collection procedures, the sample size in each study was necessarily small. The results are described both quantitatively and qualitatively.

The two samples differed in English fluency. The sample in Study 1 were six students taking an English-as-a-Second Language (ESL) course at a community college. These subjects were primarily from professional backgrounds in China, but were only moderately skilled in English. The subjects in Study 2 were 11 native Chinese-speaking graduate students at Queen's University. In each study, the subjects were asked to read an English text, to write a summary of it, and to verbalize their thoughts. (Cue dots were inserted at the end of appropriate paragraphs in the text - roughly every two paragraphs - as a reminder to comment at particular points.) Because of their limited fluency in English, the subjects in Study 1 verbalized their thoughts in Chinese; these protocols were later translated into English. The subjects in Study 2 were more fluent, and accordingly gave their protocols in English. One week later, each subject was asked to write a free recall of the text.

The history text chosen for Study 1 was written at a level judged to be slightly challenging, but within their capability (approximately Grade 7-8 level). A glossary of unfamiliar terms was provided. The text used in Study 2 consisted of a five-page article about nurses' management of children's pain, typical of texts read in an undergraduate course; no glossary was provided. The subjects in Study 1 were able to refer to the text while writing their summaries (text present summarization). Subjects in Study 2 summarized in either text present or text absent conditions. (Text absent summarization, in which subjects know that the text will be taken away before they write the summary, is supposed to encourage deep processing and thereby increase recall; see Kirby and Pedwell, 1991; Kirby and Woodhouse, 1994.)

The texts were analyzed to determine their propositional content, following Kirby and Cantwell (1984) and Kirby (1988). The propositions in the text were classified into three levels of importance: main ideas, important ideas, and unimportant ideas. The summaries and recalls were scored for the number of propositions that they contained at each level.

The summaries were also rated for depth of processing, that is the degree to which they showed that the student had integrated and transformed the information in the text (see Stein and Kirby, 1992). A four-point scale was used, on which (1) indicated a random set of ideas (with some structure within ideas), (2) represented a linear sequence of ideas (following the text), (3) showed some attempt at a relational framework, and (4) demonstrated successful application of a relational framework.

The Chinese protocols from Study 1 were translated into English, and then all protocols were scored to provide measures of the use of various processing strategies during summarization. The protocols were broken down into individual statements, which were then classified using a system described in Woodhouse and Kirby (1991). The scheme classifies protocol statements on the basis of the level or type of information addressed (e.g. main ideas, details, structural features of the text) and the type of processing activity (e.g. identifying or relating ideas, rereading, underlining text, comprehension-monitoring). In the present paper, these data were collated into seven categories. The categories grouped statements reflecting processing of specific levels of text information and different types of strategies. These categories form two groups: one describing relatively deep processing (higher-order processing of main ideas, the relating of text information to prior knowledge, and strategies used for comprehension of meaning); and the other relatively superficial processing (selection or identification of main ideas, attention to details, text inspection strategies, and strategies regarding details).

Students also completed Biggs' (1987) Study Process Questionnaire (SPQ), which assesses three approaches to learning: surface, deep; and achieving.

Quantitative Results

Approach to learning

The group of less-fluent subjects used in Study 1 obtained mean SPQ scores of 45.8 (surface), 49.0 (deep), and 54.0 (achieving). The more fluent graduate student sample in Study 2 obtained mean scores of 43.6 (surface), 51.6 (deep) and 49.5 (achieving). These scores can be compared with average scores reported for Australian university and college students (Biggs, 1987, p.63), which are 43.4, 44.0 and 40.1 for surface, deep and achieving, respectively. Both native Chinese samples are higher on deep, and much higher on achieving. These differences are consistent with other investigations which have reported higher deep scores for Asian students (e.g. Biggs, 1992; Watkins and Regmi, 1990; see also Chapter 1).

Verbalizations

The mean proportions of verbalizations in the seven categories are shown in Table 8.1.

Table 8.1
Mean proportions of verbalizations

Verbalization Category	Study 1	Study 2
Surface:		
Main idea: selection	.19	.33
Attention to details	.23	.14
Text inspection strategies	.07	.07
Detail-oriented strategies	.17	.07
Deep:		
Main ideas: higher-order processing	.07	.12
Relating prior knowledge	.06	.03
Meaning-oriented strategies	.15	.14

Note: The protocol classification scheme also coded a small number of other verbalizations, of little relevance to the task: these are not shown in this table, but, if included, the proportions would total 1.0 as expected.

For both groups, the majority of verbalizations concerned surface-level processing strategies (approximately 60%). However, the groups differed in their use of surface-level strategies. Over half the surface-level verbalizations made by subjects in Study 2 involved the identification and selection of main ideas, and there were very few verbalizations of detail-oriented strategies. In contrast, almost two-thirds of the surface-level verbalizations made by the less fluent subjects in Study 1 were concerned with details.

Deep strategies appear to be used to an equal extent by the two groups, the majority of such strategies being directed toward higher-order processing of main ideas, and meaning. The fact that both groups make deep verbalizations is particularly interesting in the context of the claim that even advanced-level second-language readers may not process L2 text in a deep or meaningful way (McLeod and McLaughlin, 1986). The present data suggest that, in a study task which requires such skills to be used (as compared to reading aloud in the McLeod and McLaughlin study), even less-proficient L2 students are able to implement some deep-level processing strategies.

Relation between approaches to learning and verbalizations

The Spearman rank correlations between approaches to learning and verbalizations are shown in Table 8.2.

Table 8.2
Spearman correlations between processing measures

Verbalization Category	Study 1 Approach to Learning		Study 2	
	Surface	Deep	Surface	Deep
Surface:				
Main idea: selection	-.14	-.54	-.07	.15
Attention to details	.51	-.51	.26	.19
Text inspection strategies	-.09	-.88*	.23	-.46
Detail-oriented strategies	.03	-.29	-.05	.46
Deep:				
Main ideas: higher-order processing	-.38	.58	-.14	-.12
Relating prior knowledge	-.64	.72	-.11	-.22
Meaning-oriented strategies	.09	.49	-.19	-.20

Note. * indicates p < .05.

It is of course necessary to interpret correlations from such small samples cautiously. In Study 1, the deep categories of verbalizations are generally positively related with the deep approach to learning and negatively related to the surface approach. Conversely, surface verbalization categories are negatively related with the deep approach to learning. The correlations obtained in Study 2 are much smaller, and there is no clear pattern of results.

Relation between verbalizations and learning products

The Spearman correlations between verbalizations and measures of summary quality and recall performance are shown in Table 8.3 for Study 1 and Table 8.4 for Study 2.

Table 8.3
Spearman correlations between processing measures and learning products, study 1 (N = 6)

	Verbalizations						
	Surface categories				**Deep categories**		
Learning product	**Main ideas-low**	**Attend to details**	**Text inspect**	**Detail strategies**	**Main ideas-high**	**Prior knowledge**	**Meaning strategies**
Summary content: main ideas	.03	.36	-.19	.49	-.23	.00	-.31
Summary content: important details	.39	.54	.00	-.06	-.46	-.77*	-.58
Summary content: other details	.23	.77*	.63	.40	-.59	-.88*	-.35
Summary depth	-.68	.00	-.52	-.26	.43	.00	.51
Recall content: main ideas	-.83*	-.61	-.75*	-.43	.84*	.74*	.83*
Recall content: important details	-.07	.70	.42	.84*	-.43	-.34	-.17
Recall content: other details	.97*	.35	.32	.08	-.72	-.55	-.97*

Note. * indicates p < .05

Table 8.4

Spearman correlations between processing measures and learning products, study 2 (N = 11)

	Surface categories				Verbalizations	Deep categories	
Learning product	Main ideas-low	Attend to details	Text inspect	Detail strategies	Main ideas-high	Prior know-ledge	Meaning strategies
Summary content: main ideas	-.39	-.14	.31	-.44	.44	.41	.77*
Summary content: important details	.10	-.33	.03	.34	.04	-.11	.29
Summary content: other details	.03	-.36	-.33	.55*	.26	.10	.22
Summary depth	-.03	-.24	.18	-.60*	.29	.44	.31
Recall content: main ideas	-.03	-.33	.05	-.67*	.30	.54*	.41
Recall content: important details	.12	-.04	-.18	.30	.16	-.09	-.01
Recall content: other details	-.45	.18	-.02	.32	.52*	.10	.47

Note. * indicates p < .05

These correlations are generally as expected: surface-level verbalizations are negatively related to successful recall of main ideas and to summary depth, and positively correlated to recall of details, whereas deep-level verbalizations are generally positively related to recall of main ideas and negatively related to recall of details. In Study 1, protocol reports of lower-level, main-idea processing (a surface category) are negatively correlated with recall of main ideas, and positively correlated with recall of unimportant details. Verbalizations about details are positively correlated with inclusion of unimportant details in the summary. Text inspection strategies (surface) are negatively correlated to recall of main ideas. Detail-oriented strategies are positively related to the recall of important details. In contrast, the three deep protocol categories are positively related to the recall of main ideas, and individual categories are negatively related to inclusion of details in the summary and recall of details. In Study 2, detail-oriented strategies are correlated positively with inclusion of details in the summary, and negatively with summary depth and recall of main ideas. The deep strategy of relating to prior knowledge is positively related to recall of main ideas, and meaning-oriented strategies are positively related to inclusion of main ideas in the summary.

The correlations between verbalizations and summary content scores are less consistent than those with summary depth or recall, though still generally supportive of the expected pattern. Two reasons for this are: (a) that subjects are summarized under two different sets of conditions in Study 2 (text absent versus present); and (b) that subjects may obtain high content scores in text present summarization (i.e. those in Study 1 and half of those in Study 2) by copying rather than by deeper processing.

Qualitative Analysis

It was argued in the introduction that students' level of fluency in L2 may influence their ability to use effective processing strategies during study. Although comparisons between the groups used in the present study must be made with great caution, examination of the protocol data generated by the two groups is suggestive of differences in the way that they approach the summarization task.

As described in the previous section, the protocols showed that both groups used deep strategies. However, examination of the protocols from the two groups suggests that there may be some differences in how these deep strategies are applied. One such difference is that subjects in Study 1 seemed to deal with the text in a sequential fashion: the protocols of a number of subjects in Study 2 indicated that they were relating information across the text. For example, subject SW (Study 2) referred back to previous points on a number of occasions as she read through the text:-

"... I don't understand, umm, why didn't the author talk about nurses' management of pain in adults? What's the point in discussing pain management only in children? I am reading the third paragraph on the second page. Now I understand why, umm, the studies were done on kids."

"... I'm reading the third paragraph on page 4. Now I can fully understand the differences between, umm, the pain, umm, management in kids and adults."

Some of the deep-level processing that might be expected to be of greatest value in the summarization task - planning and organization - was little used by the less fluent group of subjects examined in Study 1. Only two of these subjects reported such processing, e.g.:-

"I have to recall what I have read, and link all the important information together, then I can start to write." (EE).

The majority of these subjects appeared, instead, to concentrate on aspects of the text structure as the basis for their summary:-

"I have to remember some of the key words in the text, so that I can use them in my summary." (WU).

"When I am reading the text, I pay attention to particular parts of the text, like the first and last paragraphs, and the first and last sentence of each paragraph." (QN).

"I usually pay much attention to the first sentence of each paragraph and the first and last paragraphs of the text. These are the main information about the text." (RY).

Not only did subjects in Study 1 appear heavily dependent on the overall structure of the text, they also were reliant on the way it expressed ideas. These less fluent subjects frequently copied directly from the text, explaining that they were either unable to express the idea in their own words, or were not confident of their ability to do so.

"Today I used some of the words in the text, because I didn't have my own words which could express that particular idea that I wanted to convey." (PG).

In contrast, subjects in the text absent condition of Study 2 appeared to apply planning and organizational strategies more directly. In contrast to the text present conditions, text absent summarization requires that subjects rely on their recall of information to produce the summary; the subjects appeared to build their recall around the different sections of the text. Unlike Study 1, where statements of such strategies were like statements of a rule (see EE's statement above), the protocols of several subjects in Study 2 showed these strategies in action with the text content:-

"I planned it ah ... in a, in a very broad manner, ..., I pointed out in my mind the author, um, concentrated on two factors that er ..., are important in influencing nurses ..., failure in dealing with pain reduction in children. ... and then I think from those two factors, ... the subfactors .... So I planned in that way." (XL).

While the subjects in Study 2 also were aware of text structure, they appeared able to integrate this with awareness of content, and to be more analytical about its role in the text:-

"The conclusion's kind of short. I didn't expect that." (XL).

"Usually, when I read a paper like this, ..., in the first section they introduced what they talk about later, so... give you a frame of the whole paper and then I usually go through the subtitles so I have an idea what they will talk about in the whole paper. (YC).

In addition, subjects in Study 2 were more independent of the material, questioning and evaluating content:-

"Now I thinking the article just asked the question, but didn't give any answer, even suggestion." (SC).

"The next part I think that's true, uh, the three factors are true in most hospitals." (QX).

Another difference between the two groups of subjects was their use of translation. Many of the subjects in Study 1 translated parts of the text into Chinese, apparently to understand the material better:-

"I have to translate the text into Chinese in my mind while I am reading. I think it helps me get clear and complete information from the text." (PG).

Often, the apparent intention was to understand particular words or details. In contrast, subjects in Study 2 did not appear to translate during summarization. Their strategies for achieving understanding often involved working with the material, questioning and supplementing the information until they had achieved a consistent answer. Furthermore, although details sometimes provoked a search for meaning, it was often directed at a larger issue in the text, rather than at specific details.

Discussion

The small sample sizes in these studies require great caution in drawing conclusions. However, several patterns were apparent in the results and these deserve some comment. At the very least, these studies offer two case-study views of the ways some students cope with studying in L2. We offer the following interpretations as speculations in need of further confirmation. Our comments concern what the students say they are doing during study and summarization, and what effect these processes have on performance.

In spite of their varying language difficulties, both groups of subjects employed deep processing. Both groups used more surface processing, with the more fluent subjects doing more appropriate surface processing (i.e. looking for main ideas rather than focusing upon details). This supports the argument made earlier in this paper that a reasonable level of fluency provides a basis for higher level processes. The qualitative analyses also showed the more fluent subjects operating upon the meaning of the text more than their less fluent counterparts. The latter focused more upon vocabulary and text details. Surface verbalizations were more common from students with a surface approach to learning, deep verbalizations from those reporting a deep approach.

These results are not consistent with the suggestions of some (e.g. Kozminsky and Graetz, 1986) that L2 students are forced to rely solely upon surface processing, nor with those of others who conclude that L2 students tend to use deep processing as a 'top-down' way of coping with ambiguous detail (e.g. Cantwell and Biggs, 1988). Rather these results suggest that interlingual transfer and application of deep processing strategies is not automatic. Carson Eisterhold (1990) argued that a threshold level of L2 proficiency is necessary for such transfer to occur, and that such transfer can be facilitated by instruction. It is possible that such a threshold may reflect a critical point in the tradeoff between processing and storage in working memory referred to earlier: low proficiency students may be devoting most of their capacity to low level, word recognition or detailed comprehension processes. Such processes are likely to be more automatic for more proficient students, resulting in a greater capacity to engage other, higher-level, comprehension processes.

Our second concern is the effect that these processes have upon performance. In general, surface verbalizations were associated with the writing of a shallow summary, and the recall of details. Deep verbalizations were associated with the writing of a deeper summary, and the recall of more main ideas. It must be admitted that these sweeping conclusions conceal a fair amount of inconsistency, and derive from a small sample, but they are patterns which merit further investigation. To the extent that their processing is not constrained by lack of fluency, L2 subjects should be encouraged to adopt deeper learning strategies. This would be consistent with the relatively deep approach to learning which they report (on average) as their habitual style (see

Chapter 3).

Implications for Teaching

We wish to suggest two general ways in which educators can facilitate their L2 students' learning. These suggestions derive largely from the literature, but are consistent with the results of these two studies. First, strategies that compensate for lack of fluency, reducing the cognitive load for L2 students and thereby freeing up their resources for higher-order activities, will be of value. One way in which this can be achieved is through facilitating students' access to the information in text. Although it may not be possible for them to automate word recognition to the extent that L1 readers do, L2 students can develop, and benefit from, communicative competence with the discourse patterns common in academic writing. In addition to the basic grammar and vocabulary, they have a special need to learn both the vocabulary of their chosen field of study, and that used to convey the logical relations essential to understanding text structure. Beyond this, students' comprehension and recall of material can benefit from instruction in recognizing rhetorical structures used in expository text, and especially those commonly used in the student's own field.

The second approach is to ensure that students use their available processing capacity as effectively as possible. As Boyd (1991) points out, students learning English for academic purposes can benefit from instruction in relevant cognitive skills such as summarizing, that can be applied across many disciplines. Considerable evidence shows that summarizing can benefit students working in their native language, yielding an increase in both comprehension and recall. Summarization may be particularly valuable to L2 students, not only for the direct gains in learning associated with its use, but also because the task may reinforce skills in comprehension, abstraction, selection and production of L2 material. This indirect benefit may also apply to L1 students: however, it is likely that students have greater need for such practice and reinforcement in L2. We suggest that summarization must engage deeper processing to be optimally effective; merely teaching students to copy relevant sentences from text is unlikely to enhance either their comprehension or recall of the information (Hidi and Anderson, 1986; Kirby and Pedwell, 1991; Kirby and Woodhouse, 1994; Stein and Kirby, 1992). Students below the fluency threshold may need to be encouraged to adopt deeper processing strategies through translating and processing material in L1 (Campbell, 1990).

Note:

This research was supported by a grant from the Social Sciences and Humanities Research Council of Canada to the first author. The assistance of Allyson Hadwin is gratefully acknowledged.

REFERENCES

Ballard, B. & Clanchy, J. (1991). Assessment by misconception: cultural influences and intellectual traditions. In L. Hamp-Lyons (Ed.), *Second language writing in academic contexts.* Norwood, New Jersey: Ablex Publishing Corporation.

Barnitz, J.G. (1985). *Reading development of non-native speakers of English: research and instruction.* Monograph of the Center for Applied Linguistics. Washington, D.C.

Bernhardt E.B. (1991). *Reading development in a second language: theoretical, empirical and classroom perspectives.* Norwood, New Jersey: Ablex Publishing Corporation.

Biggs, J.B. (1987). *Student approaches to learning and studying.* Melbourne: Australian Council for Educational Research.

Biggs, J.B. (1992). *Why and how do Hong Kong students learn?* Education Paper 14, Faculty of Education, University of Hong Kong.

Boyd, F.A. (1991). The comprehension strategies of second language readers. *TESOL Quarterly, 20,* 463-494.

Campbell, C. (1990). Writing with others' words: using background reading text in academic compositions. In B. Kroll (Ed.), *Second language writing: research insights for the classroom.* Cambridge: Cambridge University Press.

Cantwell, R.H. & Biggs, J.B. (1988). Effects of bilingualism and approach to learning on the writing and recall of expository text. In M.M. Gruneburg, P.H. Morris & R.N. Sykes (Eds.), *Practical aspects of memory: volume 2 - clinical and educational applications.* London: Wiley.

Carrell, P. (1992). Awareness of text structure: effects on recall. *Language Learning, 42,* 1-20.

Carson Eisterhold, J. (1990). Reading-writing connections: toward a description for second language learners. In B. Kroll (Ed.), *Second language writing: research insights for the classroom.* Cambridge: Cambridge University Press.

Cohen, A., Glasman, H., Rosenbaum-Cohen, P.R., Ferrara, J. & Fine, J. (1979). Reading English for specialized purposes: discourse analysis and the use of student informants. *TESOL Quarterly, 13,* 551-564.

Cummins, J. (1985). *Theory and policy in bilingual education.* Paris: OECD

Centre for Educational Research and Innovation.

Favreau, M. & Segalowitz, N.S. (1983). Automatic and controlled processes in the first- and second-language reading of fluent bilinguals. *Memory & Cognition, 11*, 565-574.

Hague, S.A. & Olejnik, S. (1990). What L2 readers remember: is it related to their awareness of text structure? In J. Zutell & S. McCormick (Eds.), *Literacy theory and research: analyses from multiple paradigms.* Thirty-ninth Yearbook of the National Reading Conference.

Hamp-Lyons, L. (1991). The writer's knowledge and our knowledge of the writer. In L. Hamp-Lyons (Ed.), *Assessing second language writing in academic contexts.* Norwood, New Jersey: Ablex Publishing Corporation.

Hidi, S. & Anderson, V. (1986). Producing written summaries: task demands, cognitive operations, and implications for instruction. *Review of Educational Research, 56*, 473-493.

Hinds, J. (1983). Contrastive rhetoric: Japanese and English. *Text, 3*, 183-195.

Johns, A.M. (1985). Summary protocols of "underprepared" and "adept" university students: replications and distortions of the original. *Language Learning, 35*, 495-517.

Just, M.A. & Carpenter, P.A. (1992). A capacity theory of comprehension: individual differences in working memory. *Psychological Review, 99*, 122-149.

Kaplan, R.B. (1986). Some speculations about the structure of written discourse: Chinese versus English. Paper presented at the University of Hong Kong.

Kirby, J.R. (1988). Style, strategy, and skill in reading. In R.R. Schmeck, (Ed.), *Learning strategies and learning styles.* New York: Plenum Press.

Kirby, J.R. & Cantwell, R. (1984). Use of advance organizers to facilitate higher-level text comprehension. *Human Learning, 4*, 159-168.

Kirby, J.R. & Pedwell, D. (1991). Students' approaches to summarization. *Educational Psychology, 11*, 297-307.

Kirby, J.R. & Woodhouse, R.A. (1992). Measuring and predicting depth of processing in learning. *Alberta Journal of Educational Research, 40*, 147-161.

Kirby, J.R. & Woodhouse, R.A. (1994). Measuring and predicting depth of processing in learning. *Alberta Journal of Educational Research, 40*, 147-161.

Koda, K. (1990). Factors affecting second language text comprehension. In J. Zutell & S. McCormick (Eds.), *Literacy theory and research: analyses from multiple paradigms.* Thirty-ninth Yearbook of the National Reading Conference.

Kozminsky, E. & Graetz, N. (1986). First vs. second language comprehension: some evidence from text summarizing. *Journal of Research in Reading, 2*, 3-21.

Mackey, W.F. (1967). *Bilingualism as a World Problem/le Bilingualisme: phenomene Mondial.* Montreal: Harvest House.

McCrum, R., Cran, W. & MacNeil, R. (1986). *The story of English.* New York: Viking Penguin.

McLeod, B. & McLaughlin, B. (1986). Restructuring or automaticity? Reading in a second language. *Language Learning, 36,* 109-123.

Onaka, N. (1984). Developing paragraph organization skills at the college level. *English Language Teaching Forum, 22,* 14-22.

Qi, S. (1992). *A comparative case study of prior cultural knowledge in English-second- language lexical meaning-making.* Unpublished Master's thesis, Queen's University, Kingston, Ontario.

Shen, F. (1989). The classroom and the wider culture: identity as a key to learning English composition. *College Composition & Communication, 40,* 459-465.

Stevenson, H.W. & Yee, S. (1990). Contexts of achievement. *Monographs of the Society for Research in Child Development, 55,* 1-123.

Soares, C. & Grosjean, F. (1984). Bilinguals in a monolingual and a bilingual speech mode: the effect on lexical access. *Memory and Cognition, 12,* 380-386.

Stein, B.L. & Kirby, J.R. (1992). The effects of text absent and text present conditions on summarization and recall of text. *Journal of Reading Behaviour, 24,* 217-232.

Tannen, D. (1985). Relative focus on involvement in oral and written discourse. In D.R. Olson, N. Torrance & A. Hildyard (Eds.), *Literacy, language and learning: the nature and consequences of reading and writing.* Cambridge: Cambridge University Press.

Tsao, F.F. (1983). Linguistics and written discourse in particular languages: contrastive studies: English and Chinese (Mandarin). In R. Kaplan (Ed.), *Annual review of applied linguistics 1982: linguistics and written discourse.* Rowley, MA: Newberry House.

Varnhagen, K.C. (1991). Text relations and recall for expository prose. *Discourse Processes, 14,* 399-422.

Watkins, D. & Regmi, M. (1990). Approaches to learning of Australian and Nepalese tertiary students. Paper presented at the International Congress of Applied Psychology, Kyoto, Japan.

Wells, G. (1987). Apprenticeship in literacy. *Interchange, 18,* 109-123.

Yee, A.H. (1989). Cross-cultural perspectives on higher education in East Asia: psychological effects upon Asian students. *Journal of Multilingual and Multicultural Development, 10,* 213-232.

Yu, V.W.S. & Atkinson, P.A. (1988). An investigation of the language difficulties experienced by Hong Kong secondary school students in English-medium schools: I The problems. *Journal of Multilingual and Multicultural Development, 9,* 267-284.

9

How Hong Kong Students Cope With Assessment

Catherine Tang and John Biggs

Assessment and Hong Kong Culture

"The quickest way to change student learning is to change the assessment system." (Elton and Laurillard, 1979, p. 100)

The assessment tail wags the educational dog the world over (Crooks, 1988; Frederiksen and Collins, 1989; Nickerson, 1989), but Hong Kong is a place where such 'backwash' effects from assessment are particularly strong. Many of the parents of Hong Kong students are immigrants from China and are highly ambitious, if not for themselves then for their children (with the change of power in 1997 adding its own motivation). Education to these people is the perceived means of gaining upward mobility, material rewards, foreign residence, or all three. Tertiary places are gained through a series of highly competitive examinations from Secondary 5 (grade 11) onwards, which are conducted by an agency external to the school system itself. To further complicate matters, these examinations are mostly conducted in English, a foreign language to virtually all candidates.

But the Chinese have a long history of coping with examinations. For many centuries, examinations were the means by which even the poorest could gain entry into the powerful mandarin class, and appropriately enough, the traditional Chinese recipe for success is effort and diligence (see Chapter 2). Success comes to those who apply themselves to their allotted tasks unremittingly; with diligence, you can grind an iron bar into a needle, as a

Chinese proverb puts it. Hong Kong secondary teachers see their allotted task as maximizing their students' results in the public examinations (Morris, 1985). They believe that they can most effectively grind their iron bars with an expository teaching style, in which they lecture and provide notes, while the needles-to-be ascribe their own effort, and their skill in studying, as the most important contribution they can make to their own transformation (see Chapter 5 and 6). By the time Hong Kong students pass the required hurdles and enter tertiary institutions, we have a body of students who are not only highly selected academically, but street-wise in examination technique.

Given such a background, one might expect students in Hong Kong to show a propensity for surface learning. However, they do not appear to do so (Biggs, 1990), which is part of the paradox extensively referred to elsewhere in this book. It could be that Hong Kong students are Miller and Parlett's (1974) cue seekers *par excellence*. If they see examinations as typically requiring rote learning, then they will rote learn even if this is not their preferred way of learning. The quotations in Chapter 6 from interviews with Hong Kong secondary students make this conflict clear. One student thought that having to rote learn was "a disgrace to myself"; that he had been "deprived" of his "right to understand": but he continued to rote learn.

In this Chapter, we review what studies have been carried out on the effects of assessment on the learning of Hong Kong students. In particular, we probe one aspect of the paradox of the Chinese learner that may not have been adequately explored in previous chapters. Socialization in Confucian heritage cultures (CHCs) may well provide the dispositions that ease the child into the demands of the classroom; teachers in those classrooms may well instruct in ways that are more conducive to deep learning than are perceptible to round eyes wearing Western-made spectacles. But we are still left with the seemingly unarguable facts that:-

1) Hong Kong is an exam-dominated environment;
2) Exams are perceived by students to require such rote learning as to be "a disgrace to myself" (whatever those who constructed the exams may have intended); and
3) Exams in general have powerful backwash effects.

So a trace of the ubiquitous paradox remains. Are Hong Kong students immune from the long-term effects of relentless examining? Does their Confucian heritage socialization provide them with the moral fortitude, the coping strategies, or both, to enable them to survive this harsh environment?

Several issues are examined in this chapter:-

1) The nature of what it is that is being assessed; formats of testing make implicit assumptions about the nature of learning;

2) How backwash works;
3) The role and structure of assessment procedures in the Hong Kong school and tertiary sectors; and
4) Research on the effects of these procedures on the learning of Hong Kong students.

Assessment and Assumptions about Learning

What does it mean to say that we have learned something? How we answer reveals the conception we have of the nature of learning; that conception enters into decisions to do with teaching and assessing. Marton, Dall'Alba and Beaty (1993) describe an elaborate taxonomy of conceptions of learning, but it suffices here to pick up Cole's (1990) distinction between the quantitative and qualitative traditions in our educational thinking.

The quantitative tradition

In the quantitative tradition, learning is conceived as the aggregation of content: to be a good learner is to know more.

The contents of learning are conceived as discrete quanta of declarative or of procedural knowledge, the process of learning to aggregate by assimilation. The theory of learning assumed in the quantitative tradition is behaviourism, the environment reduced to sets of stimuli, to which behavioural responses are selectively linked through reinforced repetition. The curriculum is conceived as discrete units of content, such as facts, skills, and competencies, often as behavioural objectives. The competency movement, and the current concern with performance indicators, stem from the same tradition.

Implications for assessment. Assessment in the quantitative tradition involves test situations that reliably indicate whether or not the correct behavioural response to the test stimulus is in the student's response repertoire, so that the ability to reproduce previously learned content quickly and accurately becomes the criterion for good learning (Cole, 1990).

It is further assumed that the contents of knowledge are learned in binary units, correct or incorrect, and that the correct units may be summed to give an aggregate or total score that is an index of competence in what is learned. Multiple choice tests, for example, represent learning as a total score of all items correct (with or without guessing penalties), any one item being 'worth' the same as any other. In standard methods of test construction and item analysis, items are selected on the extent to which they correlate with the total test score, not in terms of their intrinsic content. Quality of content, and its integration with other content, becomes quite secondary. Even essay marking is likely to have a quantitative bias in practice. The most common procedure in marking open-ended essay responses is to award a mark for each relevant point made, and convert the ratio of actual marks to possible marks into some kind of number, which the teacher may then adjust for overall quality; the final grade is essentially arrived at quantitatively.

The quantitative conceptual framework makes assumptions about the nature of knowledge, and the acquisition of knowledge, that are simply unacceptable in the light of what we now know about human learning, although the related test technology of item analysis, test construction, and establishing reliability and validity is sophisticated and in wide-spread use.

The qualitative tradition

In the qualitative tradition, students are assumed to learn cumulatively, interpreting and incorporating new material with what they already know, their understanding progressively changing as they learn. The contents of learning are meanings, the process of learning progressive understanding of the meanings, the outcomes of learning the constructions the learner has made at any stage. The family of theories of learning that underlies the qualitative tradition is constructivism (Driver and Oldham, 1986), of which there are several modern variants: information processing theory (Shuell, 1986); student approaches to learning (SAL; Biggs, 1993); neo-Piagetian theories of cognitive development (Demetriou, Shayer, and Efklides, 1992); and post-structuralisan (Delandsheere and Petrovsky, 1994).

The curriculum in a qualitative framework defines levels of understanding that are 'reasonable' at the stage of learning in question. An immature level of response is not incorrect so much as partially correct, so what is acceptable is relative. The teacher's task is not to transmit correct understandings, so much as to help students construct understandings that are more, rather than less acceptable. Content thus evolves cumulatively over the long term, having 'horizontal' interconnections with other topics and subjects, and 'vertical' interconnections with previous and subsequent learnings in the same topic.

Implications for assessment. Whereas the logic of assessment from a quantitative point of view implies aggregating units of learning, that from the qualitative tradition is longitudinal, the aim being to discover where students stand in relation to the development of understanding or competence in the concept or skill in question. Another way of handling qualitative assessment in the case of applied or procedural knowledge is to define the application of the knowledge in terms of a situation that is ecologically valid.

Thus, a prerequisite for using qualitative assessment in the first sense is to chart the course of development of a concept or principle, so that the stages of development can be defined. This may be done on a topic by topic basis, or by using a general taxonomy that applies over a range of topics or even subjects. An example of the first is the use of phenomenography to establish the hierarchy of conceptions of understanding for each concept (Marton, 1988; Ramsden, 1988); another is the curriculum based approach of the Hong Kong Target Oriented Curriculum (TOC; Education Department, 1994). Each such approach requires that the research and development has been carried out for each topic, which involves a considerable research input. An example of the generalist model is the SOLO taxonomy (Biggs and Collis, 1982; 1989), according to which a general sequence may be assumed in the development of many concepts and skills, and that sequence may be used to guide the formulation of specific targets or the assessment of specific outcomes.

The applied or ecological approach to qualitative assessment simply situates the test in an 'authentic' setting. In a sense, this is simply saying that tests should be valid, yet so detached and quantitative has assessment become that authentic testing has become a recent catch-cry, and testing problem-solving by giving students the sort of problem they would meet in real life, rather than giving them an exam in the declarative knowledge prerequisite to problem solving, a major innovation (Masters and Hill, 1989; Wiggins, 1989).

'Teaching to the test' is usually seen to degrade teaching and learning (Frederiksen and Collins, 1989), but in either developmental or ecological models of assessment, this is precisely what teachers should do, as the tests define qualitative targets for learning and thinking.

How Backwash Works

The quotation by Elton and Laurillard at the beginning of this chapter is a pithy generalization from much collective experience. It tells us little, however, about how such backwash effects work, and in fact there is relatively little evidence to tie down the mechanisms with any certainty. One obvious factor is the kind of test constructed, but it is the *student's* perception of the test and the demands it makes that generates the effects. The student's perception of what is to be assessed may be a far cry from what the teacher *intends* to be assessed.

Teacher-based and institution-based factors in test construction

It would be simple if teachers set tasks according to the rhetoric of educational aims and objectives, but they do so rarely. First, they need the appropriate technology (Reid, 1987); do they actually know how to assess the qualitative aims of their courses? The evidence is that most teachers do not. Marso and Pigge (1991) surveyed over 300 teachers in Ohio, asking them for a copy of a recent test they had made. Of 1,000 items received, multiple-choice, true-false and short-answer were by far the most common; essay questions (only 64 received) the least. Some 72% of all items tested straight recall; the essay-type questions occasionally addressed higher levels, but the majority of even these addressed recall and comprehension only. Marso and Pigge concluded that teachers tended:-

1)   Overwhelmingly to test low level outcomes; and
2)   To attempt complex test-types only to get them wrong.

Hong Kong teachers are likely to be no better than Ohio teachers at this: possibly worse, given the relative levels of pre- and inservice training. The institution-based factors determine the latitude a teacher has to assess in the way that teacher would like to. Such factors rarely have an educational basis, and rarely do they operate in a way benign to learning. They comprise the social system of the institution (Reid, 1987), which has two aspects: (a) the informal requirements established on a collegial basis, and (b) the formal requirements of bureaucracy. An example of the first would be an agreement not to double-mark assignments because that entails an increased workload on one's colleagues, and so decide to use multiple-choice testing which obviates the need for double-marking. An example of the second would be marking quantitatively along a percentage scale in order to make life easier for administrators who need to collate grades across courses. These extrinsic factors, stemming from the social system, most often put pressure on the teacher to assess quantitatively. Examples of these factors in the Hong Kong educational scene are given in a later section.

The student's perspective

The characteristics of the test, and the context in which it is given, may provide the objective text for backwash effects, but students differ greatly in their ability to read the cues provided. 'Cue seekers' are very alert to what will tell them how best to prepare for the test, and go out of their way to optimize, while the 'cue deaf', to change the modality, seem unaffected by backwash (Miller and Parlett, 1974). Several factors are involved in testing backwash on the student's side.

Forms of understanding. When students study for an examination, they attempt to understand the material in ways that they perceive will meet requirements (Entwistle and Entwistle, 1992). The meaning of 'understanding' depends on how students perceive the examination context; understanding the content of a lecture to meet the requirements of a quick true-false test the following week will involve a different perception of understanding than that required, say, when the lecture is audited in preparation for a tutorial at which one is expected to summarize the lecture for the whole group. The expected mode of assessment creates a framework, or form of understanding, within which the student interprets and constructs the content of the course to meet the perceived need for that kind of understanding. The Entwistles found five such forms, in hierarchical order:-

1) Reproduces content from lecture notes without any clear structure;
2) Reproduces the content within the structure used by the lecturer;
3) Develops own structure, but solely to generate answers to anticipated exam questions;
4) Adjusts structures from strategic reading to represent personal understanding, but also to control examination requirements; and
5) Develops an individual conception of the discipline from wide reading and reflection.

Only the last form is directed towards understanding and applying the discipline itself, the others being determined by the examination. The Entwistles found that 'worrying'. Many of these students were in professional faculties, studying in order to practise as professionals rather than to pass exams, yet the examinations in most cases stood in the way of students achieving their own personal understandings of the content. The assessment system provided many students with a framework for understanding their coursework that was unrelated to their real reasons for taking the course!

Approaches to learning. If forms of understanding act as goals for students' efforts in study by telling them what to aim for, approaches to learning dictate how they get there.

Approaches to learning, introduced in Chapter 1, may be located at the process level, in the way originally described by Marton and Säljö (1976), as descriptions of what students *actually do* when handling an ongoing task. They may also be located at the presage level, as *likely* ways of handling a task in a given situation, which is the meaning usually addressed by questionnaire (Biggs, 1993). But whether considered at presage or process level, approaches to learning, like forms of understanding, operate in context. Even a relatively stable preferred approach to learning is responsive to a learning context, because it is derived in large part from students' perceptions of what the learning context generally requires. A learning approach must not therefore be confused, as it often is, with the context-independent 'learning style' (Riding and Cheema, 1991).

At the process level itself, Meyer, Parsons, and Dunne (1990) describe 'study orchestration', which in the actual learning situation may over-ride consistency of an individual student's general learning approach, according to what the student perceives as the particular demands of the assessment task. The first two forms of understanding would appear to bring about an orchestration of a surface theme; the third, also a surface theme but with an achieving variation in the sub-dominant; the fourth, an achieving theme with a deep variation in the sub-dominant. Only the fifth form of understanding would clearly resound in deep major.

In a comprehensive review of effects of evaluation practices on students, Crooks (1988) certainly makes it clear that effects exist, but the most interesting reports are often anecdotal (Rogers, 1969; Snyder, 1971). Marton and Saljo's (1976) study implicates the expectation of answering questions with the surface approach, but their students jumped the gun; that study was not set in the ecology of a testing situation (which nevertheless goes to show how test-sensitive some students are).

Other studies address approaches to learning in the presage sense. In one study, the lecturer warned the class that material reproduced in the exam from course materials would be penalized, but nonetheless, one group of cue seekers scored relatively higher in the written exam section than in the multiple choice; the lecturer had unconsciously marked up those who had replayed the notes (Biggs, 1973 - regrettably). However, in this study, as in many others, the propensity for rote learning was assessed at the presage level; the 'intervention' (the warning) was totally over-ridden by what the cue-seeking students would have done in any case.

When the interaction between presage and process is taken into account, results are clearer. When instructed to learn for detail, students with an orientation for surface learning (presage) obtained much higher factual recall scores than deep learners, but when instructed to write a meaningful abstract it was found they had missed the point, whereas deep learners could do so very well (Biggs, 1979). Here, tested learning quality was related to both presage and process, but the backwash was artificially created by instructions, not by the test.

Mastery learning seems to create powerful backwash, differentially read by deep and surface learners (Lai and Biggs, 1994). In this study, Hong Kong grade 10 students were taught biology conventionally and in four mastery units; it was found that on the first mastery test the students biased towards a deep approach were better than surface (as might be expected), but on the second they were equal, and they progressively diverged thereafter, the deep ending up performing poorly, and turned off by the business of incessant testing for detail, while the surface students loved it, many tasting academic success for the first time in their lives. Interviews strongly suggested that the testing format required low-level reproductive strategies, with which the surface students were happy to oblige but the deep were not.

Format of testing seems to create differential backwash. Baddeley (1991) asked physiotherapy students to read three texts related to their anatomy course on nerve function. The first two texts were tested for factual recall, and for applied understanding (what would happen if a particular nerve was severed) in a crossed design, while the remaining text was tested for both factual recall and for understanding. It was found that students did best on the type of question on the third text they had been expecting, which does suggest that format generates a backwash effect. Thomas and Bain (1982; 1984) in a series of studies found evidence both for consistency in learning across subject areas and testing contexts, but for varying mixes of reproductive and deep strategies according to multiple-choice and assignment formats of assessment. In particular, students (presumably presage deep) who perceived that memory would be helpful in the multiple-choice combined rote learning with understanding, reminiscent of the 'deep-memorizing' used by Hong Kong students (see below).

Most of the reported research sees backwash as detrimental to learning. However, the effects should cut both ways: assessment relying on qualitative criteria should induce students to use *high* cognitive level preparation strategies. One recent study on BEd students in Hong Kong strongly suggests that this is so. A portfolio method of assessment, requiring students to produce evidence of their learning to match high-level criteria, did in fact result in over one-third in a large class producing high-level products matching an 'A' grade, qualitatively defined (Biggs, in press).

In sum, then, the fact of backwash seems clearly demonstrable, even if the mechanisms creating and sustaining backwash may not be as clear as expected, given the assumed power of the effect. We are dealing with two interacting domains, from teacher and student:-

1) *Teachers'* perceptions of institutional requirements, course objectives, type of test and item required, and their technical knowledge of how to create an appropriate test; and

2) *Students'* perceptions of the form of understanding required by the test, and which meets the student's own private agenda, and the approaches and strategies needed to realize that private goal-state.

Conventional methods of assessment generally push in a quantitative direction. In fact, the longer many students are exposed to institutional learning, the more surface and less deep-oriented their approaches to learning become, not only in Australian institutions (Biggs, 1987), but also in Hong Kong tertiary institutions (Gow and Kember, 1990; Stokes, Balla, and Stafford, 1989). But it would not be Hong Kong if this generalization did not contain its own paradox also. In the school sector, the private, expatriate schools in Hong

Kong, with their elite clientele, small classes and progressive teaching methods, show an increase in deep from the middle to the end of secondary schooling; but so too, only even more pronounced especially in the case of boys, do the Anglo-Chinese or English-medium Government schools for ethnic Chinese, with their large classes and expository teaching methods.

Let us turn to the Hong Kong scene in an attempt to find out what is happening.

Assessment in Hong Kong: the Situation and Some Research

The school sector

One of the most trenchant criticisms the visiting Llewellyn Committee made in its review of the Hong Kong educational system concerned the frequency, role, and power of examinations (Hong Kong Government, 1982). The effects of assessment they saw as particularly objectionable at the end of primary school, where on the basis of an external examination each child was placed in one of five ability bands at the beginning of secondary school, which then determined which secondary school the child was likely to enter. The few lucky ones were allocated a school that optimized their chances of tertiary entrance seven years later (with its own series of hurdles), the unlucky ended up in bought places in inferior private schools, their future career options now severely limited. All bands then followed the same curriculum, and sat for the same external examinations, most set in English.

In the ten years or more since the Llewellyn Committee, little has changed. The primary assessments that are used for allocating a child into a band are now made internally rather than externally, but the pressures have if anything increased, exacerbated in Hong Kong's culture by parental social and economic ambitions in an intensely competitive situation. In fact, there is a most peculiar procedure adopted in producing the composite score which is used for banding a child; it is weighted *upwards* by the child's school mean, so that a child in a better primary school has a greater chance of obtaining a higher band secondary school than one with the same personal composite score in a worse performing school. The rationale seems to be McGregor's (1960) Theory X assumption (that is, operating on the principle that people are untrustworthy) that teachers in poorer schools will be softer in their assessments of children than teachers in higher-performing schools. One could equally of course make the Theory Y assumption (operating on the principle that people *are* trustworthy) that an academically able child who managed to get a good composite score in a poor teaching environment would be an excellent bet for a high band secondary school. As it is, the present procedure simply guarantees an elite system right down the line; ambitious parents jostle to get their tinies into a 'good' primary school from day one.

A structural feature of Hong Kong's education system, that can only exacerbate backwash, is that there is one body, the Government Education Department, to look after curriculum, teaching, and their associated infrastructure, and quite another body, the Hong Kong Examinations Authority, to control the assessment mechanisms that are publicly perceived to be the most significant in determining what goes on in secondary schools. The external examinations at grade 11 (HKCEE), grade 12 (AS level), and grade 13 (A level), are all norm-referenced, designed to select at the upper end of the distribution. The Examinations Authority is independent of the Government, being a quango self-financed on the basis of a sitting fee, which naturally discourages examinations in small enrolment subjects, cross-disciplinary subjects such as Environmental Studies (as the content is examined in other courses), and until recently parallel examinations in the mother tongue. The conception and conduct of examining is highly quantitative in the cognitive domain, and very Theory X in the affective (for example, students are allocated to examination centres in schools geographically distant from their own, and turning up at the 'wrong' centre results in a mark penalty).

The effects on teaching in secondary school were documented by Morris (1985), who found that Hong Kong economics teachers saw public examinations as requiring them to use an expository teaching style, in which they lecture and provide notes that the students duly rote learn in anticipation of the frequently predictable exam questions. T.K.W. Tang (1993) found this to be true of novice but not of expert chemistry teachers. Novice teachers held that good teaching was transmitting knowledge in preparation for the examinations and "overseeing the lazy pupils"; one novice thought that "understanding" was "being able to solve the more difficult exam questions" (T.K.W. Tang, 1993; p.50). His expert teachers, however, saw examinations not as the goal of teaching but simply as a necessary detour, their main goal being students' understanding, best constructed by interactive rather than expository teaching; in that they were right, as their students performed better.

Tang's experts were dealing with Band 1 (top stream) students. Most students, particularly in the lower bands, are not taught interactively, but in the manner noted by Morris. The effects are documented by Tommy Tang (1993), who found that of 20 grade 8 and grade 10 students he interviewed, 19 adopted a surface approach to learning, and believed that good teaching was based on transmission.

Fan (1993) compared students' approaches to writing when writing for an examination and writing at home. When students wrote for examinations, compared with writing at home, their concern for the grade they might receive became paramount; self-expression, communication, and sharing become of no account. The ideas are "either unwanted or half-baked" (Fan, 1993; p. 65), personal views are withheld for fear of offending the marker, grammatical and spelling accuracy over-ride content, model essays are memorized, and brighter students try to impress by using difficult words. Writing at home to many students is on the other hand enjoyable, more time is spent planning and revising, and the quality is much higher.

Johnson in Chapter 7 suggests that internal assessment involves an unspoken agreement between teachers and students, necessitated by the charade of testing in English when the students' grasp of English hardly exceeds the word level; teachers accordingly assess for 'comprehension' with simple, even tautologous, tests involving the recognition of no more than single words. Without such survival strategies, life would simply be intolerable in the classroom, for both students and teachers.

The picture we have of the effects of assessment on Hong Kong secondary students' approaches to learning, then, is a mixed one. The system itself is indeed exam-dominated and elitist, the primary function of which appears to be to select the top 5% or so of students for tertiary study rather than to educate the majority. It is precisely that aspect that confounds the issue; the fact that students appear to have motives and strategies that are deeper and less surface than they were in the middle of secondary school may not be saying anything about the learning environment provided by the schools, but rather about the increasing selectivity of the students. Certainly, the qualitative evidence provided by T. Tang and Fan and others makes it quite clear that the less able students are strongly influenced in a surface direction by assessment requirements.

The interesting, and encouraging, point that emerges from Fan's study of writing is that students readily isolate their strategies, writing joylessly and defensively in order to cope with examination demands, but "at home, if I like the topic, I can make it more forceful" (Fan, 1993; p69). You play the game; just do not let it get to you.

The one encouraging sign is the present situation in the development of TOC, which was implemented in a few schools in Primary 1 in 1994. This is in effect a mastery programme criterion-referenced to learning targets in terms of students' stages of growth in their understanding of the curriculum topics: a very significant and promising change of direction. TOC is however recommended only in three subjects (Chinese, English, and Mathematics) and it will be well beyond the year 2000 before it will reach secondary schools.

The tertiary sector

It is more difficult to discuss assessment in the tertiary sector in Hong Kong because each institution runs its own assessment system. The rhetoric describing objectives is usually qualitative; teaching methods vary considerably, even within the same institution, some being based exclusively on expository lectures, others being interactive and problem-based. Final assessments are similarly varied, ranging from formal examinations, to assignments, to experiential, process-oriented, activities, including peer- and self-assessment (Kuisma, 1994).

Such diversity is admirable, as far as it goes. The down side is that it does not go very far; the formal and informal social structures have their effect. One university has regulations preventing the release of examination results to students, obviously not on educational grounds, but on grounds of institutional and collegial convenience. On one occasion an academic claimed the right to use his own judgment on releasing grades, only to be told by a senior academic: "If you do it, that will force us to. That's not cricket!" And in this case he was able to invoke formal support: "Anyway, you can't. It's against the regulations".

A practice that affects Hong Kong particularly is the use of overseas external examiners, which constrains the nature of the assessment task to one that an outsider to the teaching process can handle. This tends to discourage detailed feedback, and the use of personalized assessment tasks such as portfolios, diaries, etc., or tasks involving self-assessment and peer assessment, despite their sensitivity to teaching objectives and to higher-order learning processes (Boud, 1985; Harris and Bell, 1986; Masters and Hill, 1991). Most institutions require units to be collated and levels of Honours or Distinction/Pass levels in the total programme to be determined easily. This puts almost irresistable pressure on markers, or more significantly on faculty or programme committees, to use quantitative marking schemes. It need not do so, as profiling or other qualitative schemes can be used, but in practice teachers are required to come up with a grade that can be quantified. Most teachers therefore mark quantitatively in the first place, which provides them with an inappropriate mind-set when marking: so much for this, so much for that. The problem is that in an extended piece of writing the shape of the total argument becomes lost, or at least figures minimally as just another thing to be tallied when arriving at the final grade. And of course the message to students is clear: "knowledge-tell", as Bereiter and Scardamalia (1987) put it, which is an obvious strategy if each point of information gets a mark. Knowledge-telling students then present as long a list of points as possible, as densely packed as the word limit requires. This strategy of presenting lists must be an even greater temptation to students operating in a second language discourse structure (see Chapter 7).

How then do Hong Kong tertiary students cope? We would like to conclude on a more positive note by referring to a detailed case study of a tertiary course in one tertiary institution.

A Case Study of Two Modes of Assessment

Given the effects of assessment on learning and understanding, teachers are faced with a very practical question. What mode of assessment should be used in a given course or unit: a short answer examination (ensuring coverage), or an assignment (maximizing depth of engagement)?

Integrated Professional Studies (IPS) is a preclinical subject in the Professional Diploma course in Physiotherapy at the Hong Kong Polytechnic University. IPS requires students to synthesize and integrate the theory and professional skills acquired in individual subject areas in an holistic perspective for the treatment and management of patients. Students are expected to develop high-level cognitive strategies such as critical and analytical thinking, relating, integrating, and application of knowledge.

Traditionally, assessment has been by written tests comprising short essay questions, but staff increasingly felt that case study assignments might be a more appropriate way of assessing the high-level strategies that the course is intended to address. On the other hand, as assignments address only one topic, much course content remains unassessed. An examination addresses that problem, but would that then encourage students to use low level preparation strategies?

These questions raise complex issues fully addressed elsewhere (Tang 1991); here we compare the effects of students' typical approaches to learning with those they perceive necessary for coping with a particular mode of assessment, test or assignment.

First, path analyses of two entire intakes (N = 156) were carried out, tracing the effects of students' typical approaches to learning, and their actual assessment preparation strategies orchestrated to each mode of assessment, on achievement in each of the modes, test or assignment. Second, 39 randomly selected students were interviewed to confirm how they perceived the task demands of the two formats, and what effect different strategies had on the learning outcomes.

The path analyses

Path analyses were conducted on the two intakes, with a causal model based on the 3P model (see Chapter 3). The *presage* domain was defined by the six scores on a bilingual Chinese-English version of the Study Process Questionnaire (SPQ: Biggs, 1992): surface motive (SM) and strategy (SS), deep motive (DM) and strategy (DS), and achieving motive (AM) and strategy (AS). The SPQ was administered at the beginning of the academic year. The scores give students' usual orientations to their coursework, and are not specific to any particular mode of assessment.

The *process* domain was defined by the assessment preparation strategies

(APSs) adopted by the students, using a questionnaire derived by rewording SPQ items specifically for (a) the test, and (b) the assignment. Factor analysis yielded five scales for each mode of assessment comprising six items per scale: internal consistencies varied from alphas of .55 to .60 (test), and .54 to .62 (assignment).

The *product* domain comprised three sets of scores, one for the test (the sum of the scores on four compulsory essay questions), and two for the assignment: (a) the marks awarded for the assignment, based on relevance to the question, the quality of logical argument, and on how well the main ideas or theme had been discussed, argued, and presented; and (b) a qualitative score based on the structural complexity of the assignments according to the SOLO Taxonomy (Biggs and Collis, 1982).

In the interests of space, the full path diagrams are not presented here. The effects central to the present discussion are the direct and indirect effects of the presage (usual approaches) and process (APSs) factors on the three dependent variables, test marks, assignment marks, and assignment SOLO scores. These are reproduced in Table 9.1.

Table 9.1
Direct and indirect effects on test and assignment outcomes

Source		Test (r^2=.260) Indir.	Dir.	Tot.	Ass Mark (r^2=.172) Indir.	Dir.	Tot.	Ass SOLO (r^2=.128) Indir.	Dir.	Tot.
Presage motives and strategies										
Surface	M	-	-	-	-.23	.26	-	-	-	-
	S	-	-	-	-	-.25	-.28	-	-.24	-.26
Deep	M	-	-	-	-	-	-	.10	-.14	-
	S	.18	-.15	-	-	.26	.18	-	.11	.14
Achieve	M	-	.22	.20	-	-.29	-.26	-	.22	.22
	S	-	-	-	-	-	-	-	-.10	-
Assessment preparation strategies										
APS 1		.12	.22	.34	-	-	-	-	-	-
APS 2		-	-	-	-	-.13	-	-	-.13	-.11
APS 3		-.13	.11	-	-	.12	.15	-	-	-
APS 4		.14	-.33	-.19	-	-	-	-	-	-
APS 5		-	.43	.43	-	-	-	-	-	-

Note: All printed path coefficients are significant (P < .01)

Preparation strategies and the test. Test performance was much more closely related to the process variables, the specific assessment preparation strategies, than to the students' usual approaches to learning, as can be seen from the columns reporting the direct effects (Dir.). However, the presage factors of usual motives and strategies did affect the test marks indirectly (column Indir.) because they were related to specific preparation strategies that themselves directly predicted test performance. For example, students with a deep bias chose deep-related strategies and surface bias, surface-related strategies. This sometimes had the odd effect that a direct effect from a usual approach to learning might be negative (e.g. deep strategy on test performance), but students with a deep approach might use a specific assessment preparation strategy that boosted test performance (e.g. APS 3 and APS 5). In other words, deep-biased students when handling a test in which their deepness might be a liability turn it to good effect by organizing and a strategy called deep-memorizing (see below).

Turning now to direct effects, the assessment preparation strategy with the strongest effect on the test was 'systematic organizing' (APS 5), which was adopted by students with a deep approach and high achievement motivation. The next strongest effect was negative, from a deep-related preparation strategy involving seeking relationships from the academic subjects (APS 4); the very thing the course IPS was designed to promote, interdisciplinary integration, was in fact quite counterproductive in terms of test performance, although a 'deep-professional' strategy (APS 3) was marginally productive. Finally, there was a moderately strong positive effect on test performance from a 'syllabus-bound and memorizing' strategy (APS 1), which was adopted by highly-motivated students, whether surface, deep or achieving. APS 1 seems to be a restricted surface strategy, yet it is adopted by deep or intrinsically motivated students when studying for the test.

The only presage factors relating directly to test performance were achievement motivation (positive) and deep strategy (negative).

A first reading of these results suggests that an organized surface approach, involving the systematic rote learning of strategically selected data, is an effective way of preparing for the test, in which the complication of relating to background disciplines is specifically avoided. An important question arises. If the backwash from the test is predominantly surface-related, are deep-oriented learners at a disadvantage when assessed by a test? Apparently not, because the *indirect* effects show that deep-oriented students orchestrate apparent surface strategies, such as organizing and memorizing, to do it their way. As clarified in subsequent interviews, they were motivated to understand the content, but also perceived that the test required them to memorize facts. So they did both, in the form of 'deep memorizing', going deep with a strategy that might otherwise be considered as surface.

In order to get high marks on the test, then, students need to be achievement oriented - to *want* high marks - to be systematic and organized, to focus on likely questions making sure their answers are memorized accurately, and to avoid deep or complicated issues except in so far as they relate directly to professional applications of knowledge. These students seem to be good at deriving test-appropriate strategies: as they might be expected to be, given their history in Hong Kong's schools.

Preparation strategies and the assignment. Indirect effects were minimal here, and now we see that the best predictors are from the presage domain, only two specific preparation strategies having an effect on the assignment marks (APS 2 and APS 3), and only one on the SOLO levels (APS 2).

Assignment marks were related to APS 3, a 'deep-professional' strategy, used by students who are intrinsically motivated, who want high marks, who are organized, and who avoid rote learning. In this they appear wise, because they are more likely to achieve high marks, as indeed they should as the assignment was about professional applications; APS 3 was not however related to the SOLO structure of the assignment. The other specific preparation strategy was 'cue-seeking' (APS 2), trying to identify the lecturers' expectations and writing to those rather than to the topic, a surface-related strategy that led to poorer not better performance.

Direct effects from the presage domain to performance in the assignment involved DS positively and SS negatively; and surprisingly AM was also negative. This last finding, and the general finding here that presage factors in general are better predictors of the assignment mark, are in keeping with the fact that writing an assignment is a new experience to most of these year one students. They therefore rely on their general approaches to learning, not having a repertoire of established coping strategies as they did in the test.

The path analyses do not, however, tell us how the students actually perceive the task demands of the two modes of assessment, how deep students specifically handled the task of preparing for a task, the backwash for which apparently encourages surface strategies, or how students write an assignment, the procedural details of which are unfamiliar and unclear.

To see precisely how students perceive this situation, and how they learn to cope with it, we need to turn to the finegrain of the interview data.

The interview data

Thirty-nine students were randomly selected from the two intakes and interviewed twice, once after each assessment. Their perceptions of the demands of these assessment procedures were obtained through open-ended questions about what they thought they had to do in order to do well in the assessment, and what problems they encountered in studying for the test and doing the assessment.

Perceptions of test demands. Students tended to have either a quantitative or qualitative perception of the demands of a test, each encompassing a set of cognitive strategies and other attribution factors.

Quantitative perceptions saw the test as seeking amounts of information, and as requiring low-level cognitive strategies like rote learning, memorizing and reproducing. Success was seen as requiring effort and time, and by some as requiring external factors such as luck.

Qualitative perceptions saw the test as demanding understanding and application, and hence the need to study with high-level cognitive strategies. Such students also perceived that they had an active control of the task through putting more effort in studying and to properly organize their study time and study material, but in service of the attempt to understand.

A group of students emerged whose perceptions of the demands of a test seemed to share both quantitative and qualitative characteristics. To them, studying for a test required both understanding and memorizing: a good understanding of the learning materials, and the need to memorize what they had studied and understood. Such 'deep memorization' is different from memorization achieved through rote learning without understanding of the content. The following comments from the students help illustrate this perception of requirement of deep memorization strategy:-

> "You may understand the principles, but you still have to memorize the points so that you can present all of them in a test as this is the way marking is done - by the points, so you cannot miss any."

> "There are so many things and it is not possible to rote learn everything. You must understand and try to find some common points so that it is easier to remember.... My method is to understand first and then memorize."

Other perceived demands could be associated with either a quantitative or a qualitative perception, depending on whether this organization was considered to be necessary for rote learning or for understanding: a good command of English, and some special skills and techniques, such as organization of study time and materials.

Perceptions of assignment demands. Quantitative perceptions of what the assignment required were few, mainly comprising the need for copying from journals. This was expressed as a felt need due to poor command of English.

Qualitative perceptions were varied, including: understanding the question and the content through high-level processing aiming at analyzing and interpreting; reading involved understanding, thinking and reasoning, relating to previous knowledge, to other subjects; to have one's own opinions and support them with evidence from journals; to relate to physiotherapy and to clinical practice in the real situation. Effort and time were seen as necessary for establishing a large knowledge base, and to have that knowledge organized and readily available.

Other perceptions included, as before, a good command of English in order to express ideas within the constraint of a word limit.

In sum, then, the students had clearly different perceptions of the assessment demands for each mode of assessment; surface strategies such as rote learning and memorizing were perceived to be more related to the test than to the assignment, as was suggested but not established in the path analyses.

These students were classified into surface and deep groups on the basis of the quality and cognitive level of the different preparation strategies they reported in the interviews for each assessment format. Students not demonstrating a clear classification of study approach were not included in either group. Mean differences between the surface and deep groups for the three sets of assessment scores are shown in Table 9.2.

Table 9.2
Mean difference in assessment scores between surface and deep groups

	Mean scores		
	Test	Assignment	
	(Mark)	(Mark)	(SOLO)
Surface	54.94	59.10	2.29
N	17	21	21
Deep	52.14	71.07	3.67
N	21	15	15
P	NS	<.005	<.005

The approaches as classified here are more global than the specific assessment preparation strategies identified in the path analysis, but the trend is similar. As for the test, 17 students were classified as surface and 21 as deep, and there were no differences between them on test performance (P > .05). And for the assignment, 21 students were classified as surface and 15 as deep, the difference between assignment marks and SOLO both being highly significant in favour of the deep group (P < .005).

So yet another paradox emerges. Although the assignment was perceived overwhelmingly as *requiring* deep preparation strategies, when it came to actual preparation, more students used surface strategies (21) than deep (15). Thus, the test was perceived as requiring surface-preparation strategies, but deep-oriented students could handle it equally as well, or better, than surface. The assignment was perceived as requiring deep, and those using deep strategies did better, but oddly they were in the minority. Obviously, perception of assessment demands is not enough; students need also the procedural knowledge of handling assignments appropriately. With regard to the test, on the other hand, these students had cut their academic teeth on test taking strategies in primary school; the equivalent procedural knowledge for handling the test was at the ready.

Conclusions

These results collectively show that how students cope with assessment depends in large part on what they see as the assessment task requirements, but they also need to be familiar with the task and to have coping strategies to hand. Otherwise, they fall back on their established or preferred approaches to learning. This emerged most dramatically in the interview data on the assessment, when students overwhelmingly saw deep APSs as the way to go, but in the event only a minority used them. Immediate task demands are one thing, but only those students predisposed to a deep approach could meet the perceived demands. Seeing what to do is only part of the story; you also have to know how to do it.

However, given that students will try do what they perceive as required of them, give or take some allowance for individual orientations to learning, then teachers had better make those demands as clearly as possible. Thomas and Rohwer's (1986; p. 30) claim, that "In the academic arena, ambiguity of purpose is more often the rule than the exception", may not be true here for the test, where these students seemed to have quite clear notions about good test-taking strategies, but it is certainly true for the assignment, where students were aware of the need for understanding, a broad knowledge base, and a well constructed argument, but were less sure of what these might look like or how they could achieve them. This is perhaps not surprising given their training for responding at word level in secondary school (see Chapter 7). Clearly, these students need training in assignment writing.

This review of the role and effects of assessment in both school and tertiary sectors in Hong Kong leaves at least one major impression: Hong Kong students are excellent at playing the game while remaining uncorrupted themselves. The much maligned school level examination system is probably every bit as effective at communicating surface, quantitatively loaded, backwash as it fiercest critics maintain, but the better students become highly skilled at meeting examination requirements, with their academic souls unsullied. They arrive at tertiary level with an armory of superficial strategies tuned to coping with certain kinds of assessment requirements, such as those demanded in the standard short-answer test involving point-making rather than extended argument, but they are also in possession of the deeper, more culturally located, dispositions discussed in the previous chapter, that turn them to deep learning, their way.

There are two consequences. First, when they are faced with a novel assessment format, such as an assignment involving research and an integrated argument, they have few skills to deploy ready made. They *perceive* the need for deep-related strategies, but only those with a propensity for deep-oriented learning actually engage the assignment appropriately. This clearly spells out the need for training in research and assignment writing. It is interesting in this respect that, as discussed in the following chapter, the students also have a culturally-triggered coping mechanism in the form of spontaneous collaboration.

The second consequence helps explain the sub-paradox that students maintain a deep orientation in a highly surface-oriented assessment environment. Simply, the students react to that environment specifically and contextually, the cultural dispositions maintaining an orientation to deep learning, using strategies that help them meet examination requirements while learning deeply on the side.

To close where we started, Hong Kong students are street-wise when it comes to test-taking strategies, and it is interesting to see that even deep-oriented students can handle tests using superficial strategies while retaining their integrity as learners. These results show, however, that this mode of assessment is not educationally desirable, and that if shifts are to be made, then the teaching-learning infrastructure might need to be more accommodating to students' lack of procedural wisdom.

More generally, this high-pressure quantitative assessment situation is common in Southeast Asia, and it exerts its toll. The mechanisms for coping with it - cue-seeking and target-specific sets of strategies - are ones identifiable from the Western literature. An interesting question remains. How would Western students, lacking the docility dispositions identified in Chapter 3, cope with such a situation?

REFERENCES

Baddeley, H.A. (1991). Physiotherapy students' learning strategies and worries: their relevance for behavioural science teaching. Polytechnic of East London: Unpublished Doctoral Dissertation.

Bereiter, C. & Scardamalia, M. (1987). *The psychology of written composition.* Hillsdale, NJ: Lawrence Erlbaum.

Biggs, J.B. (1973). Study behaviour and performance in objective and essay formats. *Australian Journal of Education, 7,* 157-167.

Biggs, J.B. (1979). Individual differences in study processes and the quality of learning outcomes. *Higher Education, 8,* 381-394.

Biggs J.B. (1987). *Student approaches to learning and studying.* Australian Council for Educational Research, Hawthorn, Vic.

Biggs, J.B. (1990). Asian students' approaches to learning: implications for teaching overseas students. In M. Kratzing (Ed.), *Eighth Australasian Learning and Language Conference* (pp. 1-51). Queensland University of Technology Counselling Services.

Biggs, J.B. (1992). *Why and how do Hong Kong students learn? Using the Learning and Study Process Questionnaires.* The University of Hong Kong: Education Papers No. 14.

Biggs, J.B. (1993). What do inventories of students' learning processes really measure? A theoretical review and clarification. *British Journal of Educational Psychology, 63,* 1-17.

Biggs, J.B. (in press). The teaching context: the assessment portfolio as a tool for learning. In J.B. Biggs, (Ed.), *Testing: to educate or to select? Education in Hong Kong at the crossroads.* Hong Kong: Hong Kong Educational Publishing Co.

Biggs, J.B. & Collis, K.F. (1982). *Evaluating the quality of learning: the SOLO taxonomy.* New York: Academic Press.

Biggs, J.B. & Collis, K.F. (1989). Towards a model of school-based curriculum development and assessment: using the SOLO Taxonomy. *Australian Journal of Education, 33,* 149-161.

Boud, D. (1985). *Studies in self-assessment* (Occasional Paper No.26). Kensington: Tertiary Education Research Centre.

Cole, N.S. (1990). Conceptions of educational achievement. *Educational Researcher, 19*(3), 2-7.

Crooks, T.J. (1988). The impact of classroom evaluation practices on students. *Review of Educational Research, 58* 438-481.

Delandsheere, G. & Petrovsky, A.R. (1994). Capturing teachers' knowledge: performance assessment. *Educational Researcher, 23*(5), 11-18.

Demetriou, A., Shayer, M. & Efklides, A. (Eds.) (1992). *Neo-Piagetian theories of cognitive development.* London: Routledge and Kegan Paul.

Driver, R. & Oldham, V. (1986). A constructionist approach to curriculum development in science. *Studies in Science Education, 13,* 105-122.

Education Department (1994). *General introduction to Target Oriented Curriculum (TOC).* Hong Kong: Government Printer.

Elton L. & Laurillard, D. (1979). Trends in student learning. *Studies in Higher Education, 4,* 87-102.

Entwistle, A. & Entwistle, N. (1992). Experiences of understanding in revising for degree examinations. *Learning and Instruction, 2,* 1-22.

Fan F. (1993). How examinations affect students' approaches to writing. In J.B. Biggs & D.A. Watkins (Eds.), *Teaching and learning in Hong Kong: what is and what might be.* University of Hong Kong: Education Papers No. 17.

Frederiksen, J.R. & Collins, A. (1989). A systems approach to educational testing. *Educational Researcher, 18*(9), 27-32.

Gow, L. & Kember, D. (1990). Does higher education promote independent learning? *Higher Education, 19,* 307-322.

Harris, D. & Bell, C. (1986). *Evaluating and assessing for learning.* London: Kogan Page.

Hong Kong Government (1982). *A perspective on education: report of a visiting panel.* (The Llewellyn Report). Hong Kong: Government Printer.

Kuisma, R. (1994). Peer marking of written assignments. Paper given to 11th Annual Conference, Hong Kong Educational Research Association, 26-27 November.

Lai, P. & Biggs, J.B. (1994). Who benefits from mastery learning? *Contemporary Educational Psychology, 19,* 13-23.

McGregor, D. (1960). *The human side of enterprise.* New York: McGraw-Hill.

Marso, R.N. & Pigge, F.L. (1991). An analysis of teacher-made tests: item-types, cognitive demands, and item construction errors. *Contemporary Educational Psychology, 16,* 279-286.

Marton, F. (1988). Describing and improving learning. In R.R. Schmeck (Ed.), *Learning strategies and learning styles* (pp. 53-82). New York: Plenum.

Marton, F., Dall'Alba, G. & Beaty, E., (1993). Conceptions of learning. *International Journal of Educational Research, 13,* 277-300.

Marton, F. & Saljo, R. (1976). On qualitative differences in learning - I: Outcome and process. *British Journal of Educational Psychology, 46,* 4-11.

Masters, G.N. & Hill, P.W. (1988). Reforming the assessment of student achievement in the senior secondary school. *Australian Journal of Education, 32,* 274-286.

Meyer, J.H.F., Parsons, P. & Dunne, T.T. (1990). Individual study orchestration and their association with learning outcome. *Higher Education, 20*(1), 67-89.

Miller, C. & Parlett, M. (1974). *Up to the mark.* Guilford: Society for Research into Higher Education.

Morris, P. (1985). Teachers' perceptions of the barriers to the implementation of a pedagogic innovation: a South East Asian case study. *International Review of Education, 31*, 3-18.

Nickerson, R.S. (1989). New directions in educational assessment. *Educational Researcher, 18*(9), 3-7.

Ramsden, P. (1988). Context and strategy: situational influences on learning. In R.R. Schmeck (Ed.), *Learning strategies and learning styles.* New York: Plenum Press.

Reid, W.A. (1987). Institutions and practices: professional education reports and the language of reform. *Educational Researcher, 16*(8), 10-15.

Riding. R. & Cheema, I. (1991). Cognitive styles - an overview and integration. *Educational Psychology, 11*, 193-215.

Rogers, E.M. (1969). Examinations: powerful agents for good or ill in teaching. *American Journal of Physics, 37*, 954-962.

Shuell, T.J. (1986). Cognitive conceptions of learning. *Review of Educational Research, 56*, 411-436.

Snyder, B.R. (1971). *The hidden curriculum.* New York: Knopf.

Stokes, M.J., Balla, J.R. & Stafford, K.J. (1989). How students in selected degree programmes at CPHK characterize their approaches to study. *Educational Research Journal, 4*, 85-91.

Tang, K.C.C. (1991). Effects of different assessment methods on tertiary students' approaches to studying. The University of Hong Kong: Ph.D. Dissertation.

Tang, T.K.W. (1993). Do teachers' beliefs influence students' learning. In J.B. Biggs & D.A. Watkins (Eds.), *Teaching and learning in Hong Kong: what is and what might be.* The University of Hong Kong: Education Papers No. 17.

Tang, Tommy. (1993). Inside the classroom: The students' view. In J.B. Biggs & D.A. Watkins (Eds.), *Teaching and learning in Hong Kong: what is and what might be.* The University of Hong Kong: Education Papers No. 17.

Thomas, P. & Bain, J. (1982). Consistency in learning strategies. *Higher Education, 11*, 249-259.

Thomas, P. & Bain, J. (1984). Contextual dependence of learning approaches: the effects of assessment. *Human Learning, 3*, 227-240.

Thomas, J. & Rohwer, W.D. (1986). Academic studying: the role of learning strategies. *Educational Psychologist, 21*, 19-41.

Wiggins, G. (1989). Teaching to the (authentic) test. *Educational Leadership, 46*, 41-47.

10

Collaborative Learning: the Latent Dimension in Chinese Students' Learning

Catherine Tang

Chinese as a Collective Society

Walking along the nature trails in the Hong Kong hills is an informative experience. On the trail itself, one meets walkers in singles, pairs or small parties, and they are disproportionately non-Chinese. But the picnic areas are jam-packed with a shouting and cheering mass of interactive groups, and they are entirely Chinese. Is this collectivism just a holiday phenomenon, or a cultural characteristic?

Influenced by the Confucian emphasis in inter-relatedness, the pattern of Chinese socialization has taken on a social orientation model, resulting in a dependence-emphasizing society (Yang, 1981, 1982) with a strong sense of collectivism (Hofstede, 1983). The strong tradition of filial piety and familism which encompass a non-individual collectivistic orientation amongst the Chinese has resulted in a tendency for the Chinese to put more emphasis on collective efforts by members of a group toward achieving collective goals than individual competitiveness (Ho, 1981, 1986). Studies of how the Chinese describe themselves and their perceptions of the relation between the individual self and society reveal that the Chinese are more oriented toward group-related concepts and value group-related traits and roles (Bond, 1991). They identify their 'ideal self' as being closer to their 'social self', and involve their ideal self more closely in social relationships. In summarizing recent work on Chinese values, Yang (1986) concludes that the Chinese see collective welfare and social concerns as more important than personal enjoyment and feelings.

Within a social relationship, the members are more trustful and willing to commit themselves in material resources and information, and at the same time take pride in the success of the other members.

Given these cultural characteristics, it would seem likely that small groups involving collaboration and cooperation would be a natural way to structure learning for ethnic Chinese learners. Yet within the arena of education, the institutions of learning and their infrastructures are highly individualistic. Classroom arrangements are such that the students are seated in their individual chair and desk, and assessments emphasize individual performance (Lazar, 1995). So where is collectivism in learning? In fact, collective effort in learning does occur in Hong Kong, but not often formally (but see Chapter 12). In the course of another study (see Chapter 9), it was found that many students did in fact form small groups and collaborated in preparation for their assessments. The present chapter discusses the nature and characteristics of this collaboration in learning, and its effects on the learning process and on learning outcomes.

Western Research on Cooperative Learning

The use of small groups as a way of structuring learning is not new. In the UK, the practice of grouping was advocated by the Plowden Report in the 1960s, while in the US, small group learning can be dated back to the 1970s (see for example the work of Johnson and coworkers). Contemporary understanding of cooperative learning goes beyond just a few students working together on academic tasks. Cooperative learning has come to imply a more structured learning situation, with positive interdependence within the group in which an individual student's achievement is positively correlated with the rest of the group (Johnson, Johnson and Skon, 1979). In higher education, a small group technique has been devised to combine thinking and peer teaching in medical students (Johnson, 1969), and syndicate groups are formed which enhance student cooperative effort (Collier, 1983).

Many studies comparing cooperative learning and other goal structures of student learning in competitive and individualistic situations demonstrate that cooperative learning structures tend to be superior to both of the other learning situations in promoting student achievement (Humphreys, Johnson and Johnson, 1982; Nichols and Miller, 1994; Slavin, 1983a, 1987; Topping, 1992; Webb, 1985), especially in the acquisition of cognitive skills, in learning and understanding of the content, and in conceptual and problem-solving tasks (Damon, 1984; Hooper, Temiyakarn and Williams, 1993; Johnson, et al., 1981; Johnson, Skon and Johnson, 1980; Meloth and Deering, 1992; Qin, Johnson and Johnson, 1995; Webb, 1989).

Group processes and the nature of knowledge

Group discussion is a common activity in cooperative learning. During group discussion, students develop effective cognitive strategies for problem solving through sharing ideas, exploring and thinking through the problem, clarifying thoughts, proposing and evaluating possible solutions. As the group tries to work on a common task, the discussion provides members with an opportunity for group interaction in explaining and elaborating in problem solving.

There is growing evidence that the social context of learning has significant effects on children's learning (Bruffee, 1984; Cowie, 1992). Learning in a group makes students aware of different perspectives on many controversial issues, and to form judgements through critical thinking (Cowie and Rudduck, 1988). Group interactions in explaining and elaborating require students to rehearse, organize and clarify information in order to be able to communicate with the other members, while at the same time also receive feedback about the accuracy of the information. This allows group members to formulate and appraise information from new and different perspectives, and to arrive at knowledge that is developed through a process of social construction rather than at declarative knowledge that has been taught and individually assimilated. In view of the fact that the public domain of knowledge is socially constructed and interpreted through social processes (Habermas, 1970; Lawson, 1982), it appears that the construction of knowledge in collaborative learning through social study strategies is parallel to this knowledge construction, and is situated in the social interactions within the group. Declarative knowledge that is taught and assessed is often difficult to use in order to inform interaction with the everyday world (Resnick, 1987), and this is a particularly important problem in professional education (Argyris, 1976).

Characteristics of cooperative learning

1) Task and reward structure. Slavin (1990) advocates that group reward and individual accountability are essential to the effectiveness of cooperative learning on student achievement, especially in the absence of intergroup competition (Johnson, et al., 1981). Within such a goal structure, students are rewarded on the basis of the achievement of all the other members in the group, and this motivates the students to make sure that everyone understands the materials. Other reward structures such as individual-competitive rewards where students compete for rewards, and in individualistic reward structure where individuals are rewarded only on the basis of their performance without comparison to others, may discourage contribution during collaborative group discussion because it may be

perceived as a reduction either in one's own chance of receiving a good grade or in the time available to do one's own work, respectively (Johnson and Johnson, 1975).

2) Teacher-initiated nature. Most of the cooperative learning situations described by previous studies are initiated by the teachers and the students are instructed to help each other in small groups. Other cooperative situations such as Team-Games Tournament (DeVries and Slavin, 1978), Student Teams and Achievement Divisions (Slavin, 1978), Jigsaw (Aronson, 1978) and Team Assisted individualization (Slavin, 1983b) are even more rigidly structured by the teachers, and are carried out under experimental situations. Within such learning situations, there are both student-student and student-teacher interactions.

Cooperative and collaborative learning

The above review has been concerned with formally structured ways of getting students to cooperate. This is not the same as the form of cooperation that is traditional in Chinese culture. Many writers conclude that significant results of cooperative learning on student learning are more frequently found with a highly structured and organized approach (Cohen, Kulik and Kulik, 1982; Davison, 1990; Slavin, 1990). All such work has however been about cooperative learning in Western culture. There appears to be little work reported in the literature on small group learning in a culture other than Western, or on work that is both initiated and structured by the students themselves, and is free from any influence from and interactions with the teachers. The present chapter is an attempt to fill in the gap. We look at:-

1) The nature and extent of collaborative learning;
2) Effects of collaborative learning on the learning process; and
3) Effects of collaborative learning on learning outcomes.

The Nature and Extent of Spontaneous Collaborative Learning

Thirty-nine tertiary students were randomly selected from two consecutive sets of year one physiotherapy students (N=156) at the Hong Kong Polytechnic University, and each student was interviewed after the test and assignment (see Chapter 9 for details of the study). During the semi-structured interviews, the students talked about their perceptions of the demands of the particular assessment that they had just gone through, the actual preparation strategies adopted, and their collaborative learning experience.

From the interview data, depending on whether or not collaborative learning during the preparation for the assessments was reported, the students were divided into collaborative (CO) and self-studying (SS) groups. Any possible relationship between the students' habitual learning approaches and their tendency to collaborate was explored. The interview data were further analyzed to identify different study strategies employed in the collaborative and self-studying situations. These results were then correlated with the three sets of student performance in the two assessments as described in Chapter 9.

The interview data showed that the majority of students reported the experience of CO learning. The following are some of the comments indicating this learning experience:-

"... we then got into groups of six or seven to gather information, photocopied and read the materials. After we had read the materials, we discussed again about the approach. Afterwards I started to write. We also discussed about which points were important, but eventually we decided on our own important points and then started writing."

"After we got the assignment questions, those of us doing the same question discussed how to go about doing it. We talked about what the question was asking, what sorts of journals we needed, the way of presenting, and we worked out a list. We then shared in doing the literature search and the photocopying, and we read those articles that we found. We then discussed the relevant things from each article and argued about some points."

The distribution of CO and SS students for test and assignment are shown in Table 10.1. A Chi-Square test on the distribution of these two groups of students for the test and assignments also showed that the tendency to collaborate was significantly higher in preparing for the assignments (Chi-Square value=21.41, p<.001).

Table 10.1
Distributions of collaborative (CO) and self-studying (SS) students for assignment and test (N=39)

	Collaborative (CO)	Self-studying (SS)
Assignment	34 (87%)	5 (13%)
Test	13 (33%)	26 (67%)

Detailed analysis of the interview data revealed several characteristics which distinguish the CO learning identified in the present study from the cooperative learning structures described in the literature.

1) *Spontaneity.* All the students reporting CO learning initiated the forming of study groups without any prior instruction or advice from the teachers as they perceived a felt need to do so. This spontaneous collaboration is different from the teacher-initiated nature of what has been reported in the literature.

2) *Student-centred.* Apart from forming their own groups, the students also decided the structure and types of group activities such as when to meet, where to have the group discussions, and what issues the group should discuss. Within this student-centred CO learning, there were no student-teacher interactions.

3) *Group-effort-individual-reward structure.* The reward structure of the present CO learning is different from any of the documented ones in the sense that it is an individualistic reward. Although each student's performance in either the test or the assignment was based on the collaborative effort from all the group members, the actual grade was awarded quite independently of the effort (and in fact in ignorance of the group activity).

The present form of cooperative learning is thus different from that reported so far, in at least the above three characteristics. This type of student cooperative learning method, with its characteristics and the additional element of perceived mutual benefit, is here described as Spontaneous Collaborative Learning (SCOLL).

The spontaneous nature of SCOLL may be explained from two perspectives: cultural and contextual.

The cultural perspective

As discussed in previous sections, the Chinese culture emphasizes social relationships and collectivism. This cultural preference of collectivism may have influenced these Chinese students to spontaneously form CO groups in their learning. Work with undergraduates in China confirms that the Chinese frequently involve themselves in group activities both inside the university and in the wider community (Bond, 1991). So the Hong Kong nature trail observations are more than just a holiday phenomenon, it is in fact a manifestation of a Chinese cultural characteristic. Obviously spontaneous collaboration occurs in other cultures. Goodnow (1991), for instance, refers to a tendency for students at an Australian university to form "syndicates" for working in material that is "expected or known to be on the exam" (p.47). But this spontaneous collaboration does seem particularly salient amongst ethnic Chinese (and people of most other non-Western cultures). Goodnow does not comment on the extent of spontaneous collaboration in writing assignments, but a figure approaching 90% (that found here) seems very unlikely amongst Australian or other Western cultures. Another point is that SCOLL is not indiscriminate: it is sensitive to context, being nearly three times more likely in the assignment rather than in the test (Table 10.1).

The contextual perspective

Two contextual factors seem significant in triggering SCOLL: the students' previous experience with the assessment formats, and their competency in the language used. Writing an assignment is a new experience to most of the physiotherapist students, and they did not have a clear idea of how to approach the task. So in order to accomplish the task, and especially one with an assessment element, there was a felt need to have some assistance. A discussion group would be perceived to provide a mutual support system.

The formal language of instruction of the Physiotherapy course is English which is a second language (L2) to all the students. In the preparation of the assignments, reading and comprehension of the reference materials are integral stages, and depend on at least a reasonable command of English. For those students who do not have a good command of the language, comprehension of the reference materials may be perceived as a potential difficulty requiring extra effort and assistance. Again the CO-group effort would be perceived as a source of such assistance. As the language used in group discussion was mostly Chinese except for the special and technical terms, the students found that discussion facilitated their thinking and understanding. Student-student interactions in CO learning working on a common problem provide a common ground for easy understanding of any problematic areas or mistakes that are likely to be committed, and the opportunity for easy communication as the students will share the same language.

In sum then, SCOLL may be regarded as a strategy students use in order to handle a situation in which mutual support is perceived as necessary. It is a strategy that for many longstanding cultural reasons is likely to be readily adopted by Chinese students. The need to work collaboratively is thus very much a latent dimension in Chinese students' learning.

Effects of SCOLL on the Learning Process

Previous studies on cooperative learning have focused only on outcome measures, usually in the form of productivity and performance in retention tests (Humphreys, et al., 1982; Johnson, Johnson and Scott, 1978; Slavin and Tanner, 1979). Effects of cooperative learning on students' study strategies and on higher-level learning outcomes do no appear to have been examined. In fact, most of the research effort on cooperative learning, especially those in the US has been criticized for emphasizing the structure and product of group work, rather than the process and effects of group interaction (Bennett, 1987).

In the present study, the focus of the interview data was on the actual study process that the students went through, and hence provides detailed information on a whole spectrum of assessment preparation strategies engaged in during collaborative learning.

Preparation strategies for assignment

The CO group:-

In preparing for the assignment, 87% of the students spontaneously formed study groups and worked collaboratively. The CO effort included literature search, sharing the reading of the materials and group discussion.

Literature search. The students found that a group effort facilitated the search for more information. This was particularly helpful to and appreciated by those students who did not have previous experience of carrying out a literature search. Some of them said:-

> "It is quicker to do literature search in a group because it is quicker and it offers a wider coverage."

> "I spent less time in searching for information as we did it in a group. In that case I could have more time to think and write the assignment."

Sharing the reading. Each student in the group was responsible for reading and comprehending certain reference materials which they had to present during subsequent group discussion. Most students perceived that a large amount of content knowledge was an important requirement for writing assignments, and hence the need for them to have an extensive knowledge base. Sharing the reading amongst group members was perceived as an effective way of going through and benefiting from the large amount of information as some of them said:-

"There were so many articles to read that it was not possible for me to finish reading them all by myself."

"It helped a lot as I only had to read a few of those articles."

Group discussion. The central component of SCOLL was group discussion during which the students presented the ideas that they got from reading the reference materials. The group members then contributed in discussing, arguing and sharing their own opinions. The issues discussed included the requirements of the assignment question, clarification of confusing points or unclear concepts in the references, exchanging and recruiting new ideas, and relevance of the information to the question. The following were some of the descriptions of the group discussion activities:-

"After we read the articles, we then gathered to discuss the things we read. The discussion was very useful."

"We tried to find out what the question meant, and what sort of information (ought) to be included in the assignment."

This group discussion prior to the writing of the assignment represented the students' initiative and effort in setting up their own objectives and guidelines for writing the assignments through a mutual supporting system. This experience enabled the students to be self-directive in their learning and provided them with a sense of ownership of their learning.

To examine the CO-learning strategies more closely, the students were asked to describe their learning and thinking processes during the group discussion. From the interview data, different assignment preparation strategies were identified, and the percentage of students engaging in these strategies was calculated and the results are shown in Table 10.2.

These data showed that students who were involved in CO learning did engage in high-level cognitive strategies such as analyzing, relating and application through experimenting, discussing, arguing and debating. Although some of these strategies such as sharing and exchanging ideas, criticizing and supplementing each other's ideas were specific to group learning and were thus intrinsic to CO learning, the percentage of engagement in the other deep strategies which could be developed in both learning situations was still high with the CO group. These strategies are congruent with those expected in a deep-study approach which aims at seeking meaning and understanding (Biggs, 1987; Biggs and Moore, 1993; Ramsden, 1988). Comparing the two groups of students, the percentage of engagement in these deep assessment preparation strategies was higher with the CO group.

Table 10.2
Percentage of students engaged in the different assignment preparation strategies

% Collaborative students		Surface strategies	% Self-studying students
18	-	Just copying from articles	40
		Deep strategies	
6	-	Analyze	0
6	-	Apply	0
3	-	Argue for points	0
18	-	Compare	0
12	-	Criticize each others ideas and suggest improvement	0
9	-	Find support for argument	0
9	-	Go for basic concepts	20
24	-	Interpret question requirements	20
32	-	Organize the information	80
15	-	Relate	0
12	-	Share and exchange ideas	0
14	-	Stimulate deeper level thinking	0
18	-	Supplement each other's missing points	0
9	-	Write outline and framework	0
		Unclassified strategies	
15	-	Summarize	40
35	-	Underline points	80
3	-	Write relevant and important points	0

The interview data also showed that there were differences in the thinking process during CO and SS. The following comments from the students illustrate these differences in thinking:-

"There is a welcoming challenge for the thinking process during discussion. You will start to think and query when the others give their opinions. When you are studying on your own, this won't happen, and you are more easily convinced by yourself."

"There is a difference. You tend to be subjective when you are studying on your own and go too much to the extreme. During discussion, your ideas are subjected to other people's scrutiny, criticism and suggestion for improvement, and these could be more helpful for learning. The thinking process is deeper including analyzing, relating and applications."

During group discussion, students need to explain concepts to their classmates, and this facilitates them to understand the materials more clearly and thoroughly, and also motivates each other to study. Many studies have reported that giving elaborate explanations during collaborated group discussion is positively related to achievement (Webb, 1989). In formulating the explanation and communicating with the other group members, students are engaged in a form of 'generative teaching' (Kourilsky and Wittrock, 1992) when they revisit the information in new and different perspectives by engaging in high-level cognitive processes in rehearsing, clarifying, reorganizing and integrating the information (Meloth and Deering, 1994; Webb, 1989).

SS group:

Five students (11%) did not collaborate in preparing for the assignment, and their reasons for writing the assignment all on their own were:-

"I did not discuss as I was afraid to influence and also be influenced by others. I did not want to produce the same piece of assignment."

"I prefer to finish reading everything before discussion, but that would be too late, and also I did not want to influence others and be influenced by them."

In preparing for the assignment, these students also went through the steps of searching for and reading the information. However, they also reported a higher tendency to engage in surface strategies such as direct copying from the references without any higher level processing of the information, as some of these students said:-

"I need to copy whole paragraphs from the articles... if I did not copy, I could not know what those paragraphs meant."

"I read through all the materials, underlined the useful points. I then copied and grouped the points under the headings and arranged them in order."

Although some of these SS students also tried to organize and arrange the information after copying, it seems that there was a lack in the emphasis on understanding. These is also a lack of evidence of engagement in some of the other higher level cognitive strategies demonstrated by the CO group as shown in Table 10.2.

Comparison of the thinking process during CO and SS was not possible for these SS students. However, comments from some of these students indicated the level of thinking when they were preparing for the assignment:-

"I first read through all the materials, underlined the useful points. I read through the underlined points a second time and jotted down some notes. I then wrote the assignment."

"... I then read the articles and underlined the points. I then referred back to the question and organized the way of presentation. I then did a very rough first draft by fitting the points that I underlined into the structure that I drew up while I was organizing the way of presentation. I mainly copied the points."

So for these students who did not collaborate, the thinking process seemed to focus on selection and organization of points. When these students prepared the assignment, they did not discuss their ideas of opinions with others, and there was a lack of alternative views which stimulate and challenge thinking.

Preparation strategies for the test

Out of the 39 students interviewed, only 13 (33%) formed discussion groups while they were studying for the test. The other 26 students (67%) all studied on their own.

The CO group:

For those who collaborated, most of them perceived group discussion as an opportunity to clear up some of the points in the notes, and for spotting questions through discussing past test papers. However, they were also ambivalent in their opinions of the effectiveness of such discussion:-

"Group discussion was not very helpful as we knew more or less the same things, and we were also not sure if we were 100% correct or not."

"Studying in a group is quite useful as we can remind each other of the things that we have forgotten, discuss the things that we do not understand, and also exchange knowledge."

The SS group:

The students who studied on their own seemed to think that CO effort in discussion was not helpful for their preparation for the test as some of them explained:-

"Discussion is more useful for assignments as there is so much that you need to discuss. There is not that much information for a test, so it should be all right just to study on your own."

"There is little need for discussion for the test. I know the test syllabus and I also have adequate information in hand, so I think I better use the time in studying, and I feel that I should be OK just studying on my own."

In addition, it seems that the students' perceptions of a low level requirements of cognitive process in the test might have resulted in considering CO learning inappropriate.

As for the study process, again the different test preparation strategies adopted by the two groups of students were identified from the interview data, and are shown in Table 10.3.

Both surface and deep test preparation strategies were identified in the CO and SS groups. During the interviews, the CO students described their study process as follows:-

"During discussion, we related, compared, applied and thought about the reasons. You have to know the reasons why. I studied in a group, it was easier to understand if we discussed the points together."

"You may think that you have understood a topic while you are studying, but when people raise a question in the discussion, you may find that your understanding is not accurate. So from the discussion, you can understand more or you can correct your wrong ideas."

Table 10.3
Percentage of students engaged in different test preparation strategies

% Collaborative students	Surface strategies	% Self-studying students
38	- Memorize	62
31	- Rote learn	35
31	- Recall	15
15	- Repeated studying	31
0	- Reproduce	8
0	- Study from cover to cover	31
	Deep strategies	
15	- Apply	4
8	- Compare	15
23	- Get general idea	0
8	- Reasoning	23
69	- Relate	38
46	- Visualize	38
	Unclassified strategies	
0	- Follow sequence of learning material	23
0	- Organize time	15
8	- Rewrite points	15
8	- Summarize	4
0	- Talk to oneself	4
0	- Underline points	4

Although some of the SS students also reported deep strategies such as relating, and they might try to understand, the majority of these students adopted surface strategies such as memorizing and reproducing which are congruent with those of a surface approach aiming at reproducing rather than understanding the meaning (Biggs, 1987; Biggs and Moore, 1993; Ramsden, 1988). Some of these students said:-

"I can't study in a group as I will get confused and cannot concentrate ... I have to repeat four to five times to memorize the points."

"I tried to memorize the details so that I could reproduce them later. I read from cover to cover and I did not enjoy studying."

These data showed that both surface and deep assessment preparation strategies were adopted by the two groups of students. Taking the general profile, SS students tended to be high on surface strategies such as rote learning, memorizing, recalling and reproducing, and hence could be considered to engage more in a surface study approach. On the other hand, deep strategies such as relating, visualizing and applying were more common in the CO students, implying a greater tendency for adopting a deep study approach.

Table 10.4
Analysis of variance of the test, assignment and SOLO score

	Test		Assignment		SOLO	
	Mean	SD	Mean	SD	Mean	SD
SS group	54.52	8.31	57.80	9.93	1.80	0.83
CO group	51.61	11.21	65.08	10.16	3.02	1.21
F	0.37		0.14		0.03	
P	NS		NS		0.05	

SS = Self-studying group
CO = Collaborative group

Effects of SCOLL on Learning Outcomes

Analysis of the students' performance in the two assessments did not reveal any significant difference in the mean scores of test and assignment between the CO and SS groups (Table 10.4), but the trend was that the CO group performed better than the SS group in the assignment.

For the assessment of the quality of the structural complexity of the assignments, the mean SOLO score of the SS group was 1.8, indicating an average of a multistructural level, while the mean SOLO score of the collaborative group was 3.0, indicating a relational level. This difference in the mean group SOLO scores was significant (p<.05), indicating that the CO group performed better qualitatively with better structured arguments in their assignments. To examine the strengths of the relations between the effects of the two learning situations on the students' performance, the effect size of these three sets of results was calculated, and the results showed that the effect size of assignment and SOLO scores were higher and favouring CO learning (Figure 10.1).

Figure 10.1
Effect size of test, assignment and SOLO scores between collaborative (CO) and self-studying (SS) groups

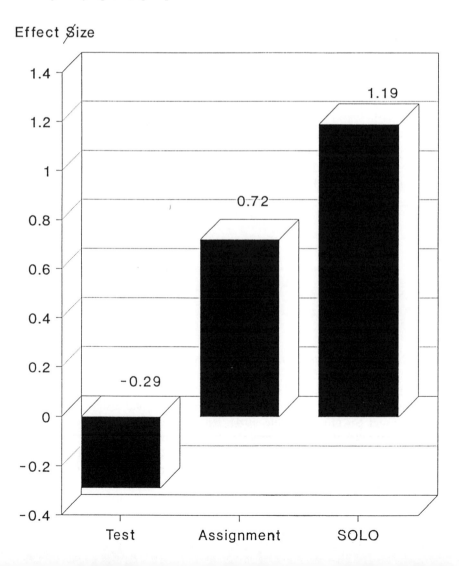

The implication of this finding is that the effect on learning outcomes was more significant for the assignment, especially for the SOLO scores. Better structural quality assignments are more likely to be related to the positive effects of SCOLL.

Implications for Teaching

To promote student collaboration, teaching method and learning tasks will have to be structured to facilitate more student-centred learning through tutorials, seminar presentation, and writing assignments. These learning tasks require students to actively participate in the teaching and learning process and hence provide opportunity for collaborative learning.

As the students in this study formed their study groups spontaneously, without any prior instruction or advice, it might be possible that some of them did not fully understand the underlying philosophy to enable them to utilize the collaborative effort. There appears to be a need to provide students with instructions or training in strategies for collaborative learning to give high-level elaborated explanation (McAllister, 1995). Although students may have ideas of peer group discussion, they may also need more instruction and guidance to help focus thoughts and activities on the task content (Meloth and Deering, 1992, 1994). Swing and Peterson (1982) demonstrated that students receiving direct instruction, role play, practice and feedback gave more explanation in small group learning. Greenwood, Carta and Kamps (1990) reported positive effects of cooperation on student learning, but at the same time cautioned the possible need for peer training and quality control, and the possible need for adaptation of curriculum materials for such an approach to learning. Even within the SCOLL situation where the collaborative effort is spontaneous, the teaching staff should adopt the role of facilitators by providing students with the procedural knowledge of how to participate and collaborate in group discussion, how to express and justify their ideas, and how to give and receive constructive criticism.

During the interviews, some students indicated the worry of unfairness if the assignments were prepared by collaborative effort as one of them said:-

"Group discussion may render the assessment unfair because we do it in a group, the things that we write in the assignment may not be our own, but rather ideas that we got from the others."

Such comments raise the question of plagiarism with collaborative learning, given that the individual receives the award after collaborative effort in the preparation of assignments. However, during the interviews, all the students confirmed that collaboration was only confined to literature search, sharing of the reading and group discussion. Each student then formed their own ideas, based albeit on the understanding and inspiration from the group discussion about how to approach and structure the assignment. The process of writing the assignment was the individual student's effort. This distinction between collaborative and individual effort was illustrated by comments such as:

> "For the assignment, we just discussed, but when it came to the actual writing, it was still our own personal ideas. Discussion was just to stimulate my thinking."

> "We discussed which points were important, but eventually we decided on our own important points and then started writing."

Although it may be overgeneralizing to say that plagiarism did not occur in collaborative learning in this present goal structure, the data from this study showed that these students did not appear to plagiarize. The author marked all the assignments, and did not detect plagiarism in those submitted by students in the collaborative group.

Conclusions

Previous research indicates that collaborative learning has positive effects on learning. The present study describes a different type of collaborative learning, (SCOLL), one that is initiated and self-structured by the students, and is effected through both Chinese cultural characteristic and the students' perceptions of the demands of the learning context and the nature of the task.

During the interactive group discussion, the students' thinking is likely to be stimulated and challenged to a higher cognitive level when they try to express their own opinions, explain and argue for their points, relate, compare and apply the information. These deep strategies facilitate the students' understanding and increase their interest in the subject, and may demonstrate one of the processes of the development of socially constructed knowledge. The positive effects of SCOLL are more apparent and strongly supported in the preparation for the assignments than for the test. Some of the deep strategies engaged by the CO students, such as arguing, criticizing each others ideas, suggesting improvements, sharing and exchanging ideas, and supplementing each others missing points are intrinsic to the particular CO-group learning context. Hence SCOLL provides a context for the development of social study strategies which facilitate a deep-learning approach. The fact that the effects of SCOLL are more apparent in the structure of the assignments rather than in the institutional marks awarded may indicate that the nature of the knowledge constructed under social conditions is different from that constructed individually in pursuit of institutional recognition and qualification.

The present findings on the effects of SCOLL on study approaches have been obtained in the context of preparation for two assessment methods, and that the format of collaboration has been restricted to group effort and individual reward. Generalization of the present findings to other learning situations must also take into consideration the respective characteristics of the context, such as students; perceptions of the task demands, and other possible alternative collaborative structures such as group effort with group reward as in the production of a single group project or a report.

SCOLL represents a latent dimension in Chinese students' learning with great potential in facilitating a deep-study approach, effort should be devoted to further explore and promote a more proper and extensive utilization of collaborative learning in facilitating and improving Chinese students' learning.

REFERENCES

Argyris, C. (1976). Theories of action that inhibit individual learning. *American Psychologist, 31*, 638-654.

Aronson, E. (1978). *The jigsaw classroom*. Beverly Hills: Sage.

Bennett, N. (1987). Cooperative learning: children do it in groups - or do they? *Educational and Child Psychology, 4*(3&4), 7-18.

Biggs, J.B. (1987). *Student approaches to learning and studying*. Melbourne: Australian Council for Educational Research.

Biggs, J.B. & Moore, P. (1993) (3rd Ed.). *Process of learning*. Prentice Hall of Australia.

Bond, M.H. (1991). *Beyond the Chinese face: insights from psychology*. Hong Kong: Oxford University Press.

Bruffee, K. (1984). Collaborative learning and the "conversation of mankind". *College English, 46*, 635-652.

Cohen, P.A., Kulik, J.A. & Kulik, C-L.C. (1982). Educational outcomes of tutoring: a meta-analysis of findings. *American Educational Research Journal, 19*(2), 237-148.

Collier, K.G. (1983). *The management of peer-group learning: syndicate methods in higher education*. Society for Research in Higher Education, Guildford.

Cowie, H. (1992). Peer commentaries on Keith Topping's review of cooperative learning and peer tutoring. *The Psychologist, 5*(4), 158-159.

Cowie, H. & Rudduck, J. (1988). *Cooperative group work: an overview*. (Vol 1 on series Learning together, working together). London: BP Educational Service.

Damon, W. (1984). Peer education: the untapped potential. *Journal of Applied*

Developmental Psychology, *5*, 331-343.

Davison, N. (1990). Cooperative learning research in mathematics. *Paper delivered at JASCE 5th International Convention on Cooperative Learning.* Baltimore Md., July 1990.

DeVries, D.L. & Slavin, R.E. (1978). Team-Game Tournament (TGT): review of ten classroom experiments. *Journal of Research and Development in Education, 12*, 39-49.

Goodnow, J.J. (1991). Cognitive values and educational practice. In J.B. Biggs (Ed.), *Teaching for learning: the view from cognitive psychology.* Chapter 3, p. 30-50. ACER.

Greenwood, C.R., Carta, J.J. & Kamps, D. (1990). The teacher-mediated versus peer-mediated instruction: a review of educational advantages and disadvantages. In H.C. Foot, M.J. Morgan & R.J. Shute (Eds.), (1990). *Children helping children.* Chichester: Wiley.

Habermas, J. (1970). *Towards a rational society.* Boston: Beacan Press.

Ho, D.Y.F. (1981). Traditional patterns of socialization in Chinese society. *Acta Psychological Taiwanica, 23*, 81-89.

Ho, D.Y.F. (1986). Chinese patterns of socialization: a critical review. In M.H. Bond (Ed.), *The psychology of the Chinese people,* (p.1-37). Hong Kong: Oxford University Press.

Hofstede, G. (1983). Dimensions of national cultures in fifty countries and three regions. In J.B. Deregowski, S. Dziurawiec, and R.C. Annis (Eds.), *Expiscations in cross-cultural psychology.* Lisse, Netherlands: Swets and Zeitlinger.

Hooper, S., Temiyakarn, C. & Williams, H.D. (1993). The effects of cooperative learning and learner control on high- and average-ability students. *Educational Technology Research and Development, 41*(2), 5-18.

Humphreys, B., Johnson, R.T. & Johnson, D.W. (1982). Effects of cooperative, competitive and individualistic learning on students' achievement in science class. *Journal of Research in Science Teaching, 19*(5), 351-356.

Johnson, A.M. (1969). *The anatomy of judgment.* Penguin Books, Harmondsworth, Middlesex.

Johnson, D.W. & Johnson, R. (1975). *Learning together and alone: cooperation, competition and individualization.* Englewood Cliffs, NJ: Prentice Hall.

Johnson, D.W., Johnson, R.T. & Scott, L. (1978). The effects of cooperative and individualized instruction on student attitudes and achievement. *Journal of Social Psychology, 104*, 207-216.

Johnson, D.W., Johnson, R. & Skon, L. (1979). Student achievement on different types of tasks under cooperative, competitive and individualistic conditions. *Contemporary Educational Psychology, 4*, 99-106.

Johnson, D.W., Maruyama, G. Johnson, R. & Nelson, D. (1981). Effects of cooperative, competitive and individualistic goal structures on achievement: a meta-analysis. *Psychological Bulletin, 89*(1), 47-62.

Johnson, D.W., Skon, L. & Johnson, R. (1980). Effects of cooperative, competitive and individualistic conditions on children's problem-solving performance. *American Educational Journal, 17*(1), 83-93.

Kourilsky, M. & Wittrock, M.C. (1992). Generative teaching: an enhancement strategy for the learning of economics in cooperative groups. *American Educational Research Journal, 29*(4), 861-876.

Lawson, K.H. (1982). *Analysis and ideology: conceptual essays on education of adults.* Department of Adult Education, University of Nottingham, England.

Lazar, A.M. (1995). Who is studying in groups and why? *College Teaching, 43*(2), 61-65.

McAllister, W. (1995). Are pupils equipped for group work without training or instruction? *British Educational Research Journal, 21*(3), 395-404.

Meloth, M. & Deering, P. (1992). Effects of two cooperative conditions on peer-group discussions, reading comprehension, and metacognition. *Contemporary Educational Psychology, 17*(2), 175-193.

Meloth, M.S. & Deering, P.D. (1994). Task talk and task awareness under different cooperative learning conditions. *American Research Journal, 31*(1), 138-165.

Nichols, J.D. & Miller, R.B. (1994). Cooperative learning and student motivation. *Contemporary Educational Psychology, 19*, 167-178.

Qin, Z., Johnson, D.W. & Johnson, R.T. (1995). Cooperative vesus competitive efforts and problem solving. *Review of Educational Research, 65*(2), 129-143.

Ramsden, P. (1988). Context and strategies - situational influences on learning. In R.R. Schmeck (Ed.), *Learning strategies and learning styles* (pp. 159-184). New York and London: Plenum Press.

Resnick, L.B. (1987). Learning in school and out. *Educational Researcher, 19*(9), 13-20.

Slavin, R.E. (1978). Student teams and achievement divisions. *Journal of Research and Development in Education, 12*, 39-49.

Slavin, R.E. (1983a). When does cooperative learning increase student achievement? *Psychological Bulletin, 94*(3), 429-445.

Slavin, R.E. (1983b). Team assisted individualization. In R.E. Slavin, S. Sharan, S. Kagan, R.E. Lazarowitz, C. Webb and R. Schmuck (Eds.), *Learning to cooperate, cooperate to learn.* New York: Plenum.

Slavin, R.E. (1987). (2nd Ed.). *Cooperative learning: student teams.* Washington D.C.: National Educational Association.

Slavin, R.E. (1990). *Cooperative learning: theory research and practice.* Englewood Cliffs, N.J.: Prentice Hall.

Slavin, R.E. & Tanner, A.M. (1979). Effects of cooperative reward structures and individual accountability on productivity and learning. *Journal of*

Educational Research, 72, 294-298.

Swing, S.R. & Peterson, P.L. (1982). The relationship of student ability and small group interaction to student achievement. *American Educational Research Journal, 19,* 259-274.

Topping, K. (1992). Cooperative learning and peer tutoring: an overview. *The Psychologist, 5*(4), 151-157.

Webb, N. (1985). Student interaction and learning in small groups: a research summary. In R.E. Slavin et al. *Learning to cooperative, cooperate to learn* (pp. 147-172). N.Y.: Plenum.

Webb, N. (1989). Peer interacting and learning in small groups. *International Journal of Educational Research, 13,* 21-40.

Yang, K.S. (1981). Social orientation and individual modernity among Chinese students in Taiwan. *Journal of Social Psychology, 113,* 159-170.

Yang, K.S. (1982). Sinicization of psychological research in a Chinese society: directions and issues. In K.S. Yang and C.I. Wen (Eds.), *The sinicization of social and behavioural science research in China.* Taipei: Institute of Ethnology, Academia Sinica.

Yang, K.S. (1986). Chinese personality and its change. In M.H. Bond (1986), *The psychology of the Chinese people.* Hong Kong: Oxford University Press.

11

Chinese Students at an Australian University: Adaptability and Continuity

Simone Volet and Peter Renshaw

Introduction

Thousands of Chinese students from Southeast Asian countries have come to study in Australian universities since the late 1980s, yet little is known about how these students adapt to the specific academic requirements of the host country, and how their approach to study compares with that of local students. Australian educational psychologists have only recently developed an interest in issues related to Southeast Asian students' learning in Australian universities, and there is still a lack of systematic and theoretically-informed research in this area.

Until recently, the only literature available in Australia on the approach to study of international students from Southeast Asia consisted of survey studies conducted by staff in the academic support services of the host universities (eg. Samuelowicz, 1987; Burns, 1991), and manuals for academic staff and students which rely heavily on personal experiences, anecdotes and unique cases to describe students' learning (Ballard and Clanchy, 1991). Although the examples that are provided in these publications usually identify students by country of origin, the overall picture that emerges out of that literature, and which is widespread among Australian academic staff, provides a stereotyped, negative and static view of Southeast Asian students' learning. These students are described as having the following features: respectful of the lecturer's authority; diligent note-takers; preoccupied with fulfilling the expectations of the lecturers; uncritical of information presented in the textbook and by the lecturers; seldom asking questions or volunteering to contribute to tutorial discussions; and unaware of the conventions regarding acknowledging quotes and referencing sources and therefore unwittingly guilty of plagiarism. No acknowledgment is made of their adjustments to the new educational environment.

The adoption of a deficit model to describe students' learning, combined with major conceptual and methodological problems in the literature, have contributed to creating a distorted view of Chinese students in Australia. The literature has failed to consider students' cognitions and behaviours in interaction with the context in which they are embedded (lack of a situated view of learning), has neglected to examine students' adjustments to the new educational context over a period of time (absence of longitudinal studies), has underestimated the magnitude of individual differences amongst the international population (lack of sensitivity to differences within and between various groups), and it has seldom systematically compared Southeast Asian students' cognitions with those of their local counterparts. Finally, the fact that Chinese learners are achieving particularly well at university in Australia has not been explained.

Overall, the rather negative picture of Southeast Asian learners provided in the literature contrasts sharply with evidence from university statistics which indicate that when English-language proficiency is not an issue (Bourne and Davenport, 1993), Asian students tend to obtain better results in their courses than local students (Burns, 1991). Many academic staff may explain the high academic achievement of Asian students in terms of stronger achievement motivation and extremely hard work compared with local students. But recent research has revealed that there is more to the explanation than simply motivation and hard work, and that the assumptions about Chinese students' learning derived from unsystematic observations and anecdotes may be inaccurate. Theoretically-grounded studies of Chinese students in Hong Kong (Biggs, 1991; Kember and Gow, 1990; Watkins, Regmi and Astilla, 1991) and more recently of Singaporean students enrolled at a Western Australian university (Renshaw and Volet, 1995; Volet and Kee, 1993; Volet and Renshaw, in press; Volet, Renshaw and Tietzel, 1994) have challenged the stereotyped view of Asian students as reproductive and surface learners, excessively focused on learning isolated facts and details, and lacking the experience and skills for interacting in group discussions.

Our research has focused on the issue of adaptability and continuity in student learning and capitalized on the unique situation created by Chinese students studying the same courses in the same institutional context as local Australian students. Our empirical studies, grounded in theories concerned with the self-regulation of learning, have emphasized the significance of cognitive, affective and contextual dimensions of learning. Specifically, we have examined students' overall study motives and strategies, their learning goals and perceptions of study settings, their participation in tutorial activities and help-seeking strategies. Distinctive features of the methodologies used in this research include the use of matched groups of Chinese and local students, short-term longitudinal designs, multiple data points, and multiple types of data including a combination of questionnaires, interviews and direct tutorial observations for converging evidence. Further insight into students' learning was obtained by asking the students from Singapore to describe various aspects of study in their home country and in Australia after one semester. The main findings from our studies in terms of adaptability and continuity are summarized below.

Adaptability and Continuity in Chinese Students' Learning at University in Australia

Our examination of the adaptability of Chinese students to study at Australian universities has focused on three salient aspects of the stereotyped view of Southeast Asian students: (a) they tend to be rote learners rather than deep learners; (b) they are highly achievement-oriented; and (c) they do not participate in tutorial discussions. Each of these characteristics will be examined in turn, for its accuracy and for evidence of adaptability and continuity in the Australian context.

1. Chinese students tend to be surface learners rather than deep learners

Implicit in the belief that students of Asian origin rely heavily on rote learning and memorization at the expense of deep approaches to learning (Ballard and Clanchy, 1991; Samuelowicz, 1987) is the assumption that their approach to study is stable across educational contexts.

The assumption of stability in approach to study is reflected in the methodologies which have been used in cross-cultural research on student learning. The most commonly used methodology is the questionnaire given at a single point in time, the most extensively used being Biggs' Study Process Questionnaire (SPQ) which assesses students' overall approach to study. A major advantage of the one-off administration of a questionnaire is the opportunity to make quick, quantitatively-based comparisons of the typical study profiles of large groups of students. However, when comparing the scores of groups of students from different countries, it is not possible to separate the impact of individual characteristics from contextual factors such as academic requirements of institutions, disciplines or countries. Kember and Gow (1990) compared their large data set from Hong Kong Polytechnic University with Biggs' (1987) large sample of Australian Colleges of

Advanced Education students to examine cross-cultural differences in approaches to study, but admitted that the departments surveyed in the two studies did not correspond very well. The investigation of adaptability and continuity in Chinese students' approach to study requires that a sample of students are studied as they face new educational demands across contexts and time, and are compared with a matched group of local students adapting to their own local university across time. The situation created by Chinese learners in Australian universities has opened up the possibility of directly addressing the issue of individual versus contextual influences on approaches to study.

According to Biggs (1994), while Western observers may have been correct in perceiving a great deal of repetitive effort with the emphasis on accuracy of recall among Chinese learners, they have been incorrect in calling this approach 'rote' learning, in the sense of learning 'without' understanding. The research conducted in Hong Kong (Biggs, 1991; Kember and Gow, 1990; Watkins, Regmi and Astilla, 1991) challenged the assumption of Chinese learners as rote learners by showing that these students in fact score lower than Western students on Biggs' overall measure of surface approach to study (the SPQ). These findings were not replicated in the Volet, Renshaw and Tietzel study (1994), since the overall surface approach scores of Singaporean students studying at a Western Australian university were higher than those of their Australian counterparts. However, the breakdown of the surface strategy subscale into more focused subscales (identified by Balla, Stokes, and Stafford, 1991) revealed no difference between Singaporean and local students on the measure of narrow focus of study (the sub-component of Biggs' surface construct which refers to learning 'without' understanding). One difference emerged, however, in the type of understanding that may be sought by Chinese students in comparison with local Australian students. The breakdown of the deep-strategy subscale into a measure of transfer (Balla et al, 1991) revealed that Singaporean students' search for understanding may take place mainly at the level of the text, and thus may not involve, to the same extent as local Australian students, attempts to relate the new information to previous or other knowledge or to make sense of the new information in the light of personal or real-life experiences. Biggs (1991) suggested that engaging in elaborative processes may be related to the language of instruction, but there may be other reasons as well, as the large majority of Singaporean students in this study considered themselves as native English speakers. Since these students were found to perform marginally better in their course of study than the matched group of local students, it can be argued that their choice of study strategies may not have been so unsuited to the demands of the learning task.

In a short-term longitudinal study (Volet and Renshaw, in press), similarities were found in the patterns of change for Singaporean and local students over one semester of academic study in the same institution. These findings support the view that the Chinese students' approach to study, like their Western counterparts, is influenced by their perceptions of course requirements rather than determined by stable personal and cultural characteristics. The data revealed that the effect of the educational context diminished both Singaporean and local students' preferences for achieving and deep approaches, while surface approach tended to remain static for both groups. With regard to study strategies, Singaporean students displayed a deep-achieving predisposition at the beginning of the semester, somewhat similar to local students and in line with previous studies, and by the end of the semester there was no clear preference for one strategy over the others. Unlike the local group, Singaporean students' deep strategies were related to deep motives, although the relationship was not as strong at the end as at the beginning of the semester. The relationship between achieving and deep motives and strategies (Biggs' desirable combination) only for the group of Singaporean students challenges the common belief among Western academics that Chinese students' high levels of study commitment is driven by a desire to get high grades without regard to the depth of understanding of the content.

Overall, these results stress the importance of distinguishing between rote learning and memorizing (see Chapter 4). Interview data from Tang's (1991) and Kember and Gow's (1990) research showed that Hong Kong students do not simply rote learn unprocessed information but attempt to understand the new information in a systematic step-by-step fashion first and once each part of the task is understood, memorize the 'deeply processed product' (Biggs, 1991). 'Deep memorizing' as a means towards understanding (Tang, 1991) might seem to be equivalent to a surface approach since students rely only on the memorization of materials provided by lecturers, but it differs from the overall surface construct because students strive to understand the materials. While memorization may be appropriate and even necessary in some situations, it should not be equated with rote learning of unprocessed information.

Further support for the distinction between rote learning and memorization was found in Singaporean students' own accounts of their learning in Singapore (Volet and Kee, 1993). Memorization was rated highly by all students but not learning word for word. Interview data revealed that students perceived different subjects (and sometimes different teachers) as encouraging different learning processes, for example, economics, history and geography as requiring memorization of facts and definitions, and literature and science as emphasizing understanding of concepts, presenting clear arguments and coming up with original thought. For Singaporean students, memorization was clearly linked to examinations. There was no indication in their comments that paraphrasing and interpreting the writings of scholars was a questionable study strategy, and thus no evidence to support the idea that "reformulating what the author had written may go against the Asian respect for the printed word" (Bradley and Bradley, 1984: 290).

Additional evidence of the importance placed by Chinese students on understanding study materials was provided by Singaporean students' rankings of 12 statements representing the possible characteristics of a 'good' student at college back home (Volet and Kee, 1993). Being able to understand the main ideas was ranked first by the overwhelming majority of students. Students did not agree, however, about the next most important characteristics of a 'good' student in Singapore. For some of them, getting the right answer and learning study materials by heart were perceived as the next most important characteristics, while for others it was the ability to evaluate different ideas and give your own opinion, as well as to develop clear logical arguments. These individual differences in perceptions stress the fact that Chinese students from Singapore do not represent a homogeneous group with regard to their prior educational experience, and that many students had to adjust to different styles of teaching already during their college studies. The prime importance given by all Singaporean students to the concept of understanding, clearly contradicts the assumption that Chinese learners are surface learners, in the sense of just trying to get by.

Converging evidence on Chinese students' search for understanding and adaptability in a new educational context was obtained using a hierarchy of learning goals rather than Biggs' SPQ instrument (Volet and Renshaw, in press). The instrument measuring goals consisted of a hierarchy of five learning goals conceptualized along an unidimensional continuum and designed for a specific unit of study, with goals representing surface and deep levels of processing as the two opposing poles of that continuum, and goals representing intermediate levels of content-processing between the two extremes. Conceptualizing goals as levels along an unidimensional continuum made it possible to use a Rasch analysis (Andrich, 1989) that provided a specific location for each student's level of goals along that continuum.

In that study there was evidence of cultural/educational differences between the two groups' levels of goals at the start of the semester, but like the Hong Kong data (Biggs, 1992), these results were in the opposite direction to the anecdotal literature, with Singaporean students' levels of goals significantly higher than those of local students. The initial higher levels of goals displayed by Singaporean students support Biggs' findings that Chinese students from Hong Kong have a more academic approach to learning (low surface, high deep) than their Australian counterparts (Biggs, 1992), and agree with Volet et al's (1994) finding that Chinese students are not different from local Australian students on the measure of narrow focus of study. These results must be interpreted with caution, since students' approaches to study do not simply reflect their levels of interest for academic endeavours, or the cultural traits of a group of individuals, or alternatively the academic demands of the institution. As stressed by Biggs (1992) a student's orientation to study represents the outcome of complex and dynamic processes affected by interactive individual and contextual factors.

The short-term longitudinal research designs of the Australian studies were particularly useful for investigating similarities and differences in patterns of change over time. The Rasch analysis (Volet and Renshaw, in press) provided not only a quantified measure of each student's level of goals for group comparisons and analyses of change over time, but also provided an indication of how each of the two cultural groups conceptualized the relationships between the stimulus items of the instrument. The comparison of students' responses at the beginning and the end of their first semester revealed that Chinese students' conceptualization of learning goals for a particular unit of study differed from those of local Australian students at the beginning of their university study in Australia, but that these differences disappeared by the end of the first semester. There was also evidence that local Australian students had changed their way of thinking in the same direction. Overall, there was a remarkable similarity in the two groups' changes over time in their perception of what cognitive processes are involved when comparing and contrasting economic theories. The similarity in the two groups' adjustments provided further support for the significant impact of course requirements and context on students' emerging perceptions and approaches to study. Similar findings are reported in a recent study by Chalmers (1994).

Another adjustment in Chinese students' learning after only one semester at university in Australia, referred to their learning goals which became more like local students'. But again the nature of these goal adjustments did not agree with the anecdotal literature, since they changed from a deeper to a more surface level. The significant relationship between the shift downwards in Singaporean students' levels of goals and perceptions of the relevance of the course content to their programme of study, provided support for the significance of students' subjective appraisals of study on their learning intentions (Boekaerts, 1992).

Overall, the combination of higher levels of goals with higher levels of surface approach to study, but not in the narrow sense, suggests that Chinese students, in Australia, as they do in their home country, place considerable emphasis on developing an understanding of the course material and that they may attempt, as suggested by Biggs (1992), to achieve understanding via the use of memorization strategies. The anecdotal claim that Chinese learners are inherently more inclined to be rote learners at the expense of deep learning was not supported in any of these empirical studies. Chinese students from Singapore, like their Western counterparts, were responsive to the demands of the new academic context, and the influence of the institutional context was registered in a similar manner for both Chinese and local Australian students.

2. Chinese students are highly achievement oriented

Another claim by Western academics is that Chinese students are highly achievement-oriented compared with Western students. It is proposed that their achievement orientation is rooted in the Confucian heritage culture, and therefore is stable across educational contexts.

The expectations of higher achievement orientation of Chinese learners have been confirmed in a number of cross-cultural studies. The research comparing Hong Kong and Australian tertiary samples (Biggs, 1991; Biggs, 1992; Kember and Gow, 1990; Watkins, Regmi and Astilla, 1991) revealed that the majority of Chinese students report themselves as higher on the achieving measures of the SPQ compared with Western samples. Similar findings were found with the group of Singaporean students at university in Australia (Volet, Renshaw and Tietzel, 1994). We found that Singaporean students reported higher achieving approach scores compared with Australian students and that these differences were maintained after one semester of study, despite a significant decrease in achievement orientation over time for both groups. Biggs (1992) argued that Hong Kong students' drive for high achievement may be related to the high competition for many fewer tertiary places and the much higher general upward mobility in Hong Kong. The same may apply to the situation in Singapore. With regard to the case of Singaporean students studying abroad, it should be recognized that these students were full-fee paying students, and therefore were expected to have a stronger motivation to achieve well in order to demonstrate to their family and sponsors back home that their investment had not been wasted. This explanation was supported by the fact that Singaporean students' scores on the achieving approach were higher than those of the Hong Kong students studying in a comparable discipline in their home country (Biggs, 1992).

The short-term longitudinal design adopted in our comparative study (Volet et al, 1994) provided further insight into Chinese learners' achieving approach to study in comparison with that of Western students. The breakdown of study approach into study motives and strategies across two occasions (beginning of study at university in Australia and after one semester) revealed that Singaporean students' achieving motives were significantly higher than those of Australian students *only after* one semester of study in Australia. These results, combined with the fact that both groups' initial achieving motives tended to be higher than surface or deep motives, suggest that at the start of their university study both Singaporean and Australian students were oriented towards obtaining high grades. This finding was not surprising given the highly competitive tertiary entrance examinations that all students had just passed to gain access to university. Group differences in achieving motives emerged only after one semester of study, with Singaporean students maintaining a relatively higher achieving approach to study compared with

Australian students, despite a significant decrease in achieving motive scores for both groups. Singaporean students' accounts of their study at the beginning and end of their first semester at university in Australia provided a possible explanation for their maintenance of high achieving motives in Australia (Volet and Kee, 1993). These students thought that there was less obvious open competition among students at university in Australia and little pressure to work hard coming from the lecturers or the tutors. They felt that, because so much money had been spent on their education, they had to put pressure onto themselves to become self-motivated and personally responsible for monitoring their own learning progress. Burns (1991) reports that 92% of Singaporean students are under considerable pressure from their families to do well compared with only 26% of Australian students feeling such pressure.

In contrast to achieving motives, Singaporean students' achieving strategies were significantly higher than those of Australian students *only at the beginning* of their study in Australia, despite a significant decrease over time for both groups. The most striking difference across groups with regard to achieving strategies, was the significant relationship (described in the first section of this paper) between achieving and deep strategies for Singaporean students and the lack of relationship for the group of Australian students. Biggs' definition of deep achievers as organized and planful in their search both for meaning and for high marks seems to apply well to the Singaporean students at university. These students are often described as working hard at night in the library, queuing up for individual assistance outside class, seeking guidelines on how to write essays in the Western style, and discussing their study with fellow students in the canteen. In our study (Renshaw and Volet, 1995) of participation in tutorials (which is discussed in more detail below) we found that Singaporean students who reported that they often proposed their own or alternative viewpoints during tutorial discussions were those displaying higher levels of achieving approaches to study. These findings suggest that the achievement orientation of the Singapore students is directed at engagement and understanding rather than high marks per se.

Further support for challenging the stereotyped idea that Chinese students' achievement orientation is directed simply at getting high grades, was found in our investigation of students' perceptions of the usefulness of five typical study settings for the achievement of low and high level goals (Volet and Renshaw, in press). The data revealed that for the achievement of low level goals (remembering information) both local and Singaporean students agreed that studying alone and attending tutorials were preferable to consulting the tutor or studying with other students. Only Singaporean students, however, differentiated the relative usefulness of the five study settings for pursuing higher forms of learning such as constructing a theoretical viewpoint. Overall, Australian students considered studying alone as the most useful form of study, regardless of whether the goal was simply to remember essential information or whether it involved theory building based on critical understanding. In contrast, both at the beginning and the end of the semester, Singaporean students rated studying alone as one of the *least* useful study settings for the achievement of a high-level goal, and tutorial attendance and consulting the tutor as the most useful study settings. Singaporean students' higher usefulness rating of study settings which involve interactions with teachers and peers seems to present a paradox. Singaporean students in Australia have the reputation of being highly motivated and performance-oriented, yet in our Western view, such an orientation is typically linked to the notion of competitiveness, itself associated with an individualistic approach. Quite the opposite emerged in this study, with Singaporean students' perception that studying alone was not the most useful form of study to achieve higher forms of learning. The importance given by these students to social exchange and communication fits better with the pursuit of higher forms of learning than does individual study.

The high value placed by these students on study settings involving interaction with academic staff may be related to their experience of participation in group discussions in their secondary school writing classes back home. Students explained in interviews (Volet and Kee, 1993) that their English teachers often set up group discussions and encouraged students to come up with ideas and points to include in their essays. Many students thought that participation in these discussions, which preceded individual essay writing, was essential for writing good essays. Through this experience, they may have realized the benefits of social interaction when a task requires the organization of ideas, concepts and opinions, such as in essay writing or critical understanding and theory building. The importance given to social interaction by our sample of Singaporean students also fits Tang's (1993) findings that Hong Kong tertiary students spontaneously collaborate to write assignments (see also Chapters 10 and 12; Volet and Kee, 1993; Volet and Pears, 1994).

Overall, the research with Singaporean students at university in Australia provided support for the higher achievement orientation of Chinese students compared with that of Western students. The great value given to academic achievement by the Singaporean students studying abroad can be explained in terms of a combination of cultural, societal and pragmatic factors, such as the traditional emphasis on education in Chinese culture (Pratt, 1992; McKnight, 1994), the fact that since independence Singapore's one party government has always placed a strong emphasis on education and academic qualifications (Smart and Ang, 1993), the high esteem in Singapore for university degrees even compared with polytechnic diplomas, and the financial sacrifices made by parents and relatives to provide quality educational experiences for the next generation, and the considerable pressures on students to do well academically. The significance of cultural and societal influences on Singaporean students' achieving approach to study is in line with Ho's (1986) claim that Chinese learners' motivation towards achievement is "rooted more firmly in the collectivist than the individualistic orientation" (p.28; see Chapter 5). One implication of our discussion is the importance of recognizing that the meaning of achievement motivation, and the way it is configured in relation to other factors (individualism and competitiveness) varies across cultures.

3. Chinese students do not participate in tutorials

Chinese students are often described by Western academics as receptive, quiet and compliant learners who do not volunteer to participate in tutorial discussions. It is believed that their apparent shyness is culturally-bound. These opinions and descriptions were evaluated in our (Renshaw and Volet, 1995) short-term longitudinal study of the tutorial participation of local Australian students and a group of predominantly Chinese students from Singapore who were enrolled in a first year economics subject at a West Australian university. The participation of the students in six tutorial groups was recorded by one of two observers (reliability was established prior to the study and checked during the data collection) over a nine-week period according to three levels of self-to-other regulated participation: 'student-regulated' participation was recorded when a student volunteered ideas, or voluntarily asked questions of the tutor or another student; 'tutor-initiated' participation was recorded when a student responded voluntarily to a question posed by the tutor or another student; and 'tutor-regulated' participation was recorded when the student was selected by the tutor to respond to a particular question, or make a comment.

Overall we found no differences in the total quantity or types of participation of the local and Singaporean students. Both groups of students engaged in tutorial discussions of their own accord, and at the instigation of the tutor. The average student from both groups engaged in only two or so instances of interaction in any tutorial, and there was evidence, in the case of the Singaporean students, that the tutors had made special efforts to include those who felt left out; we found that for the Singaporean students tutor-regulated participation was correlated positively with 'feeling left out'.

Local students predominated at the extreme high and low levels of participation; the quietest and the most interactive students in the tutorial were more likely to be local Australian than Singaporean students. Singaporean students participated in a more uniform way around the average level. It might be argued that the few local students who contributed frequently, intimidated the other students, but self-report measures of affective responses to the tutorials indicated that Singaporean and local students experienced similar and low levels of negative affect (feelings of intimidation, feeling left out, or afraid to speak). The similarity between local and Singaporean students in the overall level and types of participation in tutorials challenges the current image of Chinese students at Australian universities as being unusually quiet and unfamiliar with tutorial formats.

The interviews conducted by Volet and Kee (1993) with students from Singapore found that some of these students perceived themselves to be more reserved than local students, especially in tutorial groups where they were in a small minority. Such self-perceptions by Singaporean students are reflected in the study reported above where, on one of the four questions on self-reported participation (rather than actually observed participation), the Singaporean students rated themselves significantly lower than the local students. On similar questions regarding participation, that probed self-perceptions of offering personal opinions and alternative views in tutorials, no differences were found between local and Singaporean students. Likewise no differences were found in affective evaluations of tutorials, or feeling that the tutorial discussions went too fast. Overall these data present a picture of similarity between the groups rather than differences. It may be that the almost equivalent proportion of Singaporean and local students in the tutorial groups created an environment in which the Singaporean students felt at ease. It should be remembered also that the Singaporean students were quite familiar with tutorials prior to their study in Australia (Volet and Kee, 1993).

We found also that actual observed tutorial participation of local and Singaporean students was related to their approaches to study as measured by the reduced version of the Biggs SPQ (see Volet et al, 1994). For both groups, surface approach was related to lower levels of overall participation in tutorials, and with regard to types of participation, the surface approach was negatively related to student-regulated participation rather than tutor-regulated participation. This suggests that students with a surface approach to study chose not to initiate interaction in tutorials or respond to general questions from the tutor. Such a passive and low-profile presence in tutorials is consistent with the image of surface learners as interested in superficial understanding.

Self-reported participation was also found to relate to approaches to study. For Singaporean students, proposing one's own view, and 'proposing an alternative view', were related positively to deep and achieving approaches. This is consistent with the image of deep learners as interested in developing a personal understanding of the subject matter through the social processes of discussion and give-and-take argument. It suggests also that learners with an achieving approach use tutorials as a setting to acquire as much knowledge as possible so that they can achieve high grades.

A concern expressed by academics at Australian universities is the extra demands made by fee-paying overseas students for assistance outside the formal academic context of tutorials, lectures, and so on. In our observational study (Renshaw and Volet, in press) we examined this issue by asking the students to report where they would seek assistance if they could not understand an aspect of a tutorial. Both the Singaporean students and the local students indicated a similar preference for checking the textbook as the best way to clarify a misunderstanding, but Singaporean students gave higher rating to social sources of assistance, such as asking friends, or consulting the tutor after the tutorial. This finding may reflect a more thorough approach by the Singaporean students who are prepared to consult both the textbook, check with friends, as well as approach the tutor if necessary. Overall the Singaporean students would rather seek assistance without involving the tutor directly (that is, from the text or from a friend). This challenges the view that Chinese students are dependent on the tutor, and always prefer to seek the correct answers directly from the academic authority.

Conclusion

In conclusion, our research on the issue of adaptability and continuity in Chinese students' learning at university in Australia provides evidence that they adapt to meet the requirements of the new educational environment while at the same time maintaining a high-achievement orientation throughout their academic study.

Our short-term longitudinal studies, theoretically grounded in theories of self-regulation of learning and using multiple types of data, provide converging evidence of adjustments in Chinese students' learning goals, approaches to study and even conceptualizations of learning. The patterns of change in these students' learning after one semester of study in Australia, were similar in nature and direction to those of local Australian students, reflecting the impact of contextual influences on all students' study.

Overall, these results are consistent with the research conducted in Hong Kong by Biggs and colleagues (1992; this volume), but challenge much of the anecdotal literature on overseas students' learning. The shift in Chinese students' approaches to study from a deeper to a more surface level *after* one semester at university, combined with evidence of these students' concern for understanding the study materials before memorizing for examination purposes, contradict the claims that Southeast Asian students are predominantly rote learners and that their approach to study is culturally-bound and therefore stable across educational contexts.

Further evidence of Chinese learners' adaptability was found in the observations and self-reports of Singaporean students' participation in tutorials. Although their overall level and type of participation was not significantly different from that of local Australian students, evidence from interviews in their accounts of study of an awareness that Asian students in general tend to be more quiet than local students. The Singaporean students we interviewed (Volet and Kee, 1993), perceived Asian students to be initially quieter in tutorial discussions, due (in the opinion of these students) to the higher pace and louder conversational style of class interaction compared with Singapore, combined with new culturally-bound social conventions, such as the acceptability of interrupting someone to express your own opinion. These students thought that it was only a question of adaptation and transition to a different educational system and they recommended that Western academics not take for granted that Asian students are and will always be quiet. Certainly our observational and self-report data on participation provide no grounds for such an assumption - the Singaporean students were not highly interactive but neither were the local students. In fact the quietest and most reserved participants in each tutorial tended to be locals.

Chinese learner achievement orientation to study at university in Australia was stable and consistently higher than that of local students. The converging evidence from questionnaire and interview data was consistent with the anecdotal accounts from the overseas students' literature and with the cross-cultural studies comparing Chinese and Western students' approaches to study in their respective home country - that students from Southeast Asian countries place a consistently high value on academic achievement. There was evidence in our studies, however, that Chinese students' high level of achievement orientation, which was explained in terms of cultural, societal and pragmatic factors, was accompanied by a search for comprehension of the materials. Evidence of a relationship between the deep and achieving approaches to study of Singaporean students, and their awareness of the significance of study settings involving interaction with academic staff for achieving higher forms of learning, questions the stereotyped idea that Chinese learners' high achievement orientation is mainly directed at getting good grades.

Based on studies with Singaporean students predominantly of Chinese origin, it has been argued in this chapter that Chinese learners at university in Australia display a number of desirable study characteristics. They demonstrate a strategic adaptability in their attempts to meet the new educational requirements, and an advantageous and wise continuity in maintaining a high academic orientation. The case of Chinese students from Singapore however may be unique among the group of other Chinese learners, since they were taught in English throughout their schooling and considered English as their first language. In contrast, Chinese students from Hong Kong enrolled in TAFE (Technical and Further Education) colleges in Australia reported greater language-related difficulties in their study in comparison with overseas students from other Southeast Asian countries such as Malaysia and Indonesia (Volet and Pears, 1994). We recognize the special needs of students with language difficulties, and the demands they make on limited academic services. Our short-term longitudinal research has been able to track change and stability in approaches to study of Chinese students for whom English was no problem, and thereby has enabled some insight to be gained into Chinese students' approaches to study without the confounding effects of language and different contextual demands, which had not been possible in previous cross-cultural studies.

REFERENCES

Andrich, D. (1989). A probabilistic item response theory model for unfolding preference data. *Applied Psychological Measurement, 13*, 193-216.

Balla, J.R., Stokes, M.J. & Stafford, K.J. (1991). *Using the Study Process Questionnaire to its full potential*. Technical Report No 1. Educational Technology Centre, City Polytechnic of Hong Kong.

Ballard, B. & Clanchy, J. (1991). *Teaching students from overseas: a brief guide for lecturers and supervisors*. Melbourne: Longman Cheshire.

Biggs, J.B. (1987) *Student approaches to learning and studying*. Hawthorn, Vic.: Australian Council for Educational Research.

Biggs, J.B. (1991). Approaches to learning in secondary and tertiary students in Hong Kong: some comparative studies. *Educational Research Journal, 6*, 27-39.

Biggs, J.B. (1992). *Why and how do Hong Kong students learn? Using the learning and study process questionnaires*. Education Papers No.14, Faculty of Education, University of Hong Kong.

Biggs, J.B. (1994). What are effective schools? Lessons from East and West. *The Australian Educational Researcher, 21*, 19-39.

Boekaerts, M. (1992). The adaptable learning process: initiating and maintaining behavioural change. *Journal of Applied Psychology: An International Review, 41*(4), 377-397.

Bourne, H. & Davenport, T. (1993). Factors impacting on the academic performance of international students: a progress report. In Barthel, A. (Ed.), *Cultural diversity and higher education: has it made a difference? Should it make a difference?* (pp. 25-31) Conference proceedings. University of Technology, Sydney.

Bradley, D. & Bradley, M. (1984). *Problems of Asian students in Australia: language, culture and education*. Canberra: Australian Government Publishing Service.

Burns, R.B. (1991). Study and stress among first year overseas students in an Australian university. *Higher Education Research and Development, 10*(1), 61-77.

Chalmers, D. (1994). Local and overseas students' goals and management of study. *Issues in Educational Research, 4*(2), 25-56.

Ho, D.Y.F. (1986). Chinese patterns of socialization: a critical review (pp. 1-37). In Bond, M.H. (Ed.), *The psychology of the Chinese people*. Oxford: Oxford University Press.

Kember, D. & Gow, L. (1990). Cultural specificity of approaches to study. *British Journal of Educational Psychology*, *60*, 356-363.

McKnight, A. (1994). Chinese learners of English: a different view of literacy? *Open Letter: Australian Journal for Adult Literacy Research and Practice*, *4*(2), 1994.

Pratt, D.P. (1992). Chinese conceptions of learning and teaching: a westerner's attempt at understanding. *International Journal of Lifelong Education*, *11*(4), 301-319.

Renshaw, P.D. & Volet, S.E. (1995). South-east Asian students at Australian universities: a reappraisal of their tutorial participation and approaches to study. *Australian Educational Researcher*, *22*(2), 85-106.

Samuelowicz, K. (1987). Learning problems of overseas students: two sides of a story. *Higher Education in Research and Development*, *6*, 121-133.

Smart, D. & Ang, G. (1993). *Medium-term market opportunities for Australian education: a survey of Hong Kong.* Asia Research Centre of Social, Political and Economic Change. Murdoch University, Western Australia.

Tang, K.C.C. (1991). *Effects of different assessment procedures on tertiary students' approaches to learning.* The University of Hong Kong: PhD Dissertation.

Tang, K.C.C. (1993). Spontaneous collaborative learning: a new dimension in student learning experience? *Higher Education Research and Development*, 115-130.

Volet, S.E. & Kee, J.P.P (1993). Studying in Singapore - studying in Australia: a student perspective. *Occasional Paper No.1*, Murdoch University Teaching Excellence Committee, Murdoch.

Volet, S.E. & Pears, H. (1994). *International students in Technical and Further Education colleges (TAFE) Western Australia: past students' reflections on their TAFE experience and attitudes towards educational exchange between their country and Australia.* Murdoch University / TAFE International (WA). Perth: CCTN.

Volet, S.E. & Renshaw, P.D. (in press). Cross-cultural differences in university students' goals and perceptions of study settings for achieving their own goals. *Higher Education*.

Volet, S.E., Renshaw P.D. & Tietzel, K. (1994). A short-term longitudinal investigation of cross-cultural differences in study approaches using Biggs' SPQ questionnaire. *British Journal of Educational Psychology*, *64*, 301-318.

Watkins, D., Regmi, M. & Astilla, E. (1991). The-Asian-learner-as-a-rote-learner stereotype: myth or reality? *Educational Psychology*, *11*(1), 21-24.

12

Peer Tutoring and Learning Outcomes

Sam Winter

An Introduction to Peer Tutoring

The purpose of this chapter is to present evidence of the effectiveness of peer tutoring in the Hong Kong classroom. Peer tutoring occurs whenever one student teaches another (whether of the same age, younger or older). It has a long history, reaching back at least as far as the early nineteenth century experiments of Lancaster and Bell (detailed in Salmon, 1932). Its appeal has grown in the West over the last 20 years. This may be due in part to the increasing evidence regarding the effectiveness of the approach, but also because it has been seen as a cheap means of delivering education in an era of successive recessions and governments committed to tight public-spending policies. Since 1970 the number of books and research articles in peer tutoring has increased tremendously; Goodlad and Hirst (1989) were able to find over 1,000 publications relating to peer tutoring in the 14 preceding years.

Peer tutoring is often discussed in the context of cooperative learning (e.g. Topping, 1988). The first may be viewed as a subset of the second, insofar as peer tutoring (a) is guided by a cooperative value (that the success of others is as important as one's own success); (b) involves students actively working together to achieve a shared learning goal; and (c) requires the teacher to become a manager of learning rather than a provider of instruction. However, the static 'tutor' and 'tutee' roles and tutor-training procedures characteristic of many peer-tutor projects set them apart from many other cooperative learning formats (e.g. those described by Slavin, 1987).

Peer tutoring has been found to be an effective method of tutoring across a range of subject areas, age and ability levels. Projects commonly focus upon the learning needs of the tutee. In these projects the tutor's role may be regarded as philanthropic. Consequently, such projects are often described as 'tutorial service' projects (Fitzgibbon, 1978). However, a large body of evidence indicates that tutors gain as much as, or more than, those who are being tutored. Consequently, 'learning-by-tutoring' projects, focused on the learning needs of the tutors, have become more popular in recent years. Whoever (tutor or tutee) is the focus of a project, there is evidence to suggest that gains for both parties extend beyond academic outcomes into attitudinal and behavioural areas.

A wide range of ages and abilities are represented in the peer-tutoring literature. Published research represents most age levels (e.g. the use of preschoolers as tutors in Lobato, 1983), and ability levels (e.g. the use of low-achieving, handicapped and behaviourally disordered students as tutors in Eiserman, 1988; Scruggs et al., 1985). Similarly, a wide range of instructional domains are represented in the peer tutoring literature. While reading is perhaps the best represented area (see Mathes and Fuchs, 1991, for a review of research solely in this area), peer tutoring has also been extended into mathematics instruction, traditional secondary school subjects such as science education, social studies, and foreign languages, as well as more generalized academic abilities such as spelling, study skills and essay writing. Less commonly, projects have focused on non-orthodox curriculum areas such as sign language, drug education, sexuality and birth control, and the 'country code', as well as a variety of learned social behaviours.

Published projects involving peer tutors vary greatly in terms of the type and amount of training offered to the tutors, and the degree to which the activities of tutors and tutees are programmed ('structured').

Peer Tutoring Outcomes and Factors Related to Outcomes

Educational gains are commonly reported for both tutees and tutors. The research also indicates that peer tutoring can bring about attitudinal, behavioural and social gains for both parties. Among such benefits reported for tutors are improvements in school attendance rates, self-concept, interpersonal relationships, attitudes towards tutees, the subject being tutored, school and teachers, improved motivation to succeed, better work habits, and improved behaviour in class and at home. Among affective, attitudinal and behavioural gains reported for tutees are improvements in social status, self-concept, academic motivation, school attitudes and classroom behaviour. While much of the above data on affective outcomes is qualitative and anecdotal in nature, there are notable exceptions (e.g. Haggerty, 1971, and Robertson, 1971).

Hartley (1977), Cohen et al. (1982), Cook et al. (1986), Levin et al.

(1987), Mathes and Fuchs (1991) and Hattie (1992) have all employed meta-analytic and related techniques to amalgamate research data on tutoring outcomes and factors that are associated with those outcomes.

First, these studies together confirm what has long been apparent to practitioners that learning outcomes for tutors and tutees are impressive across a wide range of age ranges, ability levels and subject domains, and that there are (albeit less predictable) affective, attitudinal and behavioural gains to be made also. For example, Cohen et al. (1982) report a meta-analysis of 65 studies of tutoring (from 500 available studies in the literature). These studies covered a range of tutored subject areas, involved actual classrooms, experimental and control groups, and objectively measured outcomes. Cohen and colleagues were also careful to avoid studies which had 'tutored to the test'.

Cohen and colleagues' findings regarding outcomes for tutees were as follows. Of the 52 studies which reported achievement outcomes for tutees, 45 reported superior gains for tutees over controls, and in 19 cases the superiority of tutoring was statistically significant. The average effect size for the 52 studies was 0.4. In eight studies which assessed changed attitudes towards subject matter, all reported that tutees made positive gains, although only in one was the change statistically significant. Average effect size for the eight studies was 0.29. In seven out of the nine studies which assessed self-concept, the tutees made positive changes. Average effect size for the nine studies was 0.09.

Findings regarding outcomes for tutors were as follows: 38 studies assessed achievement gains, of which 33 showed that tutors made gains larger than controls. In 10 of these the gains were statistically significant. The average effect size was 0.38. In four out of five studies investigating attitude to subject matter there was evidence of positive changes, although the change was statistically significant in only one case. In 12 out of 16 studies looking at self-concept, positive changes were reported; in four of them the change was significant.

Secondly, three of the studies indicate that peer tutoring is both more effective (Hartley, op.cit., Levin et al. op.cit., Hattie, op.cit.) and more efficient (Levin et al., op.cit.) than other forms of educational interventions.

For example, Hattie (1992) synthesized 134 meta-analytic studies of the effects of educational innovations. These 134 meta-analyses generated 22,155 effect sizes and represented 7,827 studies based on between five and 15 million students. The mean effect size for educational outcomes from peer tutoring was 0.5. This effect size was the second largest identified for methods of instruction, behind reinforcement (effect size 1.13) and equal with mastery learning. By comparison, the mean effect size for achievement outcomes for educational innovations was 0.4. Peer tutoring therefore appears to be a comparatively affective innovation. Turning to affective outcomes, peer tutoring was associated with a mean effect size of 0.34. Only one method of instruction exceeded this effect size: mastery learning, with an effect size of 0.69. For comparison, the mean effect size for innovations was 0.2.

Thirdly, there are surprisingly few factors that appear reliably to predict successful tutoring. The two studies that are relevant here are those of Cohen and coworkers, (op.cit.) and Mathes and Fuchs (op.cit.). Cohen and his colleagues examined a number of factors that might be associated with learning outcomes for participants in tutoring projects. For tutors, only one factor appeared to be significant: focus upon mathematics. For tutees, rather more factors appeared to be associated with successful outcomes: (a) short projects rather than long ones, (b) focus on a low-level (basic skills) subject area; (c) focus upon mathematics (rather than reading); (d) evaluation by way of locally-developed tests (as opposed to nationally standardized ones); and (e) unpublished work (in contrast to published work or dissertations). They also found structured (rather than unstructured) tutoring to be moderately predictive of large effect sizes for tutees.

The superiority of short projects over long ones (at least for tutees) is easily understandable; short projects have an innovatory flavour which influences the enthusiasm and motivation of all concerned. More surprising is the superiority (in terms of both tutor and tutee outcomes) of maths over reading programmes in view of the preponderance of the latter; a preponderance that continues some 11 years after Cohen et al's article. Surprising too are the superior outcomes of unpublished projects (vis-à-vis published work) in view of the commonly held assumption that more successful projects have a better chance of being published.

Perhaps surprisingly, Cohen and colleagues found that tutor and tutee learning outcomes were unaffected by (among other things) the presence or absence of training for tutors, the age levels of the participants, any tutor-tutee age-differential, and the ability of the tutee.

Mathes and Fuchs (1991) examined 11 studies involving peer tutoring in reading with students who had reading disabilities. All of the studies met stringent 'best evidence' criteria. From patterns in the data they concluded that effect sizes were larger for: (a) projects occurring in mainstream classrooms than was the case for special education (effect sizes of 0.42 and 0.27 respectively); and for (b) projects involving handicapped students as tutors rather than tutees (0.42 and 0.30). However, they admit that these conclusions may result from the fact that handicapped students in mainstream settings, as well as those chosen as tutors, are often more able than those in special settings or those who are tutored. Interestingly, the data also indicates that: (a) cross-age and same-age tutoring are of similar effectiveness (0.38 and 0.32); (b) 'expert' tutors perform similarly to tutors whose attainments are similar to those of the tutee (0.36 and 0.34); and (c) classwide and individual tutoring appear to be equally effective (0.36 and 0.35). The negative findings on age and ability differentials confirm those of Cohen et al. (op.cit.).

Peer tutoring and Chinese Students

Writers in this volume and elsewhere have remarked upon the value placed upon collectivism in Chinese culture. Hofstede (1983) defines collectivism as a preference for a tightly-knit social framework in which members can expect others to look after them in return for total loyalty. Often described more simply as a concern for the group rather than for the individual, it rests on an awareness that individual humans primarily exist in relation to others (Bond and Hwang, 1986), as well as traditional Confucian concerns for filial piety and familism, collective welfare and social concern rather than personal enjoyment (see Chapter 10), and for social harmony in general (Bond and Hwang, op.cit.).

The importance placed by Chinese culture upon the individual in relation to the social group is evident throughout the literature. Ma (1988) suggests that collectivism is actually incorporated into invariate stages of moral development among Chinese children and adolescents. Certainly, Chinese socialization practices emphasize sharing, cooperation and acceptance of social obligations, and deemphasize competition and aggression (research reported in Ho, 1986). Also relevant is Chiu's (1987) comparative study of Taiwanese, Chinese-American and Anglo-American mothers' rearing practices which found that the former two groups promoted comradeship, sharing and dependency much more than the latter group. On similar lines, Domino and Hannah (1987) reported that stories written by young Chinese students contained many more references to teamwork and cooperation than was the case for their American counterparts.

The importance of social groups outside the family appears to increase as students grow older. Ma and Chan's (1986) research with older primary school children suggests that the peer group is of great significance. Lau and Wong's (1992) research with secondary school students reveals that true friendship is valued higher than any other value except freedom. Within tertiary education Chinese students interact in larger groups than their American counterparts (Wheeler, 1988), place a strong importance on social values generally and on conformity in particular, deferring to authority readily (research reported in Yang, 1986). Yang also reports that they aspire, above all other possible ways of living, to incorporate group participation into their lives. In a possibly related finding, Lau and Gruen (1992) report that a strong stigma is attached to loneliness in Chinese culture.

Collectivist values seem to generate a readiness to cooperate with others on tasks. Wheeler (1986) notes that a greater proportion of interaction among Chinese students is task-related (as opposed to recreational) as compared with

American counterparts. A frequently cited study by Li, Cheung and Kau (1979) indicated that, as Chinese children grow older, they show increased readiness to cooperate on a task. The opposite is the case for American students (Madsen, 1971). Most interestingly, the readiness to cooperate survives under conditions where rewards are dispensed on a competitive basis. Tang's research (see Chapter 10) underlines how ready Chinese students are to collaborate, on an informal and spontaneous basis, even when rewards (course grades) are allocated on an individual basis. She even suggests that they may have a 'need' to work together. The old Chinese proverb 'friendship first, competition second' seems to ring true even in urbanized Hong Kong.

Not only do Chinese students like to work together, they also appear to do very well when they do. Salili (see Chapter 5) notes that Chinese students work harder together than when working alone. The writer's research with tertiary students (Winter, 1996) confirms this view, revealing academic-engagement levels above 90% in cooperative learning conditions. Tang (Chapter 10) reports that students who collaborate with others display high achievement. Once again, personal research (Winter, op.cit.) confirms this, suggesting that Hong Kong tertiary students who learn cooperatively perform better in exam conditions in which they are asked to apply what they have learned.

Notwithstanding the above, statements about Chinese collectivism may need qualification on at least five grounds. First, modern ethnic Chinese live in great numbers in economic, political, social and cultural contexts ranging from the mainland, Hong Kong, Taiwan, Singapore, Malaysia, Thailand and Indonesia in Southeast Asia to places further afield such as Australasia, North America and Britain. Writers such as Mak (1990) and Cheung and colleagues (1992) have therefore questioned the degree to which there is a uniform Chinese culture. The same may be true for its most central values, including 'collectivism'.

Second, the collectivistic values displayed by Chinese may be somewhat context specific. Ho and Chiu (1994) analyzed the values expressed in 2,000 popular Chinese sayings, and found that collectivism and anti-individualism predominate in only one out of the five areas examined: achievement.

Third, cultural values are relative. A number of writers suggest that, in a world-wide perspective, Chinese may not be especially collectivist, but rather that Americans (who tend to provide a reference point in modern social psychological research) are unusually individualistic (Ho, 1986). On similar lines, it has been pointed out to the writer by an eminent anthropologist (G. Evans, personal communication) that the Balinese tend to regard the Chinese as very individualistic.

Fourth, there are signs that social changes may be eroding traditional collectivist values. Wang, Oakland and Liu (1992) report that single children produced under China's one-child policy exhibit more behaviour problems and less cooperativeness than do those in multi-sibling families. Yang (1986) also notes research indicating that social conditions may impact on collectivism.

Lastly, writers such as Lau (1992; also Lau and Wong, 1992) point out that Chinese collectivism may be an instrumental rather than a terminal value: reflecting merely a way of getting things done in Chinese culture, and of achieving one's personal (often highly individualistic) goals. There is a parallel here with the educational value so often ascribed to the Chinese. Yang (1986) and Salili (see Chapter 5) both note that, for Chinese, education may not be valuable in itself but in terms of what it can achieve (terminal values). The paradox is that these terminal values are often seen as socially-oriented (collectivistic) rather than individualistic.

Turning now to human-heartedness, it is clear that values such as concern for others, generosity and compassion are important values in Chinese culture. Research by the Chinese Culture Connection (1987) indicates that Hong Kong rates fourth among 22 countries for this value. On similar lines Yang (1986) reports research suggesting that Chinese people value benevolence highly (at least compared with Americans). For his part, Ma (1988) even suggests that compassion is enshrined in stages of moral development in Chinese culture.

For human-heartedness too there remains a question regarding its uniformity across all Chinese cultures. Singapore ranked relatively low for human-heartedness in the Chinese Culture Connection research cited earlier. Singapore is a less uniformly Chinese society of course, and it may be argued that the finding reflected the impact of other cultural groups on the data.

Finally, when considering the highly-pressured nature of teaching in Chinese (and other Asian) classrooms, it is worth noting that there is a price for the teacher to pay. For example, Wong (1989) noted that 40% of Hong Kong secondary school teachers plan to leave the profession, and that job dissatisfaction was related to stress. Chan and Hui (1995) report that, of all sources of burnout, the strongest was the feeling of being 'used up at the end of the work day'. One suspects that this feeling stemmed directly from the didactic teaching methods commonly used in classrooms, and that peer tutoring might allow teachers a way out of this unfortunate trap.

In summary then, cooperative learning approaches such as peer tutoring conceivably have much to offer in the Chinese educational context. On one hand, they appear to draw upon values of collectivism and human-heartedness in Chinese culture. On the other hand, they offer an alternative to the more traditional teacher-centred pedagogy that dominates classrooms and possibly contributes to teacher exhaustion and burnout.

In practice, relatively little published work exists in this area. There are scattered reports regarding the use of study groups with Hong Kong secondary students (Lai, 1993) and tertiary students (Chapter 10). Tang's research into spontaneous collaboration suggests that Chinese students often prefer to work together. Everyday experience confirms this. Older siblings help their younger siblings at home, or work together with classmates on homework, often (in

Hong Kong anyway) occupying the telephone line for long periods. They also respond enthusiastically when given a chance by their teachers to work in groups (see Biggs, 1990).

More structured work involving peer tutoring (with students in fixed roles as tutors or tutees) appears to occur quite frequently in mainland China (see Sheridan, 1990, and Potts, 1994). It is also quite common in Hong Kong (witness the widespread secondary school 'Big-Brother-Big-Sister' schemes). However, such work is often relatively unsystematic and unevaluated. The projects to be described in the next section represent attempts to inject slightly more rigour into the enterprise by ensuring training for tutors, monitoring of tutor performance, and evaluation of outcomes. They are grouped according to their focus on English or Chinese literacy skills. Additional Hong Kong projects are described in Winter (1995).

Studies of Peer Tutoring in Hong Kong

There now follow short accounts of five peer-tutoring studies recently conducted in Hong Kong. They represent reasonably systematic attempts at peer tutoring insofar as they all involved training for tutors, monitoring of tutor performance, and evaluation of outcomes. In this sense they are to some extent unrepresentative of peer tutoring as it normally occurs in Hong Kong. The five projects fall into the area of English or Chinese reading and are presented according to the language involved (see Table 11.1 for a description of the main features of these studies).

Peer Tutoring in English

Hui's Study

Hui, an Educational Psychologist working within the Hong Kong Government Education Department, has organized a number of peer-tutor projects to improve English reading skills of lower form pupils in Hong Kong Secondary schools. In each of her projects the first language of both tutors and tutees has been Cantonese.

In a 1985 pilot study she taught as Form Six tutors to use a tutoring technique known as 'paired reading' (Morgan and Lyon, 1979). Paired reading (PR) involves a set of procedures for: (a) listening to a tutee read; and (b) reading alongside the tutee. It has been used successfully elsewhere in the world as a basis for peer-tutoring projects (e.g. Winter and Low, 1984). The tutors then used PR for four weeks with a group of Form One pupils requiring remedial help in English. Tutees were allowed to read from a book of their own choice. Because tutees were reading in a second language (L2) tutors were taught to encourage understanding of each passage, for example by summarizing its meaning before the tutee began to read.

Table 11.1
Five Hong Kong peer-tutoring studies: main features

	Hui	Winter	Ma	Chan	Pang
Tutor age level	15-18	16+	16+	10-15	16+
Tutee age level	12+	12	12+	10-15	14
No. of pairs	36 max	23	41	30	35
Type of project	ts	ts	ts	ts/lt	ts
Control/Comparison gp.	n	y	n	y	y
Project Length (wks)	8	6	8	4	6
Total Tutoring (hrs)	8	15	10	7.5	10
Timing of sessions	ln	ln	ln	as	ln
Tutoring method used	pr	pr	ppp	pr	pr
Incentives	--	n	y	y	y
Objective evaluation	y	y	y	y	y
Motivation problems	--	y	y	--	y
Attendance problems	--	y	y	--	y
Compliance problems	--	y	--	--	--

Notes:

(a) This table is compiled on the basis of information readily available to the author.
(b) Tutor and tutee age levels; for indication only.
(c) Type of project: ts = tutorial service, lt = learning by tutoring.
(d) Timing of sessions: ln = lunch, as = after school.
(e) Tutoring method used: pr = paired reading; ppp = pause, prompt, praise.
(f) Control-comparison group, objective evaluation, incentives, motivation problems, attendance problems, compliance problems: y = yes, n = no, -- = no information

The project evaluation was generally positive, and led to a larger 1986 study. This involved three secondary schools for whom Hui was providing a support service, and incorporated a number of changes, some of which were based upon what had been learned in the pilot study. In each school up to 12 tutors aged 15- to 18-years were trained to work daily for 30 minutes with 12-year-old children needing remedial help. Tutees were allowed to read from a subject textbook of their own choice. Tutors employed an independent reading mode technique to listen to tutees reading. If a tutee made an error or hesitated on a difficult word then the tutor supplied the correct word. Tutors noted errors which tutees made during reading, and set aside time for teaching the tutees to read and spell these error words correctly. Tutors employed probes to evaluate the success of their instruction. The project continued for six weeks, and was evaluated favourably by tutors, tutees and classteachers.

For more details of Hui's work see Winter (1989).

The North Point study

Twenty-three Form One pupils in a government-aided secondary school in an area of Hong Kong island were invited to join a peer-tutoring scheme as tutees on the basis of their English performance during the first term of the academic year. Form Four pupils were invited to volunteer as tutors for eight school weeks. Sufficient volunteers were selected to provide one tutor for each tutee.

Tutors and tutees met at a social gathering after school hours and were matched together in pairs by the school social worker. All pairs were same-sex. Tutors were then trained to use a modified form of PR, as follows:

1) Allow your tutee to read something he/she has chosen.
2) If a word is difficult then read it for him/her.
3) If many words are difficult then (a) read part of the book to your tutee and then ask him/her to re-read it or (b) read one sentence each.
4) At all times you must show interest by (a) listening carefully to what your tutee reads, (b) talking and asking questions about the tutee's book and (c) praising success.

Tutors watched a demonstration of these tutoring procedures being applied, and were then asked to employ them in pairs in a role-play situation. Tutors were given personal folders in which they were to keep written guidelines for tutoring, and record sheets for scoring the punctuality and learning attitudes of their tutees.

Tuition took place twice a week for eight school weeks. All tutors and tutees met at the same time and place. Each session took place during lunch recess and lasted about 30 minutes. Tutees were given the responsibility of bringing their chosen books to all tutoring sessions, together with a dictionary to be used if needed. Tutors had the responsibility to bring their folders containing written tutoring guidelines and record sheets.

A teacher at the school supervised tutors and tutees during tutoring sessions. The two biggest problems encountered were attendance and compliance. Average attendance for the 23 tutees was around 12 out of 17 sessions. Seven tutees missed over half the scheduled sessions. A few were late in attending. A number of tutees repeatedly brought homework assignments or test revision material to the tutoring sessions, and requested the tutor to help them complete these tasks. A number of tutors complied with these requests, even though both tutors and tutees had been told that the project sessions were to be used solely for the purpose of reading English books.

Tutees' English abilities were assessed before and after the project through the group Hong Kong English Attainment Test (HKAT) Series 3 (for Primary Six pupils). A control group of 21 Form One pupils of approximately the same English abilities sat the HKAT alongside the experimental group but received no special treatment during the project. Complete pre- and post-project test results were obtained for 42 pupils, 21 in the experimental group and an identical number in the control group. The test marker did not know to which group the pupils belonged.

Among tutees, boys gained an average of 4.6 months, in comparison with boys in the control group who made a mean gain of 3.7 months over the six weeks of the project. However encouraging these figures were they failed to reach statistical significance. The gains for girls were not so striking. Girl tutees made a mean gain of 3.8 months, compared with girls in the control group who made a mean gain of 3.9 months. One of the more striking findings of this project was that boys made larger gains than girls despite lower levels of attendance; boys averaged 6.7 sessions absent versus 4.1 for girls. However, the association between attendance figures and reading gains was non-significant statistically.

Winter (1989) noted that the absence of significant effects in this study may be the consequence of several factors. In addition to a small sample and short pre- to post-test period (factors which make it difficult to obtain statistically significant results in any experiment), there were problems of (a) infrequent tutoring (twice per week as compared with daily tutoring in Hui's study quoted earlier), (b) poor attendance, and (c) poor compliance with tutoring guidelines.

Ma's 1993 study

Ma (1993) reports a peer-tutored project in a secondary school which had recently decided to transfer to an English medium of instruction for all secondary classes. The aim of the project was to enhance participants' English reading ability and interest in reading English. Tutees were all volunteers from English remedial classes in Form One. Tutors were recruited on a volunteer basis from Form Four.

The reading materials for the project were composed of (a) passages from Form One English textbooks and (b) lyrics to English language folk songs. The passages numbered 20; one for each tutoring session. Tutors were given copies of the material, together with tape recordings of the material being read, in order to allow tutors the chance to prepare for tutoring.

Tutors were taught to use a 'pause, prompt and praise' method (McNaughton et al, 1981). Like PR, this technique has been used successfully in peer-tutoring studies elsewhere (e.g. Wheldall & Mettem, 1986). Tutors praised tutees as often as possible for correct reading. They paused for more than five seconds or until the end of the sentence wherever the tutee made an error. If necessary the tutor supplied a prompt as follows. If the error did not make sense then the tutor prompted with a clue about the meaning of the sentence. If the error made sense then the prompt focused on the look of the word. If the tutee failed to attempt the word then the tutor prompted him to read on to the end of the sentence or begin at the start of the sentence again. Where a prompt failed to elicit the correct word the tutor simply supplied the word to the tutee.

Forty-one pairs of students participated in twenty lunchtime tutoring sessions lasting 20 to 30 minutes each and spread over a period of eight weeks. Participants were free to arrange other times to meet if they wished, as long as they covered all 20 passages. The project organizer (Ma) met once with small groups of tutors to offer support during the project.

During each session the tutor noted up to five errors made by the tutee. At the end of the session tutors asked tutees to practise the pronunciation and spelling of those words as a homework assignment. At the start of the following session, tutors asked tutees to read and spell the assigned words. Any words that were still difficult were practised and tested again. Tutors made written notes of progress in learning these difficult words.

By the designated end of the project only 22 pairs had finished all 20 sessions. Another six had finished at least 15 sessions. Eleven pairs had finished less than ten sessions. All tutees who had covered all 20 passages earned an attendance certificate, all their tutors earned a commendation letter from the Principal.

In week three of the project a reading test was drawn up using a passage not yet covered in the tutoring sessions. Thirty-three tutees available for the test read the passage without assistance while tutors recorded the number of errors. They made an average 19.72 errors. The same passage was employed as a test at the end of the project. Twenty-one tutees available on that day made an average 11.62 errors. Of these 21 students, 17 made fewer errors than they had on the first test.

A number of tutors reported improved attitudes, confidence and reading ability among their tutees. Several felt that their own reading ability had been improved.

Ma reports difficulties in trying to maintain the interest of the participants over the eight weeks of the project. These difficulties arose from: (a) a clash of timing between the project and other extra-curricular activities; (b) a lack of communication between tutors and tutees, so that one party was not informed when the other was absent; (c) late-comers among those who went home for lunch; and (d) insufficient support for tutors from the project organizer.

Ma suggests that peer-tutor programmes have a better chance of success if: (a) their timing avoids clashes with other activities (he questions whether lunchtimes are appropriate); (b) the numbers of participants are held to a more easily manageable figure; or (c) tutors and tutees are given more regular monitoring and support.

Peer Tutoring in Chinese

Chan's 1987 Study

Chan (1987) compared the effectiveness of (a) peer tutors supervised by student teachers and (b) student teachers acting as tutors using PR to promote Chinese reading skills. Thirty Hong Kong students aged ten to 15-years were recruited on a volunteer basis from Primary grades Four to Six of a day/residential school run by a Society of Boy's Centres. The school assisted boys who had displayed social and emotional problems at home and in previous schools. The majority also displayed basic skill deficits.

The pupils were tested on two local normative tests: the Graded Chinese Word Recognition Test and the Hong Kong Attainment Test 4C3. The ten most able were assigned to act as peer tutors, the remaining 20 pupils were split at random into two tutee groups. One group was tutored by the peer tutors and the other was tutored by a group of volunteer student teachers from a local Government College of Education.

Student teacher and peer tutors separately received one-and-a-half-hours of training in the use of PR techniques. After a short introduction to the idea of tutoring, each group was shown a video recording which demonstrated PR. They then received verbal instruction in the use of the technique, were given a summary handout and were then required to practice the technique in role play with a partner. A model pair was selected to further demonstrate the use of PR to the rest of the group.

Tutor-tutee pairs worked together for 15 sessions of 30 minutes taking place at school after normal working hours over a period of four weeks. Tutees chose books from a stock of 86 selected by Chan herself.

Tutors received support and incentives. Peer tutors were supervised by a group of student teachers during the project and received a selection of stationery rewards for collaborating in the project. Student teacher tutors received travelling expenses, a souvenir and a record of service to be placed in their college file.

At pretest the mean word recognition performance of each tutee group was at the P1-P2 level, whilst that of the peer tutors was at P2-P3. At post-test word recognition gains for both sets of tutees were roughly equivalent to a four-month gain. Peer tutor gains were rather smaller. On the Attainment test, a rather broader test of literacy, all three groups made substantial gains.

Pang's 1993 study

In what is perhaps the most carefully conducted peer-tutor study so far reported in Hong Kong, Pang (1993) reported a project at a coeducational secondary school in which he was placed as a trainee Educational Psychologist. His study sought to improve Chinese reading ability and attitudes among students in the bottom 20% of the ability range.

Thirty-five Form Two students (aged around 14 years) were recruited as tutees by way of a wall poster, oral notices and information sheets. Thirty-five other low-achieving Form Two students acted as a control group.

Nineteen Form Four students, all 'capable readers' (and all, incidentally, girls) were chosen to be tutors. Tutors took part in a training and role-play practice session designed to ensure that they were able to use the following modified PR technique:-

1) The tutor reads aloud with the tutee, allowing the tutee to set the pace.
2) If, when the two are reading together, the tutee hesitates or makes a mistake the tutor tells the tutee the correct word. The tutee repeats the word before continuing.
3) If the tutee signals that he wants to read alone then the tutor should stop reading aloud and should follow the tutee reading alone.
4) If, when reading alone, the tutee hesitates or makes a mistake then the tutor should tell him the correct word, make him repeat it, and then read aloud with him until he next signals.
5) Whenever the tutee reads a difficult word or sentence, corrects his own mistake or signals to read alone, then the tutor should praise him.

Tutees read from newspaper materials of their own free choice from those provided by their tutors and the researcher. All newspaper materials read by tutees were displayed on a Bulletin Board in the covered recreation area of the school.

There were 20 sessions each of 30 minutes' duration over a period of six school weeks. All sessions took place during the lunch hour. Tutors and tutees were rewarded with magazines after ten sessions if they had managed full attendance. At the end of the project tutors were awarded a certificate of contribution and tutees were awarded a certificate of attendance. Pang met with the tutors every week to receive feedback from and offer feedback to them.

Project evaluation was by way of:-

1) A 200 character inventory consisting of eight sentences drawn from newspapers was employed at pre- and post-test. This inventory was used for testing word recognition and recall. Tutors tested word recognition by asking the students to read the inventory. Chinese subject teachers tested word recall by dictating the inventory for students to write.

2) A checklist on reading interests and habits, was also employed on a pre-test post-test basis. This checklist investigated students' interest in reading newspapers, the time they spent doing so, and the difficulty they experienced when engaged in the activity. Similar questions were focused on textbooks, in order to assess the degree to which any changes in reading habits transferred to materials not used in the project.

3) Two questionnaires (one each for tutors and tutees) were completed post-test, which focused on students' experiences of, and their perceptions about gains from the project.

Pang presents pre- and post-test data for the 32 tutees whose attendance was 90% or more, and for the 31 control students who were available for both pre- and post-tests.

Tutees made statistically significant improvement in word recognition. The mean gain in accuracy on the 200 word inventory was 5.03 for the tutees and 3.06 for the control group. These figures are significantly different at the 0.05 confidence level. Tutees also made significant improvement in word recall. The mean gain was 5.97 for the tutees and 2.00 for the control group. These figures are significantly different at the 0.05 confidence level.

Tutees reported an increased amount of time spent reading newspapers. They reported spending a mean additional 21.97 minutes reading newspapers compared with a decrease of 4.23 for control subjects. The difference between these figures is significant at the 0.05 level.

Tutees reported increased interest in reading newspapers in their spare time. The mean change in rating on this item was +0.72 compared with -0.46 for the control group. Both represent statistically significant changes from pre-test, although in clearly different directions.

Tutees reported decreased difficulty in reading newspapers. The mean change in tutees' rating on this item was +1.12 compared with -0.26 for the control group. The figure for the tutees represents a statistically significant change. This is not the case for the control group.

There were no signs of transfer of improved reading attitudes and habits to textbooks in terms of the three variables studied: time spent reading textbooks, interest in doing so and difficulty experienced when doing so.

Of the 30 tutees who commented on the effects of the project, the following expressed a view that it had been helpful/very helpful: 28 in regard to reading skills; 26 in regard to reading habits; and 23 in regard to reading interests.

Of the 14 tutors who expressed a view on the project, the following felt that the project had been helpful/very helpful for tutees: 13 in regard to reading skills; 12 in regard to reading habits; and 13 in regard to reading interests. The following felt that it had been helpful/very helpful for themselves: 14 in terms of reading skills, 9 in terms of reading habits; and 14 in regard to reading interests.

Sixty-three percent of tutors reported some sort of difficulty during the implementation of the project. By comparison, tutees seemed to have an easier time, only 37% reporting difficulties. Fourteen percent of tutors and tutees felt that they had not received sufficient support and reward during the project.

Twenty-three percent of tutors felt that tutoring sessions were too long, while a substantial 48% of tutees held the same view. Relatively few students believed that the sessions were too short (15% of tutors and 21% of tutees). A similar pattern emerged with regard to the duration of the entire project. Some 14% of tutors believed that the project was too long, while a substantial 38% of tutees shared the same view. Relatively few students felt that the project was too short (7% of tutors and tutees).

Seventy-eight percent of tutors and 69% of tutees felt that this sort of project should be implemented further in their school.

Discussion

The five studies described above represent a small sample of what can be attempted through peer tutoring. They all took place out of class-time with relatively small numbers of students. The projects also reveal emphases upon (a) cross-age tutoring involving adolescent tutors working with younger tutees, (b) in a tutorial service capacity that focused on the needs of the tutees. They were all relatively short (eight weeks or under) and structured projects, important factors in view of the fact that these seem to be more effective than longer or unstructured ones (Cohen et al., 1982). They were all concerned with reading skills (the most popular area for peer-tutor research, but, as demonstrated by Cohen et al., op.cit., not necessarily associated with the most dramatic outcomes). Most involved a modification of the PR technique.

Notwithstanding the narrow range represented, these studies indicate both the potential benefits and problems associated with peer-tutoring projects. On one hand, they suggest that peertutoring can result in improved achievement and attitudes. On the other, together they confirm that peer-tutoring projects are difficult to organize in a way that ensures continuing high motivation, attendance and compliance among participant students.

Difficulties in these areas clearly beset several of the studies reported. With regard to motivation, Pang reported that around 1/4 of tutors and 1/2 of tutees felt that a 30 minute tutoring session was too long. Similarly, 1/7 of tutors and over 1/3 of tutees felt that the six-week project was too long. Note that they held these views despite an overwhelming opinion among them that they had gained from the project and that more such projects should occur.

With regard to attendance, the North Point study revealed an average attendance around 70%. Extrapolation from Ma's data indicates an attendance rate around 77%. Pang indicates that a minority of students in his study also displayed attendance problems.

With regard to compliance, several students in the North Point study clearly acted on the belief that it was more valuable to be tutored on actual class- and homework than it was to be tutored on general English. Several tutors complied with tutees' requests to focus their tutoring on that area of concern instead.

These difficulties underline the importance of: (a) clear communication with tutors, tutees and staff regarding the nature of the project and its aims; (b) regular supervision and clear accountability procedures for students and staff who are supervising them; and (c) incentives for attendance and compliance.

They also underline the importance of incorporating peer tutoring into ordinary class-time. In this connection, it should be noted that Ma and Winter, whose projects both operated during lunch recesses, found that students resented being denied that normal lunchtime recreation enjoyed by other students.

The view of Winter (1989) and Ma (1993) that peer tutoring should be part of the school time-table is one that raises difficult issues for educationalists in a place like Hong Kong. Teachers and Principals faced by a crowded school timetable that cannot easily accept another subject, may rightly ask the question "what other timetabled activity must we cancel?". The risk is that the answer will be "none" and peer tutoring will remain an extra-curricular activity. Accordingly, peer tutoring's best chance of being brought 'out of the cold' may rest in its adoption by subject teachers as a method to be used in class among same-age peers during their standard lessons, so that it is not another activity inserted into the school timetable, but is instead an activity which teachers can incorporate into their ordinary class teaching, alongside all their other instructional techniques. In short, the argument is that peer tutoring needs to be taken out of after-school 'Big-Brother-Big-Sister' schemes and placed into ordinary classroom instruction. To ensure that peer tutoring becomes part of the daily experience of Hong Kong students, the approach being recommended depends on a large numbers of teachers being favourably disposed and knowledgeable about the approach; this has implications for initial and in-service training. As we have seen, the research evidence suggests that the potential in terms of outcomes (achievement and otherwise) for the tutors and tutees is substantial.

REFERENCES

Biggs, J. (1990). Asian students' approaches to learning: implications for teaching overseas students. Paper delivered to 8th Australasian Tertiary Learning Skills and Language Conference, Queensland University of Technology.

Bond, M. & Hwang, K.K. (1986). The social psychology of Chinese people. In Bond, M. (Ed.), *The psychology of the Chinese people*. Hong Kong: Oxford University Press.

Chan, D.W. & Hui, E.K.P. (1995). Burnout and coping among Chinese secondary school teachers in Hong Kong. *British Journal of Educational Psychology, 65*, 15-25.

Chan, K.C.L. (1987). Paired reading: a comparison of the effectiveness of student teachers and peers in the tutoring of poor Chinese readers in a primary school in Hong Kong. The University of Hong Kong. MEd Dissertation, University of Hong Kong.

Cheung, P.C., Conger, A., Hau, K.T., Lew, W. & Lau, S. (1992). Development of the Multi-trait Personality Inventory (MTPI): comparison among four Chinese populations. *Journal of Personality Assessment, 5*(3), 528-551.

Chinese Culture Connection (1987). Chinese values and the search for culture-free dimensions of culture. *Journal of Cross-Cultural Psychology, 18*(2), 143-164.

Chiu, L.H. (1987). Child rearing attitudes of Chinese, Chinese-American, and Anglo-American mothers. *International Journal of Psychology, 22*, 409-419.

Cohen, P., Kulik, J. & Kulik, C. (1982). Educational outcomes of tutoring: a meta-analysis of findings. *American Educational Research Journal, 19*(2), 237-248.

Cook, S., Scruggs, T., Mastropieri, M. & Casto, G. (1986). Handicapped students as tutors. *Journal of Special Education, 19*(4), 483-492.

Domino, G. & Hannah, M.T. (1987). A comparative analysis of social values of Chinese and American Children. *Journal of Cross-Cultural Psychology, 18*(1), 58-77.

Eiserman, W. (1988). Three types of peer tutoring: effects on the attitudes of students with learning disabilities and their regular peers. *Journal of*

Learning Disabilities, *21*(4), 249-252.

Fitzgibbon, C.T. (1978). An examination of the literature on tutoring. Report No.117, Center for the Study of Evaluation, UCLA, California.

Goodlad, S. & Hirst, B. (1989). *Peer tutoring: a guide to learning by teaching.* Kogan Page, UK.

Haggerty, M. (1971). The effects of being a tutor and being a counselee in a group on self-concept and achievement level of under-achieving adolescent males. Dissertation Abstracts, 1976, 37, 2.733A-734A. University Microfilms, 76-18, 626, PhD Michigan State University.

Hartley, S. (1977). Meta-analysis of the effects of individually paced instruction in mathematics. Doctoral Dissertation, University of Missouri.

Hattie, J. (1992). Measuring the effects of schooling. *Australian Journal of Education*, *36*(1), 5-13.

Ho, D.Y.F. (1986). Chinese patterns of socialization: a critical review. In Bond, M. (Ed.), *The Psychology of the Chinese People.* Hong Kong: Oxford University Press.

Ho, D.Y.F. & Chiu, C.Y. (1994). Component ideas of individualism, collectivism and social organization: an application in the study of Chinese culture. In Kim, U. et al. (Eds.), *Individualism and Collectivism.* London: Sage.

Hofstede, G. (1983). Dimensions of national cultures in fifty countries and three regions. In Deregowski, J.B., Dziurawiec, S. & Annis, R.C. (Eds.), *Expiscations in cross-cultural psychology.* Lisse, Netherlands: Swets and Zeitlinger.

Lai, E. (1993). Cooperative learning in a Geography class. In Biggs, J.B. & Watkins, D.A. (Eds.), *Learning and teaching in Hong Kong: what is and what might be.* Educational Papers 17, Faculty of Education, The University of Hong Kong.

Lau, S. (1992). Collectivism's individualism: value preference, personal control, and the desire for freedom among Chinese in mainland China, Hong Kong and Singapore. *Personality and Individual Differences*, *13*(3), 361-366.

Lau, S. & Gruen, G. (1992). The social stigma of loneliness: effect of target person's and perceiver's sex. *Personality and Social Psychology Bulletin*, *18*(2), 182-189.

Lau, S. & Wong, A.K. (1992). Value and sex-role orientation of Chinese adolescents. *International Journal of Psychology*, *27*(1), 3-17.

Levin, H., Glass, G. & Meister, G. (1987). Cost-effectiveness of computer-assisted instruction. *Evaluation Review*, *7*(1), February, 50-72.

Li, M.C., Cheung, S.F. & Kau, S.M. (1979). Competitive and cooperative behaviour of Chinese children in Taiwan and Hong Kong. *Acta Psychologica Taiwanica*, *21*, 27-33.

Lobato, D. (1985). Preschool siblings of handicapped children: impact of peer support and training. *Journal of Autism and Developmental Disorders*, *15*(3), 345-350.

Ma, H.K. (1988). The Chinese Perspectives on Moral Judgment. *International Journal of Psychology*, *23*, 201-227.

Ma, H.K. & Chan, S.W. (1986). Attitudes towards other people in adolescents. *Educational Research Journal*, *1*, 63-67.

Ma Y.K. (1993). A peer-tutoring project in a Hong Kong secondary school. Unpublished Paper, Faculty of Education, The University of Hong Kong.

Madsen, M.C. (1971). Developmental and cross-cultural differences in the competitive and cooperative behavior of young children. *Journal of Cross-Cultural Psychology*, *2*, 365-371.

Mak F.L. (1990). Chinese culture and psychiatry: the emperor's new clothes. Inaugural lecture from the Chair of Psychiatry, The University of Hong Kong, January.

Mathes, P. & Fuchs, L. (1991). The efficacy of peer tutoring in reading for students with disabilities: a best evidence synthesis. Vanderbilt University, Nashville, USA. ERIC ED 344 352.

McNaughton, S., Glynn, T. & Robinson, V. (1981). Parents as remedial reading tutors: issues for home and school. New Zealand Council for Educational Research, New Zealand.

Morgan, R. & Lyon, E. (1979). Paired reading: a preliminary report on a technique or parental tuition of reading retarded children. *Journal of Child Psychology and Psychiatry*, *20*, 151-160.

Pang, C.W. (1993). A paired reading project for low achievers in Hong Kong. MEd Dissertation, The University of Hong Kong.

Potts, P. (1994). Reforming special education in China. In Potts, P., Armstrong, F. & Masterson, M. (Eds.), *Equality and diversity 2: national and international contexts for practice and research*. London: Routledge.

Robertson, D. (1971). The effects of an intergrade tutoring experience on Tutor self-concept. Paper presented at the Annual Conference of the California Educational Research Association. April, ERIC ED 059 769.

Salmon, D. (Ed.) (1932). *The practical parts of Lancaster's 'Improvements' and Bell's 'Experiment'*. Cambridge University Press, UK.

Scruggs, T., Mastropieri, J. & Richter, L. (1985). Peer tutoring with behaviorally disordered students: social and academic benefits. *Behavioural Disorders*, *10*(4), 283-294.

Sheridan, E.M. (1990). Primary Chinese language instruction in the People's Republic of China. *Reading Psychology*, *11*, 141-150.

Slavin, R. (1987). Cooperative learning and the cooperative school. *Educational Leadership*, November, p.7-13.

Topping, K. (1988). *The peer tutoring handbook: promoting cooperative learning*. Croom Helm, UK.

Wang, F.E., Oakland, T. & Liu, D.H. (1992). Behavior problems exhibited by

Chinese children from single- and multiple-child families. *School Psychology International*, *13*, 313-321.

Wheeler, L. (1988). My year in Hong Kong: some observations about social behaviour. *Personality and Social Psychology Bulletin*, *14*(2), 410-420.

Wheldall, K. & Mettem, P. (1986). Behavioural peer tutoring: training 16-year-old tutors to employ the 'pause, prompt and praise' method with 12-year-old remedial readers. In K. Wheldall, F. Merrett & E. Glynn (Eds.), *Behaviour Analysis in Educational Psychology*. Croom Helm, UK.

Winter, S. (1989). Paired reading projects in Hong Kong: second and Chinese language applications. *School Psychology International*, *10*, 25-35.

Winter, S. (1995). Student interaction and relationships. In Biggs, J.B. & Watkins, D.A. (Eds.), *Classroom learning: educational psychology for the Asian teacher*. Singapore: Prentice Hall.

Winter, S. (1996). Cooperative learning in teacher education: a south-east Asian case study. Submitted to Studies in Higher Education.

Winter, S. & Low, A. (1984). The Rossmere peer tutor project. *Behavioural Approaches with Children*, *8*(2), 62-65.

Wong, T.H. (1989). The impact of job satisfaction on intention to change jobs among secondary school teachers in Hong Kong. *Education Journal*, *17*, 176-184.

Yang, K.S. (1986). Chinese personality and its change. In Bond, M. (Ed.), *The psychology of the Chinese people*. Hong Kong: Oxford University Press.

13

Improving Student Learning Through Action Research into Teaching

Lyn Gow, David Kember and Jan McKay

Introduction

The difficulties encountered in effecting change in teaching practices at the tertiary level have been a continuing concern to researchers and practitioners in higher education. In this chapter we describe a three-year project which investigated the extent of self-managed learning at the Hong Kong Polytechnic University. We will concentrate on the final phase of our project, which was still in progress at the time this chapter was written, in which we are testing initiatives in action research projects which we hope will do more to encourage independent learning.

The project had its birth in the many anecdotes that greeted us as newly-arrived academics in Hong Kong. The anecdotes suggested that Hong Kong students relied heavily on rote learning and memorization and that they were more passive and less interactive in class than typical 'Western' students. Some of our colleagues described their Hong Kong students as lacking in the skills of self-management. There was an element of contradiction, though, because many of our new colleagues maintained that their students were good, or even excellent. It was moreover suggested that they were keen and competitive, and could produce good work in projects. At that time, there appeared to be little research evidence to clarify this confusing picture and to determine whether students from Hong Kong or other parts of Asia were more prone to rote-memorization than their Western counterparts (see also Chapters 3-6).

Student Survey

The conflicting descriptions of Hong Kong students and the lack of research evidence provided the incentive to start investigations. The study consisted of three main stages, the last of which is still in progress. In the first stage of the study, carried out in the 1988-89 academic year, a survey of students' approach to study with the Study Process Questionnaire (SPQ, Biggs, 1987; see also Chapter 1) was conducted. Parallel studies in other institutions in Hong Kong are described in this book.

Our conclusions from this first phase were that the Hong Kong students are inherently no less inclined to use a predominantly deep approach than their counterparts elsewhere and might even be marginally more inclined to do so (Gow and Kember, 1990; Kember and Gow, 1990; 1991). Similar inferences were drawn in the parallel studies. It appeared to us that in Hong Kong there is a balance of students with propensities towards surface and deep learning approaches, and similar tendencies to be influenced by their learning context, as for students elsewhere.

Semi-structured interviews during the first phase of our study had suggested a number of contextual variables which were discouraging students from adopting a deep approach (Gow and Kember, 1990). The interviews revealed evidence of surface-assessment demands, heavy workloads, didactic teaching styles and lack of intrinsic motivation. Each of these contextual variables can be related to a wider literature which suggests that they can influence students to adopt a surface approach to study tasks.

Anecdotal observations of rote learning, in Asian students, may therefore be explained more by the nature of the curriculum and the teaching environment than as an inherent characteristic of the students. It is possible that some of the anecdotes result from self-fulfilling prophecies (Rosenthal and Jacobson, 1968). Lecturers believe that their students adopt predominantly rote-learning strategies so set surface level assessment items. Their expectations are fulfilled when the students adopt reproductive strategies to complete the surface-level tasks.

In a study of Malaysian students, Zubir (1988) classified them as either lecturer-oriented or self-oriented, though suggested that many were capable of both. The author found that the learning orientation of the students was strongly influenced by the teaching approach.

Lecturer Phase

The second phase of the study concentrated on the lecturing staff. Semi-structured interviews were conducted individually with 39 full-time lecturing staff to determine their views on educational goals, the reasons some students fail to achieve the course objectives, the changes they would like to make to their teaching, the barriers standing in the way and strategies they could use to overcome these barriers. Transcripts were analyzed independently by three raters and themes extracted. There was a mismatch between the interviewees' perceptions of the goals of higher education and what they were trying to do in practice. While they stated that the goals of higher education were to encourage novel problem-solving, independent learning and intrinsic interest, in reality they felt that the courses they taught focused narrowly on preparing students for specific technical posts. A desire to make changes to teaching was expressed by many lecturers, though barriers such as lack of resources and student resistance were advanced.

Based on the responses of lecturers, we developed a questionnaire to determine whether categories of lecturers' viewpoints about teaching and learning, once identified, in the interviews, were reproducible in a larger sample. The questionnaire contains a number of statements, derived from the interviews, about the goals of higher education, reasons why these goals may not be achieved, ways in which teaching and learning might be improved, constraints on change and attributes of good academics. The questionnaire has been administered at the Hong Kong Polytechnic University as well as at the City University of Hong Kong. From the data it was possible to identify two orientations to teaching: transmission of knowledge and facilitation of learning. Departmental mean scores on the two orientations were found to correlate with longitudinal data from the student surveys with the SPQ. Departments which scored highly on transmission of knowledge tended to discourage deep approaches to study by their students, whereas departments more strongly oriented towards facilitation of learning seemed to wean students away from surface approaches and there was evidence of greater use of deep approaches (Gow, Kember, and Sivan, 1992).

The interviews and questionnaire data from the lecturing staff suggested that staff development initiatives to encourage self-managed learning should attempt to:-

1) Bring practice into line with lecturers' espoused goals of higher education;
2) Persuade staff to accept responsibility for teaching and learning outcomes;
3) Deal with constraints to change;
4) Work with course team or departmental groups capable of initiating changes; and
5) Provide on-going assistance and advice on implementing innovations.

Action Research

Drawing this conclusion was one thing, discovering a way to do something about it was not so easy. Eventually, after a number of blind alleys and false starts we have arrived at a mechanism for assisting teaching staff to evaluate their teaching and implement changes which aim to encourage independent learning. The medium we arrived at is action research, which involves lecturers in attempting to improve their own teaching through cycles of planning, acting, observing and reflecting. Educational practices are regarded as social practices to be changed through collaborative action.

Lewin (1946) is believed to have been the first to use the phrase action research to describe a process of social research leading to social change, characterized by active participation and democratic decision making. It has subsequently seen wide adoption in the school sector and in teacher education, following the work of Stenhouse (1975), who advanced the idea of teachers as researchers. Extensive discussions of the place of action research in education are provided by Carr and Kemmis (1986) and McKernan (1991).

Interestingly, both of these books focus almost exclusively on the school sector. There are few references in the literature to action research as a form of educational development and curriculum change in higher education. In Kember and Gow (1992) we discuss the characteristics of action research and advance reasons why we believe it to be eminently suitable as a form of both educational and staff development in higher education. In this chapter we will concentrate on the more practical concerns of initiating and supporting action research projects in higher education, using one project as an example.

Initiating Action Research Projects

To provide an incentive to begin an action research project we offer interested lecturing staff support in carrying out such a programme. The nature of the support varies from project to project, but has included: clarifying initial ideas; suggesting relevant literature; helping to plan the project; devising methods of evaluation; acting as sounding boards and critical friends; helping with proposals for funding; becoming involved in the teaching; contributing to writing up projects; and providing moral encouragement when the going gets tough. To assist with the projects we had the services of a full-time Research Fellow and later won funding for an additional research associate.

When helping to initiate and in providing guidance with projects, there is a danger of behaving as a conventional staff developer which implies some element, at least, of external involvement and/or direction setting. Action research, though, is based upon collaboration, participation, democratic decision-making and emancipation through critical self-reflection.

Stenhouse (1975, p.159) discusses the relationship between the researcher and teacher in school-based action research programmes. He concluded that the most promising way of overcoming the social and psychological barriers to teacher participation was through mutually supportive cooperative research between teachers and full-time researchers. Carr and Kemmis (1986, p.161) feel that the relationship between researcher and teacher is important. The researcher should become a 'critical friend' helping the insider to make wise judgments in the process of educational transformation. Stenhouse (1975, p. 142) believed that proposals should be presented as provisional specifications to be tested rather than unqualified recommendations. This orientation or approach seems highly appropriate for higher education staff who are often sceptical of didactic pronouncements.

Initially, it was far from easy to get projects started. It has become easier as the idea of conducting action research has become better known around the institution. The momentum and impact provided by initial projects has provided the spur for the genesis of others.

After a salutary experience (where we possibly pushed a little hard), we have become more cautious in our role as facilitator. We now insist that projects we support are derived from the concerns and suggested changes of those we are facilitating. We found this approach resulted in a gestation period before projects commenced, as it required a degree of initial attitude-change. Staff within the institution had become used to a more didactic or prescriptive style of staff development, so expected us to initiate change. However, perseverance eventually paid off and we now have more than ten action research projects in progress.

We have explored three strategies for initiating projects without being overly directive:-

1) We established informal contacts with colleagues, because of interest in the initial phase of the project, over periods from six months to two years.
2) We conducted a series of workshops to advertise the concept of action research in education, with the expectation that participants would start an action research project following the workshop.
3) Through the process of curriculum development and accreditation, projects were developed with the theme of developing and implementing some aspect of the new or revised curriculum.

The informal contacts largely arose out of the first phase of the wider project. Some lecturers became interested in discovering more about the learning approaches of their students. Often a latent concern was aroused. Feedback sessions, reporting results from the study, were held for most of the departments whose students were investigated. At these sessions, the interest seemed to be heightened because the research discussed was on the department's own students. It could certainly not be dismissed as a foreign theory, irrelevant to the local context or culture.

These experiences did point to an indirect benefit to an institution of supporting educational research on its own students. The direct effect on teaching and learning of the first phase of the project is less easy to establish than that of the smaller-scale action research projects. However, if interest and awareness had not been heightened by the initial surveys, there would probably have been little momentum to generate the programme of action research projects.

The contacts made with colleagues, when research results were discussed, revealed some who took a particular interest in an innovation and were prepared to implement it through an action research project. In some cases, innovations were, and are being, carried out with individual classes or lecturers; in others, departmental initiatives involving substantial change in the total departmental learning-environment, for a specified group of students, are being tried. All innovations are being monitored.The second initiation strategy was through workshops on action research. Several were held for individual departments which had been actively involved in the initial phases of the project.

A further workshop, on small-scale action research projects in education, was advertised in the same way that lecturers are invited to participate in other staff-development workshops in the institution. The advertising for the workshop suggested an expectation that participants would become involved in an action-research project following the workshop. The expectation of some initial enquirers, however, seemed conditioned by previous workshops which normally expect little commitment beyond the workshop session. There was a significant fall-off between responding to the advertisement and actually becoming involved in a project.

A booklet on action research for small-scale educational projects was developed to accompany the workshops. The booklet and workshops dealt briefly with the nature of action research and covered the phases of planning, action, observation and reflection. The cyclical nature of action research was stressed. An overview was given of a number of techniques for making observations and gathering data. A lecturer, who was already involved in action research, described her project. The workshops were deliberately kept short but provided ample opportunity for discussion and raising questions. They were not meant to be comprehensive courses in educational research; rather brief introductions to the concept of action research and invitations to participate in a supported project.

Following the workshops, it was possible to form a number of groups, either by discipline or by a similar concern. On-going support was offered to the groups by the authors acting as critical friends. The full-time research fellow for the overall project provided assistance to the groups by keeping records, performing literature searches, acting as a classroom observer, conducting interviews, and offering advice and support. Regular meetings were held by the groups to discuss and reflect upon progress. A diary or journal was maintained for each project, in which was recorded important points to emerge from the meetings, action taken, and observations of the participants. White (1988) believes that all participants in action research projects should keep journals, the contents of which are shared with other group members to establish dialogue and promote reflection.

Initiation through course-development processes is the strategy we have used least because of the origins of action research from a research project and because none of us are formally associated with the course accreditation process within the Polytechnic. One project did begin because of the need to develop a course, achieve accreditation, and to successfully implement the innovatory features.

Although our particular circumstances have constrained opportunities to initiate action-research projects through course-development requirements, some projects which began in other ways have led to involvement in the development of new courses or to substantial revisions to existing courses. A good example is given in the case study which follows. The relationship between the action research projects and the processes of curriculum development and review are discussed further in the reflective section which follows the case study.

Case Study

To allow a better understanding of the nature of the activities, one action research project is described in some detail. The project was initiated by Jan McKay, the Clinical Coordinator for the Radiography Section of the Optometry and Radiography Department. The project was the topic for McKay's doctoral thesis. For this section there will be a shift from the collective 'we' to a more personal 'I' as McKay describes her experiences.

The case study to be described was initiated because of the concern I felt that there was little or no connection made between the theoretical and clinical aspects of the programme for student Diagnostic Radiographers. These students, who spend approximately half of the total programme time in the clinical situation, were never expected, or encouraged in any way, to develop links between the two elements. The necessity for such a large involvement in clinical practice is because of the nature of the profession. Students can only 'practise' on each other to a certain degree within the Polytechnic, as radiation cannot be used for diagnostic purposes in an indiscriminate manner. Experience in equipment manipulation, skill acquisition and image analysis can be gained in practical classes, but lack of patient contact is similar to teaching chemistry

without the use of a laboratory. I discovered that the gap between theory and
clinical experience was a recognized problem within the medical profession.
Balla (1989) and Coles (1989) have both noted that the separation of theory
and practice is particularly obvious in the medical area which has traditionally,
and still has in many instances, separate experiences in the teaching of theory
and development of clinical practice.

The importance of developing a graduate who has the professional abilities
to function appropriately, which should include the proper climate in which the
transfer of learning from theory to clinical practice is encouraged, is expressed
in the following quote from Tarico, Holland and Altmeir (1989):

"Diagnostic radiology has mushroomed to include computed tomography,
ultrasound, and, most recently, magnetic resonance imaging. Performing
effectively in these areas requires a broad base of knowledge, a wide array
of technical skills, and a serious commitment to professionalism. In
addition, the technologist must interact skillfully with many persons
including patients, radiologists, clinical specialists, other allied
professionals (p. 134)."

The first three cycles of my study were aimed at improving the transfer of
learning from theory to clinical practice, and took place over one year. The
project has since widened to include curriculum development and
implementation, as the programme was upgraded from a Professional Diploma
to a Bachelor of Science. The main emphasis in this chapter will be on the first
three cycles and how implications from them have influenced the development
of the degree programme.

Comments from external examiners' reports, and from senior staff
members within the profession, indicate that new graduates have a solid
grounding in theoretical knowledge, but often show little ability to demonstrate
the relevance of this theory to the clinical situation. The aim of this study has
therefore been to attempt to enhance, in a group of second year Diagnostic
Radiography students:-

1)   Understanding and integration of theoretical learning;
2)   Application of theoretical learning to the clinical situation; and
3)   Critical decision-making on clinical practice.

The changes were conducted using the action research model described
earlier and, in accordance with this model, there were several phases, each one
being reflected upon and reviewed before the implementation of the next.
Changes were made, if and when they were deemed necessary.

It is not usual in action research to have an experimental and control
group, but, as the class is normally divided into two distinct and separate

groups, one group participated in the changes described, while no change was made to the teaching of the other group. The groups are randomly formed at the commencement of the first year and comparison of the academic entry status of the students showed no difference between them. Both groups completed the clinical training programme as it is prescribed for the course.

Prior to the commencement of the intervention, both groups were asked to complete the SPQ (Biggs, 1987), and their marks from end-of-year examinations for the previous year were noted.

The project comprised three cycles, each cycle relating to a period of clinical practice. It commenced in October 1989, and included the academic year and the summer-time clinical placements between the second and third academic years, finishing in October 1990.

The students of the experimental group were asked to make written evaluations of the clinical placements they attended. Guidelines were given for the evaluations which were designed to encourage the students to look at clinical practice within the various clinical settings they attended in relation to the theory they have covered, and to encourage integration of information from different subject areas. Also, a reading reference list was given to encourage students to gain information from a wider range of sources. It comprised an annotated list of articles relevant to the students' stage of training from five professional journals, covering the range of second-year subjects.

At the completion of each clinical-practice period, students were brought together in small groups to discuss their experiences and evaluations on the placements attended.

My original plan was to bring students together for four tutorials each, one for each placement they attended in the block. The groups were comprised of members who had attended the same, or similar, placements in terms of the nature of work undertaken. Students brought to the groups the evaluation reports they had written up during the clinical block.

Lessons Learnt from the First Cycle

Discussions with my colleagues and reflection upon the first series of tutorials produced the following conclusions:-

1) It is not necessary, and may even be detrimental, to bring the students together for so many discussions, as the same issues were raised on several occasions.
2) The numbers attending each group were variable, from 8 to 14. A group size of eight was much more satisfactory in terms of participation of all members of the group.
3) Comments made on evaluation reports were of only limited value to the

discussion groups as they were collected at the beginning of the sessions and could not then be previewed.

4) Discussion centered around either:-

a)   Incidents raised by the members of the group; or
b)   Questions posed by myself.

The level of discussion was relatively low for all the group sessions and I found myself involved in a considerable amount of questioning to provide a focus for discussion.

Lessons Learnt from the Second Cycle

The second cycle of tutorials was subsequently rearranged in the following manner:-

1) I collected and read the evaluation reports prior to the commencement of the discussion;
2) Each student attended two tutorials, each group comprising eight members;
3) The composition of members of each group was independent of placements attended, and was different for each tutorial.

Discussion areas were those raised by individual members, and also points raised for discussion by myself according to comments made on the evaluation reports. The overall level of discussion within the groups was increased from the first cycle. Prior access to the evaluation reports made my interjections more of a prompting element rather than a focus of direction as in the first cycle.

Lessons Learnt from the Third Cycle

The third cycle of tutorials closely followed that of the second, particularly with regard to:-

1) The early return of reports;
2) The number of tutorials attended by each member, and the number of members in each group; and
3) The different mixture of members for each group.

The major difference between the second and third cycles was the manner in which the discussions took place. Students still raised individual items, but my perusal of the evaluation forms had highlighted several broad areas of discussion which could be posed in a problem-solving context. Members were asked to formulate answers to the problems posed. The general level of discussion was increased from the second cycle, the increase being greater for some groups than others.

Results of the Study

It was not anticipated that such a study, which spanned one year of the three-year programme, and in only one area of the training (which is assessed in terms of pass/fail, rather than level of grade), would show large changes. Accordingly, no significant change was noted in those areas which are most likely to be influenced by the formal, overall teaching/examination process of the course. These areas included:-

1) No significant change was noted in the SPQ scores. The SPQ was administered pre- and post-intervention, and no significant difference was noted between the two groups on either occasion.
2) There was no appreciable difference between the two groups in terms of end-of-year examination scores both pre- and post-intervention.

However, one post-test administered to the two groups showed an appreciable, valid difference. The post-test was in the form of three open, problem-solving type questions which related directly to the clinical situations the students encountered during the second year of training, and so required the adaptation of theoretical learning to specific situations. An example of the questions given is:

"Think back to the experience of ONE of your general clinical placements and discuss how you feel the equipment you used aided or limited the quality of the examinations taken. In your discussion, take patient care, radiation protection/dosage and film quality into account."

The test was scored using a modified version of the SOLO taxonomy (Biggs and Collis, 1982) which measures quality of learning as opposed to being a quantitative measure. The SOLO taxonomy gives five categories upon which the level of learning is judged. I found after the first assessment of the post-test that a significant number of answers seemed to fall between two of the given categories. The SOLO taxonomy was therefore modified to be able to reflect this group more accurately. The best way to demonstrate this is to give an example of the different levels of answers given to the above question.

1) *Prestructural*

Patient Care. Actually it mainly depends on the radiographers. How they treat the patients. Equipment, of course [is] important. e.g. drip stand, steps for patient to climb up to the couch. But the most important thing is the attitude of the radiographer. This [is] also affected by the work load of that hospital.

Radiation Protection. Equipment is very important in radiation protection. Whether the X-ray tube output is consistent, lead rubber is sufficient and not torn or dirty. These always aid the exam's quality.

Dosage. Again, consistence of X-ray output. Exposure given by radiographers (which depends on the experience of the radiographers) always affect the quality very much.

Film quality. Processing is a an important factor affecting the film quality. New cassette and screens also very important.

2) *Unistructural*

There was one time that I saw an NPC [Naso-pharyngeal Carcinoma] case done on an X-ray couch because that hospital [doesn't] have a skull unit. During the examination, the patient must [assume] a difficult posture in order to [cooperate with] the technique. Fortunately it is a smart patient. Although he's smart but it's [necessary] to repeat the examination and I think it may not be the cause of the overcouch technique but [a] skull unit may help in a certain extent.

3) *Multistructural*

A&E Department in XX Hospital:
X-ray machine has programmed exposure factors of different projections. The exposure factors can vary according to different patient conditions. It saves time in deciding exposure factors and thus the examination time. Sensors used in different projections is programmed, it also can vary according to the situation. It reduces radiation dose to patient and reduces chances of repeating due to wrong exposure factors being used. Lead sheet reduces radiation dose to patient and reduces scatter radiation. Immobilization device helps to reduce movement unsharpness.

4) *Relational*

A&E Department in XX Hospital:
X-ray couch with floating top, and level can be raise[d] and lower[ed]:-
- good for patient with bad condition, i.e. he can sit on the couch more easily

- transfer of patient is more efficient, i.e. level of couch may change to that of stretcher.
- however, the change in level of couch results in difficulties in adjusting. FFD [focus to film distance] (which change[s] every time after transfer of patient) it may increase error, i.e. shorter FFD is used, overexposed. Longer FFD is used, underexposed.
[leading to] repeat of film increase dosage.

The X-ray has autosensor. Since the centering of [the] bucky must be center[ed] to the center of [the] film no displacement of the film in the bucky is allowed, increased technical error. Quality of [the] film decreases because sometimes the current centering cannot be used.

A significant group of answers that did not appear to conform to the categories given above, fell between (3) and (4). The answers implied a higher level of learning than that described in (3) but did not properly reflect (4). Another category, (3.5), was used which described the level of learning as:-

3.5) *Multistructural with clinical relevance*

The learner picks up more and more relevant features, does not integrate them but shows relevance to clinical practice rather than repetition of classroom teaching. An example of this category is given:-

"In the XX Hospital, it is newly equipped with new, sophisticated machine, it is a floating top X-ray couch and the level of the couch can be adjusted. All the exposure factors are computerized and it can [be] used only by touching the screen and turning the wheel."

"This X-ray couch is particularly convenient for patients especially for those who do not walk too smoothly and it can [be] convenient for us when there is a need to transfer patients, as far as patient care is concerned, it is quite good."

"However, since it is quite new, not all the radiographers are sure about the exposure factor[s] and usually there may be a need to repeat hence increasing the radiation dosage. Both the cones and the diaphragms are accurate enough to protect the patient."

"As far as if the exposure factors are correctly handled, the film quality is high as long as the tube is quite new."

"But one [thing is] that each individual radiographer adjusts the couch-level to suit their height and there seems to be no standard and they usually do not exactly take the FFD accurately, and this may affect the film quality. Also the wheel and the screen is so sensitive that only a small slight touch will change the readings, sometimes with a busy day, it [does] cause problems to us."

To test the validity of the scoring, a number of scripts were selected from both groups which covered the range of scores. These were anonymous and were marked independently by a colleague on the same programme.

The initial correlation between the two markers for the three questions ranged from 0.64 to 0.88. After discussion on individual questions where the score given was significantly different between the two markers, some changes were made by both markers. The correlation between the two then ranged from 0.89 to 1.00. Scores between the two groups were compared by t-tests and showed that the differences between experimental and control groups were statistically significant in all three questions (see Table 13.1).

Table 13.1
Differences between experimental and control groups on the three questions

	Mean Scores		
	Question 1	Question 2	Question 3
Experimental Group (N=26)	2.94	2.90	3.42
Control Group (N=27)	2.52	2.35	2.22
Significance of Difference (P<)	.01	.01	.000

Reflections

The intervention has demonstrated that a change is possible and that students can be encouraged to integrate knowledge and use it for problem-solving, within the context for which the learning is intended.

To promote integrated, problem-solving learning in a more generalized fashion, it would seem to be necessary to promote change within the whole structure of the training programme. It is evident that change within one aspect of the programme will not support generalized change throughout. For example, no student read any of the articles included on the reading list, though encouragement to do so was given during each series of discussion groups. This is one measure which has produced no change. The reasons for this failure could be seen as institutional in that these students have high lecture-contact hours (approximately 26 hours per week) and are not encouraged to read beyond the information given in lectures, or the handouts which accompany them. The examination process in place for the Professional Diploma would seem to reward knowledge based learning rather than evidence of wider reading and research.

What may be seen as a reinforcement of these comments are some of the replies given to a question posed by a lecturer, teaching the same group of students, in a professional subject area. This subject has a high-lecture element, a much smaller practical, or laboratory, element and no tutorials. Lectures for the year are 96 hours, and and an additional 32 practical hours. Students were asked to comment at the end of the year on the way the subject had been taught. This exercise was undertaken independently of the action research study. Nearly all students either expressed the fact or agreed with the statement that large sections of the course were boring. Reasons given are:-

1)   Too slow;
2)   Techniques not the same as, or do not relate well to those used in Hong Kong;
3)   Too simple, material already covered elsewhere;
4)   Not enough radiographs; and
5)   Insufficient discussion on some problem areas.

Students requested:-

1)   Case studies at the end of each topic;
2)   Slides of the relevant radiographs etc;
3)   Writing/rewriting of some of the lecture notes, including more diagrams;
4)   Complete operating theatre techniques, including those using contrast media;
5)   Include IVU and basic biliary examinations;
6)   Break the class into small groups for discussion and questions;
7)   More questions both as part of the handout, and also during the lesson, could these questions be directed to small groups of 4-6 students;
8)   More time to read the handouts before they are discussed; and
9)   More information on when a radiograph is deemed to be unacceptable due to positioning, and how to recognize both the positioning fault and how much correction is necessary.

Degree Development

The Professional Diploma programme was originally scheduled to be upgraded
to a BSc in October 1991, but was deferred for a year because the programme
that was developed did not meet the criteria for a degree programme. Some of
the comments made in the Report of the Internal Validating Panel (1991) were
as follows:-

> "The panel expresses disappointment that in both the documentation and
> the subsequent discussion, the CPC [Course Planning Committee] has
> neither evidenced the level of maturity and preparedness appropriate to
> offering the course at degree level nor demonstrated as a course team that
> they have coherently worked through the key issues including the
> development of an adequate theoretical basis, achievement of integration,
> both vertically and horizontally and in the balance between theoretical and
> clinical work."

> "The panel considers that the proposed degree course is too practice-
> oriented and there is insufficient theoretical basis evident in the course
> curriculum to ensure that the apprehension of theory and its application in
> practice in a professional context will be of a form and level appropriate
> to a degree course."

> "The course was rather heavy in class lectures. The planning team was
> advised to elaborate the approach for encouraging student centered learning
> and the provision of means for developing the intellectual traits of students
> up to degree level cited in the general and specific course aims."

The development of the initial programme was such that the comments
from the panel can be understood easily. The Course Planning Team never met
on a regular basis. One meeting determined the planning and timing of course
material, with small adjustments at later stages to ensure a balance of the
number of subjects taught over successive years. The material included in the
programme was virtually identical to that of the Professional Diploma with
some changes in the names of subject titles. Individual subjects were developed
independently of other subjects, and without any discussion on content and
integration. The Course Leader believed that students demanded to be 'spoon
fed' and was uncomfortable with the idea of establishing student centered
learning measures into the programme.

Some time after the deferment of the initial programme I was asked to take
on the position of Course Leader designate with the task of planning a new
programme which took into account the comments of the original Validation
Panel. One of the first and most important tasks that I saw in this development

process was the need to establish a course 'team' where the members of the section involved would ultimately know that they had all contributed and, indeed, would feel they had 'ownership' of the programme that developed.

Information from the action-research study has been useful for the subsequent development of the degree programme. It has provided the encouragement needed to open up the teaching/learning pattern, and the confidence to know that students are capable and able to meet the challenge.

The training programme aims to:-

1) Encourage integration of learning to provide a well-rounded understanding of the profession;
2) Establish the relevance of theoretical learning to the clinical situation; and,
3) Develop problem-solving abilities.

As a means of meeting these criteria the programme has a number of features, identified through the action research:-

(a) Final year subjects, under the broad heading of Professional Subjects, are integrated from the first two years' study.
(b) The lecture hours have been considerably reduced and the use of tutorial classes has been widely developed. Material within subject areas has been rationalized so that students can expect to undertake background reading for specified topics where the learning is factual and well explained in texts. A real effort has been made to make the style of teaching/learning relevant to the required outcome.
(c) Considerable effort has been made to ensure that Clinical Studies are integrated into the Professional Subjects, and are an assessable element of the programme at each stage. No period of clinical experience is undertaken without the theoretical component having been covered first, the aims and objectives of each stage of clinical practice are clearly stated and the assessment element is relevant to the expected learning outcome.
(d) The number of hours spent in clinical training have been reduced by approximately 40% from the Professional Diploma programme. A reduction in clinical practice hours may not be considered an appropriate step to take to enhance the integration of theoretical learning into the professional context, but, it has been carefully planned to ensure students are appropriately prepared for their clinical placements to gain maximum benefit from the experience. A consequence of the reduced clinical hours is that other components of the course can be spread over a longer period.
(e) The degree programme ensures that first year students have completed the professional studies programme before proceeding into clinical placements. The professional subject in year one has a reduction of lecture hours and an increase in practical hours so that students, prior to their first clinical

block, have already developed a level of procedural and manipulative skills that have traditionally been developed in clinical practice. Second and third year degree students will have clinical experience in specific areas of practice only upon the completion of the theory in their professional studies.

To assist in the implementation of these changes the academic staff realized it would be necessary to undertake an in-house programme of staff development. A workshop on action research was held to enable staff to initiate action research projects within their individual subject areas to confirm the ability of the students to assume responsibility for their own learning. Evaluation procedures have been developed for monitoring the changes that the alteration of teaching patterns can make. A team-building exercise has been implemented, including the development of skills in tutorial teaching, problem-solving courses, case studies and project management. This, we hope, will assist us to develop our abilities and confidence in conducting the more open-style learning process. Also, a week-long Clinical Instructors Workshop, incorporating Polytechnic and clinical staff, has been conducted. This was the first time such a venture had been undertaken, and it was seen as 'ground breaking'. An half day clinical workshop has followed this to coincide with the first-year students proceeding to their first clinical placements.

Comments made by the Internal Validation Panel (1992) of the current degree programme were encouraging and recognized the changes that had developed within the planning group. Their views were supported by comments made in the Validation Report of the Hong Kong Council for Academic Accreditation (1992) which recommended the implementation of the BSc in Radiography:-

"The panel found the proposal well-documented and comprehensive. It commented on the courage of the staff to embark on such a new venture while taking up the challenge of a degree-level course. The proposed innovative approach to clinical training and academic studies represents a radical departure from the programmes in Radiography elsewhere. However, the staff members have demonstrated themselves as a coherent and determined team."

"Their efforts in blending the various interested parties together and in integrating their inputs in the planning stage of the BSc course are to be congratulated. Panel members were particularly impressed by the positive attitude of the students towards education and their profession as well as their enthusiasm for the new degree. They enjoyed the open discussions with the course team and the supportive conversation with members of the external planning groups and employers."

The degree programme is now in its first year of operation and, while it is too early to give any particular evidence of improvement in student learning, encouraging details from informal discussions with lecturers on the course have been received.

Critical Reflections

To evaluate the effectiveness of action research for educational development in higher education, we have to consider both the success of each individual project and their collective value in promoting change and educational development within the institution. In reference to the case-study project described above five levels of reflection can be identified:-

1) Students reflect with fellow students on their evaluations of the clinical placement.
2) Students reflect with McKay as to how effectively they utilized their theoretical training in the clinical setting.
3) We reflect, together with staff in Diagnostic Sciences, on the effects of the revised clinical-placement programme.
4) We reflect on the effectiveness of action research as a strategy for educational and staff development and curriculum change.
5) We negotiate with institutional management to establish support for action research projects as an on-going activity within the institution.

The remainder of this chapter focuses on the final two levels of reflection. We discuss the suitability of action research as a medium for curriculum change and educational development. The described case study is used as an example where appropriate.

Research or Educational Development?

The status of the projects as research or educational-development activities has been queried on a number of occasions. Initially the tactic was to use whichever description we felt the questioner wanted. When requesting funds for research staff to assist with the projects the proposal was presented to the Research Committee with the stress on the research aspect and the promise of publications. One of the writers, David Kember, is employed as an educational developer. Initially the wider project was regarded by his unit as a research project which he was encouraged to participate in, but only in time available after completing assigned 'educational-development' activities. In time the overall project developed in the direction of the smaller-scale action research projects and there was growing recognition within the Unit that these were educational development activities and did answer a Polytechnic need which had not previously been addressed. There is now acceptance that the majority of his time is devoted to these activities. Also, the Research Committee now accepts that there is both a research and an educational development aspect to the projects as recent funding for a Research Associate was shared between the Research Committee and the Educational Development Fund.

The participants all seem to have envisaged the projects as both research and educational-development activities. There is no doubt that all participants have a strong interest in teaching as the projects are voluntary and the onus is on potential participants to suggest the topic for the project. The participants, though, are also aware of the potential rewards from publications so these provide incentives for participation.

Action Research or Research?

For convenience, the projects have all been described as 'action research' though in some cases they might be attributed to other paradigms. Some could be classified as following an interpretive approach and will, no doubt, produce results which could be written up as a pure-research study.

We feel that research into teaching and learning within the courses taught by the lecturer(s) will promote useful reflection upon the teaching and learning processes. If the results are reported to and discussed with departmental colleagues, then it is difficult for them to ignore the findings. Most lecturers habitually ignore the work of educational researchers as it can be conveniently dismissed as irrelevant or inapplicable to their discipline or courses. When the study is on students in courses they teach and was performed by their colleagues, then it clearly cannot be rejected for these reasons. We have therefore taken an eclectic approach to supporting projects. We have supported any proposal which seemed likely to result in a meaningful reflection upon teaching and learning within a course, or which aimed to improve some aspect of the teaching. On reflection, we feel that this policy has been more helpful, realistic and workable than any attempt to impose selective guidelines as to what is or is not truly action research. We suspect that such policies would prove unworkable, as many projects have taken quite unexpected twists and turns.

Development of Research Expertise

Some projects seem to be functioning as mediums for developing participants' research skills. This is a staff-development function which has always been incidental to the educational development aims, but the projects do appear to contribute to a need which has become very apparent. The Polytechnic was, at the time of writing this chapter, seeking to acquire university status so academics were under pressure to publish. As a high proportion come from vocational backgrounds and/or are in disciplines with little research tradition, many have limited research expertise. Some project participants have viewed action research into their own teaching as a way of satisfying the demand to perform research while still concentrating on teaching, a role in which they are comfortable and are committed to. With some participants, the role of critical friend thus takes on elements akin to the role of a supervisor of research students.

Widening the Circle of Involvement

Educational developers are invariably faced with high ratios between themselves and the number of academics in an institution - far higher than any staff/student ratios. Activities which require intensive involvement with relatively small numbers of academics can be difficult to justify, unless they have a snowball effect on others. In this respect, action research shows promise in that there is recognition that educational innovation requires social change which is best achieved through collaborative action.

McKay's project started with the concern of an individual with one component of a course. It now involves all members of the section, to some extent at least, and the entire course is being influenced. We believe that this project provides a clear demonstration that a mechanism does exist for widening the circle of involvement.

Retrospect

The chapter, up to this point, was written well before the final publication date. In these intervening years, action research has firmly established itself in Hong Kong as a mode of educational development. From the tentative beginnings described in this chapter, several grants were obtained to support action research projects in the Hong Kong Polytechnic University. A substantial grant was then obtained from the University Grants Committee for the 'Action Learning Project'. This is an inter-institutional project supporting over 50 action research projects across the seven universities in Hong Kong.

The extensive participation in these projects show clearly that action research may be an import from the West, but it fits perfectly into the local culture. It is also apparent, from both the case study described in this chapter and from other projects, that action research is an appropriate mechanism for transforming curricula to allow the Chinese learner to adopt a deep approach to learning. In the case study the students originally suffered from a curriculum designed on the assumption that Hong Kong students needed to be spoon-fed and were only capable of rote-learning. Through an action research approach it was possible to change both the curriculum and many of these underlying attitudes. Given a curriculum which allowed initiative to flourish, the students soon showed that not only were they capable of a deep approach - they actually preferred learning in that way.

REFERENCES

Balla, J.I. (1989). Changing concepts in clinical education: the case for a theory. In Balla, J.I., Gibson, M. & Chang, A. (Eds.), *Learning in medical school*. Hong Kong: The University of Hong Kong Press.

Biggs, J. (1987). *Student approaches to learning and studying*. Melbourne: Australian Council for Educational Research.

Biggs, J. & Collis, K. (1982). *Evaluating the quality of learning: the SOLO taxonomy*. New York: Academic Press.

Carr, W. & Kemmis, S. (1986). *Becoming critical: education, knowledge and action research*. Brighton, Sussex: Falmer Press.

Coles, C. (1989). Elaborated knowledge: towards a theory for undergraduate medical education. In Balla, J.I., Gibson, M. & Chang, A. (Eds.), *Learning in medical school*. Hong Kong: The University of Hong Kong Press.

Gow, L. & Kember, D. (1990). Does higher education promote independent learning? *Higher Education, 19*, 307-322.

Gow, L., Kember, D. & Sivan, A. (1992). Lecturers' views of their teaching practices: implications for staff development needs. *Higher Education Research and Development, 11*(2), 135-149.

Hong Kong Council for Academic Accreditation. (1992). *Validation report: B.Sc. Radiography*. Hong Kong.

Hong Kong Polytechnic. (1991). *Report of the internal validating panel for the B.Sc. in Diagnostic Imaging*. Hong Kong.

Hong Kong Polytechnic. (1992). *Report of the internal validating panel for the B.Sc. in Radiography*. Hong Kong.

Kember, D. & Gow, L. (1990). Cultural specificity of approaches to study. *British Journal of Educational Psychology, 60*, 356-363.

Kember, D. & Gow, L. (1991) A challenge to the anecdotal stereotype of the Asian student. *Studies in Higher Education, 16*(2), 117-128.

Kember, D. & Gow, L. (1992). Action research as a form of staff development in higher education. *Higher Education, 23*(3), 297-310.

Kember, D. & Gow, L. (1993). Problems with implementing goals in higher education: a Hong Kong case study. *International Journal of Educational*

Development, 13(2), 113-124.

Lewin, K. (1946). Action research and minority problems. *Journal of Social Issues, 2*, 34-46.

McKernan, J. (1991). *Curriculum action research.* London: Kogan Page.

Rosenthal, R. & Jacobson, L. (1968). *Pygmalion in the classroom.* New York: Holt, Rinehart, and Winston.

Stenhouse, L. (1975). *Introduction to curriculum research and development.* London: Heinemann Education.

Tarico, V.S., Holland, M.H. & Altmaier, E.M. (1989). Clinical effectiveness in radiology technology students: an empirical perspective. *Journal of the American Society of Radiologic Technologist, 59*(2), 134-141.

White, L. (1988). Writing journals as part of the learning process. In Kemmis, S. & McTaggart, R. (Eds.), *The action research planner.* Geelong, Victoria: Deakin University.

Zubir, R. (1988). Descriptions of teaching and learning: a Malaysian experience. *Studies in Higher Education, 13*, 139-150.

OVERVIEW

14

The Chinese Learner in Retrospect

John Biggs and David Watkins

Several recurrent themes and implications for theory and practice involving the Chinese learner have been raised in this book. But before considering these, we need to come back to the question raised in the Introduction: who is this 'Chinese Learner'?

The best answer to that seems to lie in the notion of a Confucian-heritage culture (CHC; Ho, 1990). The viability of that idea is acknowledged both by individuals from within that culture and by outsiders who have studied it. It may be difficult to define that culture precisely (Wang, 1991), but its usefulness in accounting for otherwise puzzling phenomena (such as our so-called 'paradox of the Chinese learner') is clear. While most of our research evidence derives from studies of Hong Kong students, evidence from studies conducted in other Chinese cultures, such as Singapore and mainland China, confirms our belief that our Hong Kong students indeed represent a general 'Chineseness', deriving from the Confucian heritage itself, that allows us to understand Chinese learners better, wherever they are in the world. Many Western educators fail to comprehend the conceptions of learning and related constructs deriving from this heritage, leading them to misunderstand their Chinese students. For example those Australian tertiary teachers discussed in Chapter 3. The extent to which these findings apply to non-Chinese CHCs, such as Japan, Korea, and Vietnam, is too early to tell, but many of the results reported here are consistent at least with research into Japanese students (Hess and Azuma, 1991; Stevenson and Stigler, 1992; Sue and Okazaki, 1990). Be that as it may, our discussion here centres on the Chinese segment of CHCs.

In discussing who the Chinese learner is, we also need to address the question of who the Chinese learner is not. The Western misperception, the Chinese-learner-as-rote-learner, is the most obvious but not the only case of cultural astigmatism. When CHC people are viewed through the lenses of familiar Western polarities, the focus becomes blurred and even distorted. In the West, such polarities as memorizing versus understanding, intrinsic versus extrinsic motivation, achievement motivation as an ego versus a social motivation, collective versus an individual orientation, controllable attributions (effort, skill) versus uncontrollable (ability) attributions, are useful: not surprisingly, because they were derived in the West. But these same contrasts appear to create paradoxes when applied to CHC students.

In trying to reconcile and clarify these issues, we hope, first, to add to our knowledge of the Chinese learner. Second, we explore what this might mean for Westerners teaching overseas Chinese students, with respect to beliefs about learning, relations with teachers, language difficulties, and conceptions of writing and the problem of what is plagiarism and what is not. We close, then, on these practical notes. But first we address the issue of Western misperceptions.

Western Misperceptions of the Chinese Learner

Memorizing and understanding: the role of repetition

The first feature of typical Chinese (and other Asian) learners that evidently strikes the Westerner is the apparent tendency for rote learning. This has been discussed at length in Chapters 3, 4, and 5 and mentioned substantially in several other Chapters in various contexts: culture (Chapter 2), development (Chapter 6), language (Chapters 7 and 8), and most notably, assessment (Chapter 9).

Hopefully, this book has laid to rest the myth that Chinese learners are especially given to rote learning, where 'rote' is understood in the dictionary definition: "the mere exercise of memory without proper understanding of, or reflection upon, the matter in question" (Shorter *OED*, 1992). However, some questions remain, one in particular being the role of memorizing in understanding. It is undoubtedly true that students in CHC systems use *repetition* as part of their learning strategies a good deal more than Westerners do. But the reason for this is less clear. Is it because of cultural factors, as suggested in Chapter 2? Is it because of perceived task demands, for example those of assessment (Chapter 9), or those of coping with a second language (Chapter 8)?

Marton, Dall'Alba and Tse suggest in Chapter 4 that CHC students learn repetitively in the belief that memorization can lead to understanding. But does this mean that memorizing is a means of at least *deepening* understanding, as argued in Chapter 4, or that memorization is a *precondition* for understanding, which seems to be the interpretation of Hess and Azuma's (1991) "repetition as a route to understanding" derived from studies of Japanese students. Let us retrace Marton et al.'s hierarchy of memorization and understanding.

Mechanical memorization is clearly *rote* learning: a blind process that excludes understanding. But Marton's "memorization with understanding" has two components. The first, "memorizing what is understood", is clearly related to Tang's (1991) "deep memorizing", a strategy used particularly for examination preparation and is not particularly CHC, being used by students everywhere (e.g. Thomas and Bain, 1984). Kember and Gow (1990) postulate a 'narrow' approach, which appears to have aspects of both deep and surface. This approach is characterized by the sequence "understand-memorize-understand-memorize..." on tasks that are clearly defined by the lecturer. Kember and Gow attribute this partly to the need to reduce processing load when working in L2, and partly to a transfer of Confucian 'filial piety' to the teacher or lecturer; i.e. part task demand, part cultural. The parsimonious explanation is that their narrow approach is not a different approach, culturally defined, so much as a strategic use of a deep approach (see below).

Marton et al's second category, "understanding through memorization", is however more problematic. It could mean that the act of memorizing itself creates the understanding: that there is only one dimension to learning, with memorizing continuously leading to understanding. However, it could also mean that memorizing is a route to understanding (Hess and Azuma, 1991): that while memorizing does not create understanding, it is a useful precondition for it. However, such a belief - or strategy (it appears to be both) - is universal, being determined by the requirements of particular tasks rather than by cultural factors themselves.

For example, the nature of learning to read and write text with a character system is a more complex, memory-dependent task than is reading and writing with an alphabet system. Nevertheless, as Kirby (1988) says, reading in an alphabet system still requires automatic mastery of the lower-order decoding skills before comprehension at the sentence and main idea levels can take place. This is so simply because of working memory limitations: the lower order skills need to be mastered to the point of automaticity so that there is sufficient space to derive meanings involving the simultaneous processing of whole sentences. Another example is understanding a complex piece of music. Repeated hearings are necessary before the meaning begins to emerge, but this repetition is not creating the meaning so much as creating recognizable sign-posts or markers within or between which listeners then structure their interpretation and meaning. This last process, creating the interpretation, is experientially different from that of creating the sign-posts, by means of which one comes to recognize the phrases and structure of the music.

The issue thus gets back to whether or not there are two sets of processes:

memory-related and understanding-related. Certainly Marton et al.'s subjects seem to think that there are. Even in the "understanding through memorization" group, the subject on page 80 says memory and comprehension "are closely related... and promote each other", and (2:14, p.81): "...each time I repeat, I would have some new idea of understanding". This seems clearly to imply separate but related processes, both of which are miles away from rote learning.

The developmental sequence described in Chapter 6 captures the early stages of this conception. The stage one students may or may not distinguish memorizing from understanding, but as far as schoolwork is concerned they ignore the latter, and use simple rote learning, without understanding, in order to get through their day. Even Watkins' top level student at stage four saw understanding simply as a more efficient way of memorizing verbatim for examination purposes. These students did not use memorizing for understanding, but rather the opposite; they aim to understand in order to memorize more effectively, a mnemonic only. Deep memorizing (Chapter 9) is a sophisticated reversal of this; the students have already made sure they understood, as they need to for their own deep purposes, and then as a separate exercise, for assessment purposes, they rote learn.

In sum, there is a lot of 'noise' to cut through before the meaning can be apprehended so that repetition is necessary to reduce the proportion of noise to message. Learning to read and write in any system is such an example, but a character system requires this repetitive strategy even more than does an alphabet system. Thus, the difference between those who use a lot of repetition in learning for understanding, and those who learn for understanding without much repetition, derives from perceived task demand, which differs between cultures. Thus, the Chinese learner is not so very different from the Western learner; what differs are the perceived demands of common tasks learners from each culture typically face in their home environment. Chinese learners come to use repetition strategically more often than Westerners do in their attempts to understand their world.

For example, let us examine Volet and Kee's (1993) finding (see also Chapter 11) that initial differences between local Australian students and newly arrived Asian (mostly Singaporean) students in Australia in their approaches to learning disappeared at the end of their first semester. The Asians had rapidly adapted; their study approaches were "highly responsive to the demands of a specific learning situation rather than determined by inherent characteristics of individual or cultural groups" (Volet and Kee, 1993: p.3). When the Singaporeans were asked what were the 12 most important ways of studying (a) in Singapore and (b) in Australia, "Being able to read and understand main ideas" was the first perceived task demand in both places, but "Always aim to get the correct answer" and "Learn lecture material by heart" were perceived as the second and third most important strategies in Singapore.

After one year in Australia, these strategies were seen as least important, while "Evaluate different ideas and give own opinion" jumped from low priority in Singapore to second highest priority in Australia. Obviously, there is no rigid rote orientation amongst at least these CHC students, or even a predilection for a repetition strategy. What strikes us is not a preference for repetition, but their *cue consciousness*, driven by a need to perform well in whatever assessment tasks are set (Chapter 9); they are highly motivated to do well in their set tasks, and are alert for cues that help them do so. At the same time it can be argued that the tendency of Western educators to equate 'memorization' with 'rote memorization' has lead to an unwarranted neglect of the rote of memorization in the development of high quality learning outcomes (see Chapter 4 and 6).

Intrinsic and extrinsic motivation

"To offer a prize for doing a deed is tantamount to saying that the deed is not worth doing for its own sake". So said A.S. Neill (1960: p.162), headmaster of *Summerhill*, a school as unConfucian as could be. But Confucius, untrammelled by the rigid categories of Western thought that see extrinsic motivation as undermining intrinsic (Deci, 1975), saw rather that "there are golden houses and beautiful girls in books", as Lee reminds us in Chapter 2.

Thus, Western ways of categorizing motivation - extrinsic, intrinsic, and achievement - do not travel well, at least not to the Orient. More important than trying to categorize motivation is the existential 'felt need' that drives students to study; "the tendency to find academic activities meaningful and worthwhile, and to try and get the intended academic benefits from them" (Brophy, 1986: p.8). Westerners have seen intrinsic motivation as the only way of defining what is "meaningful and worthwhile", and therefore the deep (intrinsic) motive as the precursor of the deep strategy (Biggs, 1987). The Chinese learner may sees things more pragmatically. Rather than waiting for those internal conditions to be right, the deep strategy may be activated by a head of mixed motivational steam: personal ambition, family face, peer support, material reward, and yes, possibly even interest. Even more basic are those very Confucian "internal dispositions (that) create a sense of diligence and receptiveness" (Hess and Azuma, 1991: p.7) that would certainly help make academic activities "meaningful and worthwhile", in a way that leaves the more familiar American concept of intrinsic motivation standing. In short, the familiar extrinsic/intrinsic polarity collapses.

Achievement motivation: ego versus social

Neither is the CHC concept of achievement motivation identical to Western concepts (see Chapter 5), as it involves both collective and individual frameworks (Holloway, 1988; Salili, 1994). In Western countries, achievement motivation is interpreted as individual competition by those whose need for success dominates their need to avoid failure (Atkinson, 1964); those wired up this way find taking on all comers and winning as very ego-enhancing and rewarding. The individualist conception is paramount. But in Asia, standards of excellence and of what constitutes success may be determined both by the individual and by "significant others, the family, the group, or the society as a whole" (Yang, 1986: p.114). Further, the "pressure on students to study hard and do well in examinations, which is notorious in Hong Kong, may be present regardless of the educational level of the parents" (Ho, 1986: p.30); as in Japan, parents see their child's achievement as a matter of family 'face' much more so than Westerners do.

There are several points here. First, we see that CHC conceptions of achievement are multiple, even holistic. It is not either-or, but both-and. Second, the strict individuality in the West is merged in a superordinating collectivism that derives from Confucian notions of order and stability; in return for obedience and loyalty to the collectivity, principally the family, the individual is given security and face, but when those duties have been fulfilled, the individual is encouraged to pursue his ('his' is used advisedly) own interests (Ho and Chiu, 1994).

Collective versus individual orientations

Thus, the notion of collectivism goes quite beyond achievement motivation itself. In China, social relations between teacher and student, and student and student, are as complex as one might expect in a collectivistic culture. Students live on campus in dormitories, and unsurprisingly this environment facilitates a tremendous amount of collective activities, including academic discussions, study groups, and the like (Chan, 1993). The teachers live on campus too, often in the same building as their students, giving rise to much teacher-student interaction outside the classroom, and although teacher-student relations may be strongly hierarchical as compared with those in the West, they are also typically marked if not by warmth then by a sense of responsibility and mutual respect. This is perhaps another area where Western observers see only part of the picture. Ginsberg's (1992) observations that the lecturer is the authority, "a respected elder transmitting to a subordinate junior" (p. 6), may in itself be true, but the model of teaching is not so much one of simple transmission as one based on much interaction, in a complex and mutually accepting (if not warm) social context.

In CHCs generally, students spontaneously collaborate outside the classroom; in Hong Kong, over 80% in one Hong Kong tertiary class where this was monitored, resulting as it happened in better structured and higher quality assignments (Tang, 1993). This figure is far greater than the extent to which Western students would be likely to collaborate over assignments and other work-related matters. Organized peer learning can work well in Hong Kong schools (Lai, 1993; Winter, Chapter 11), but it is seldom attempted, although in Japan and other CHCs there is a great deal of class discussion (Hess and Azuma, 1991; Stevenson and Stigler, 1992). Hong Kong secondary school students would in fact prefer a more collaborative learning environment which they consider would promote the deeper, more achievement-oriented approach to learning that they would prefer (Chan and Watkins, 1994).

Internal attributions: controllable versus uncontrollable

Related to the above discussion are cross-cultural differences in attributions of academic successes and failures (see Chapter 5). While Western subjects consider ability, which they perceive to be uncontrollable, to be a major cause of academic success, Chinese students are far more likely to ascribe their performance to be due to controllable factors such as effort and study methods.

This is consistent with the value placed on effort and endurance in CHCs; success achieved through hard work is valued more highly than that gained by high ability in Confucian heritage, but not in Western, culture. Ability itself is perceived by Chinese teachers, parents, and students as an attribute that can be modified by effort. The upshot is that Chinese students are much more likely to accept personal responsibility for their successes and failures than their Western counterparts, which of course is the other side of the responsibility to the collective. However, this can have both positive and negative consequences. While their attributions encourage them to work harder and harder thus maximizing their likelihood of academic success, they are likely to feel guilty and to be blamed by their teachers and parents if failure results (see further discussion below).

The Chinese Learner in Hong Kong

The majority of research reported in these chapters is based on students in Hong Kong. While we have argued that Hong Kong students are in many key aspects representatives of a CHC, they are also unique, caught between the conflicting values and educational philosophies of British colonial and traditional Chinese society. Further, concerns about the political transition of

Hong Kong from British to Chinese rule in 1997 have created an educational context with difficult adjustment problems for both teachers and students (Postiglione and Leung, 1992). Two of the more serious of these problems will be highlighted below.

Teaching and learning in an second language

The situation in Hong Kong, where the great majority of students change from Cantonese to English as the language of instruction when they enter secondary school, has long been recognized as causing educational difficulties, not surprisingly when many students and even teachers have a low English-language proficiency. Large classes (40+), and a strongly teacher-centred approach, provide limited opportunities for the students to speak in English, and indeed most students fear being asked to speak in English, so that little emphasis is placed on the expressive registers of speaking or writing in English. Teachers use Cantonese frequently, usually to explain English terms, because that is the only language that the students understand and use outside the classroom. Writing in English is not even required in most school and some public examinations, because multiple choice or other objective testing is frequent.

As discussed in Chapter 7, both students and teachers have to resort to various strategies to cope. There is often an unwritten agreement between the students and teachers that the teachers will only ask questions that the students' limited English can handle no matter what the curriculum requirements of the subject. But students cannot escape English as it is the language of both their texts and tests, and the English standard required is well above the level of proficiency of most students. Hence the various strategies that enable students to survive without really understanding what they are reading. Not surprisingly, students who are not confident in their use of English typically adopt surface approaches to learning (Watkins, Biggs, and Regmi, 1991).

Unfortunately, the Hong Kong Government's most recent attempt to introduce Chinese more widely as the medium of instruction for those students least proficient in English seems to be meeting with little success. Both schools, and particularly parents, still see English proficiency as necessary for future success either abroad or in Hong Kong, where most tertiary institutions still officially use English as the medium of instruction.

Given the context, it is surprising how well Hong Kong students perform, even in English, according to international comparisons (Johnson and Cheung, 1991). This provides evidence yet again for the striking adaptiveness of the Chinese learner. This picture is now becoming increasingly complicated by the 1997 transition back to Chinese rule. It seems likely, officially at any rate, that the language of instruction will eventually become Putonghua (Mandarin). At the same time, Hong Kong's position as "Window on the West" will logically demand the maintenance of English as a medium of instruction in at least some of the tertiary institutions, if not in secondary schools. This is a situation that will require all the adaptiveness Hong Kong students can muster.

The assessment system in Hong Kong

As argued in Chapter 9, Hong Kong education is strongly influenced by the highly-competitive public examination system. Hong Kong parents perceive that educational success is the road to a better life for their children and their family in general, so they are particularly anxious that their children do well at school. The Confucian belief that any child can do well if only he or she tries hard enough means that failure is seen by both parent and child as the fault of the child who has disgraced the family. Such attribution to effort and motivation to succeed drastically increases the pressure on students. It works well in some cases, but can be hugely injurious in others. When combined with a norm-referenced examination system, where only the top 20% can succeed in reaching tertiary level, teaching becomes focused and ruthless, particularly when teaching and examining are carried out in a second language (L2), so that Hong Kong students are under considerable academic stress early on in their school careers. A recent case where a three-year old was consistently beaten for not doing enough homework is unfortunately not unique. The guilt and shame of not being able to cope academically has led to depression and suicide of even pre-teen age children (see Chapter 3). But those who survive such a system have the motivation and coping strategies to succeed anywhere in the world, and they do (Flynn, 1991; Sue and Okazaki, 1990).

The Chinese Learner Abroad

Classrooms everywhere, Western rhetoric notwithstanding, require the qualities of diligence, conformity to task requirements, at least some reference to attributions to effort and strategy, respect for authority, submitting to group rules, and the like (McCasland and Good, 1992). These are of course the dispositions in which CHC students are socialized so well. The Hong Kong classroom environment we have just described would be intolerable without these dispositions; Western classrooms make similar demands only more gently. It is no wonder that CHC students do so well in them.

This is not to say there are no problems. There are real problems of course to do with language, and the related one of coping with culture shock and homesickness. These social difficulties naturally impel already collectivistically-inclined international students to work and live in their own ethnic groups, which in turn brings charges of unwillingness to adapt, even of hostility to, and from, the host culture. Western students are likely to resent the way in which overseas CHC students form tight groups, whether for academic purposes or not. But surely it is a natural tendency for expatriates anywhere to club together in a foreign culture; this is very evident in Hong Kong professional circles as it is with Australians in London or Americans in Canada. Moreover, a large majority of international students claim they *want* to mix with Australians but feel that "Australian students stay in groups and it is difficult to join these groups or make friends" (Mullins, Quintrell, and Itancock, 1995; 218).

Language and social adaptation aside, CHC students move from an academic culture based on a set of values and expectations that are congruent with their general socialization, to an environment lacking familiar support structures. Not all the study skills that CHC students have developed in their own environments, such as good receptive learning skills in the classroom and collaborative learning with peers outside the classroom, are equally adaptive in the overseas ecology, with different classroom methods. Peer back-up becomes more frequently social and recreational rather than task-related, and because of their restricted social contacts, elaboration of content in the mother tongue is much less likely than at home. Nevertheless Volet and Renshaw's Singaporean students showed an amazing adaptability which (apart from language, which was not an issue to most of these Singaporeans) does indeed seem characteristic of CHC students.

Some beliefs that may not travel

Some CHC beliefs can lead to misperception of the Western context and need correcting. These are well-known and need only brief mention here. CHC students, for reasons that vary in different particular countries, have problems with writing. One major problem we have already discussed: Hong Kong students tend to have good receptive skills, listening and reading, but poor expressive skills, speaking and writing. But at least these students have their attributions going for them: belief in effort and strategy, and a high degree of achievement motivation. Further, Chapter 8 reports several ways in which deep processing can be encouraged in students working in a second language.

In a different category are problems involving plagiarism. Some CHC countries, China in particular, are only beginning to recognize international copyright conventions, so plagiarism to students from these countries is an unappreciated concept. Of course, they need to be made to appreciate it, from day one. But what appears to be plagiarism often occurs as a result of writing in a second language. Students who want to make a point particularly clearly see paraphrasing the source as a strange thing to do when the source itself makes the point better than they ever could reword it in an imperfectly mastered language. When the teacher and marker is also the author of the source, the student is obviously not deliberately trying to mislead as to authorship, although there *might* be a different question of 'patting the horse's bum', as a Cantonese phrase robustly puts it. But that syndrome is universal, as is the cure. The point is that it looks like plagiarism to a Western teacher when it obviously is not. Of course, such issues can also be raised by a Chinese student to excuse their conscious plagiarism!

Essay writing may present problems because some CHC essay structures do not follow the Western convention of presenting a balanced argument and drawing one's own conclusions (Ballard and Clanchy, 1984; Ginsberg, 1992). In Chinese writing, the introduction is often historical and discursive to recall 'past lessons', not the focused review the Western essay requires; the body contains much direct quotation from respected sources. Such beliefs and expectancies are not genetic, and have to be replaced. It helps if Western teachers are aware of the nature of these problems, and see that this sort of thing is based on misunderstandings, not on a deliberate attempt to mislead. The work reported in Chapter 11 shows that a reorientation to Western task demands typically occurs surprisingly quickly.

There are two major implications. Western educators need, first, to be aware that students may arrive with conceptions of task requirements that are inappropriate in a Western setting. The 'criminal' offence of plagiarism frequently reduces simply to a misunderstanding. The second implication follows immediately. Task requirements need to be made absolutely clear. What is tacitly understood by local students may not be so clearly understood by overseas students; recall that "Always acknowledge source of information" was seen as the lowest priority rule of studying in Singapore (Volet and Kee, 1993), but also recall that after a semester in Australia these students saw that as much more important.

Relations with teachers and classroom behaviour

As we saw in China and other CHCs, students' relations with teachers are hierarchical. Many Western teachers see a hierarchical teacher-student relationship as 'cold', and in these politically correct times take active steps to develop a 'warm' egalitarian relationship. CHC students, used to a hierarchical relationship do not readily take to a first name relationship with their teacher, or to challenge and argue with them (Barker, et al. 1991). If that is the price of a 'warm' relationship, they would rather withdraw. Both sides need to realize that that space has at least two-dimensions: warm-cold, and hierarchical-egalitarian. Hierarchy need not destroy warmth, but on the other hand neither does warmth necessarily create a comfortable working relationship. The hierachical relationship in CHC cultures may or may not be warm in Western terms (that is a different issue), but it is marked by its own positive interpersonal affect: respect and acceptance, which may certainly in the course of time and with some individuals become marked by genuine warmth (Wong, 1995) but respect is the functional affect, doing service in an hierarchical society what warmth does in an egalitarian one. To insist on the tokens of warmth from the outset is to CHC students distasteful. To do so is rather like writing a writer-based text, egocentrically written for the benefit of the writer, not the reader (Flower, 1981); teaching, like writing, should be reader-based.

It is in this light that we could interpret the attitudes of those Australian teachers who perceived the classroom behaviours of CHC students as undesirable: passive, not discussing in class, not asking questions (Samuelowicz, 1987). Blaming students for not being what teachers would like them to be is unhelpful (Biggs, 1993). The blame may not even be accurate. Some evidence does support the allegation that Chinese students are passive. Barker and colleagues (1991), in the University of Queensland, found that ethnic Chinese from Hong Kong, Malaysia, and Singapore, were less likely to participate in tutorial discussions and express their opinions. On the other hand, Renshaw and Volet (1994) found that Singaporean students participated around the group average, whereas Australians tended either to be dominant, or to be silent throughout. The research evidence is unclear, even on a point on which opinion is strong.

It is possible that a self-fulfilling prophecy exists. If CHC students are strong on cue-seeking, they will be particularly sensitive to what they perceive as demands to be met. In fact, there is often a wide gap between the qualities lecturers *say* they want from their students, and the tasks they *set* them to do, which frequently encourage question-spotting, and rote memorization of facts and theories considered important by the teachers (e.g. Bowden, 1988; Entwistle, 1984). If lecturers then complain about CHC students' inability to criticize, or their lack of breadth, it is possible that CHC students are simply responding more closely than Western students to what they see as required of them. Lecturers may be perceiving what they have created.

Language difficulties

This area is of course the most obvious source of difficulty, and is seen as such by both teachers and students (Samuelowicz, 1987). Studies of L2 acquisition overwhelmingly endorse immersion as a highly effective approach to language learning (Cummins, 1979). Immersion is particularly important for overseas students, whose previous language experience is largely restricted to the input registers of listening and reading, with little extended writing and less talking required in the academic mode, and are then expected formally and informally to operate in all four registers. Students need to build up automaticity in the lower-level language skills so that they can devote working memory space to content concerns (Cantwell and Biggs, 1988), and this is only likely to happen when students are required to live and think in L2. This is consistent with the claim in Chapter 8 of a threshold level of L2-proficiency being required before deeper-level processing is possible.

There are actually two issues here: (a) the need for a supportive linguistic context, and (b) the need for a collaborative context in which to work. At home, the two coincide, but overseas, the collaborative context is usually not the work context. With the increasing tendency for overseas students to live in rented houses off-campus rather than in university halls of residence, this separation is exacerbated. It may be possible for teachers to organize group work in classes that would require overseas students to work collaboratively with native speakers of English, thereby satisfying both content and language-learning needs but usually resulting in dominance of the groups by native speakers who are quicker on the draw and get in first. It is this, rather than cultural differences as such, that almost certainly explains the differences in the findings of Barker and colleagues (1991) and Renshaw and Volet (1994) about tutorial participation; the latter worked with Singaporean students, whose English was extremely good. It would thus be more accurate, more profitable, and less ethnocentric, to target the issue of tutorial participation in linguistic rather than in ethnic terms.

Study skills training

Given their motivation and attributions to controllable factors, overseas students would appear to be ideally placed for training in study and writing skills. As noted, CHC students seem to have spontaneously developed study skills that are adaptive in their own environments. They have developed good receptive learning skills in the classroom, elaborative learning being carried out with peers outside the classroom. Standard questionnaire profiles on approaches to study present an unusually healthy picture (see Chapter 3).

Overseas countries present a new ecology, with different classroom methods; peer back-up is more frequently social and recreational rather than task-related; and because of their restricted social contacts, elaboration of content in in their mother tongue is unlikely. There would seem to be a strong case for intervention, not so much in direct study-skill training, but in more metacognitively-oriented approaches that help students come to terms with their context (Biggs, 1988). Instruction to develop understanding of the discourse patterns commonly found in academic literature, and the expectations Western academics have of academic writing and plagiarism-related issues would be particularly valuable. L2 students can also be helped to use the processing capacity they possess as efficiently as possible. Teaching summarization skills may be particularly salient in this respect, as is reported in Chapter 8, Chapter 7 also reminds us of the need to ensure the grammatical competence in L2 of such students. This is too often neglected in courses for overseas students.

Implications for staff development

The conclusions reached in this book are that overseas CHC students are just as capable or even more capable of high-quality learning outcomes than their Western peers. However, the L2 context and mutual misperception between teacher and student can lead to mutual misunderstandings. The CHC students, particularly those educated in educational contexts such as Hong Kong, are highly cue conscious. That is, they are very achievement oriented and alert to cues from their lecturers and from the assessment system itself as to what is needed to succeed in a particular course. On occasions they may falsely interpret the need for quantity rather than quality in learning outcomes and perform accordingly.

Perhaps more commonly, their teachers may misinterpret the cognitive processes the students are actually adopting. While this can, of course, happen with any student, it is more likely to happen with students from a Confucian heritage culture, where basic processes such as memorizing and motivation take on a somewhat different meaning.

What this implies is that staff development may be needed to assist Western lecturers to see learning through the eyes of their students, particularly those from a different culture. The action research approach described in Chapter 13 is a valuable way of encouraging such a perspective. Of course, Chinese students (just as Western students) do not all study the same way. However, we believe that there are sufficient commonalities among CHC students and sufficient differences between them and Western students to have made our task of understanding the cultural, psychological, and contextual factors that have shaped their approaches to learning worthwhile. We hope this book will contribute to the reader's understanding of these issues also.

REFERENCES

Atkinson, J.W. (1964). *An introduction to motivation.* New York: Van Nostrand.
Ballard, B. & Clanchy, J. (1984). *Study abroad: a manual for Asian students.* Kuala Lumpur: Longmans.
Barker, M., Child, C., Gallois, C., Jones, E., & Callan, V. (1991). Difficulties of overseas students in social and academic situations. *Australian Journal*

:hes to learning and studying. Australian
ch, Hawthorn, Vic.

f metacognition in enhancing learning.
n, 32, 127-138.

) practice: a cognitive systems approach.
d Development, 12, 73-86.

nge in teaching practice. In Ramsden, P.
' perspectives. London: Kogan Page.

udents. Occasional Paper No. 101. Institute
nigan State University.

. Effects of bilingualism and approach to
ıll of expository text. In Gruneberg, M.M.,
ds.), Practical aspects of memory: volume
iplications. London: Wiley.

earning of medical and business students in
ne University of Hong Kong: M.Ed.

tion. New York: Plenum.

perspectives on learning. In Marton, F.,
N. (Eds.), The experience of learning.
es Press.

strategies for writing. New York: Harcourt

Flynn, J.F. (1991). Asian Americans: achievement beyond IQ. Hillsdale, NJ:
Erlbaum.

Ginsberg, E. (1992). Not just a matter of English. HERDSA News, 14(1), 6-8.

Hess, R.D. & Azuma, M. (1991). Cultural support for schooling: contrasts
between Japan and the United States. Educational Researcher, 20(9), 2-8.

Ho, D.Y.F. (1986). Chinese patterns of socialization: a critical review. In Bond,
M.H. (Ed.), The psychology of the Chinese people. Hong Kong: Oxford
University Press.

Ho, D.Y.F., & Chiu, C.Y.F. (1994). Component ideas on individualism,
collectivism, and social organization. In Kim, U., Triandis, H.C.,
Kagitcibasi, C., Choi, S.C. & Yoon, G. (Eds.), Individualism and
collectivism: theory, method, and applications (pp. 137-158). Thousand
Oaks, CA: Sage.

Holloway, S.D. (1988). Concepts of ability and effort in Japan and the US.
Review of Educational Research, 58, 327-345.

Johnson, R.K. & Cheung, Y.S. (1991). Reading literacy in Hong Kong in
Chinese and English: a preliminary report on the IEA study. Paper read to
Annual Conference, Institute of Language in Education, December 15-17,
Hong Kong.

Kember, D. & Gow, L. (1990). Cultural specificity of approaches to study. *British Journal of Educational Psychology, 60,* 356-363.

Kirby, J.R. (1988). Style, strategy, and skill in reading. In Schmeck, R.R. (Ed.), *Learning styles and learning strategies.* New York: Plenum Press.

Lai, E. (1993). Cooperative learning in a geography class. In Biggs, J. & Watkins, D. (Eds.), *Learning and teaching in Hong Kong: what is and what might be* (pp. 177-188). Hong Kong: Education Papers No. 17, University of Hong Kong.

McCaslin, M. & Good, T.L. (1992). Compliant cognition: the misalliance of management and instructional goals in current school reform. *Educational Researcher, 21*(3), 4-19.

Mullins, G., Quintrell, N. & Hancock, L. (1995). The experiences of international and local students in three Australian universities. *Higher Education Research and Development, 14,* 201-232.

Neill, A.S. (1960). *Summerhill.* New York: Hart.

Postiglione, G. & Leung, Y.M. (1992). *Education and society in Hong Kong.* Hong Kong: Hong Kong University Press.

Renshaw, P.D. & Volet, S.E. (1995). South-east Asian students at Australian universities: a reappraisal of their tutorial participation and approaches to study. *Australian Educational Researcher, 22,* 85-106.

Salili, F. (1994). Age, sex, and cultural differences in the meaning and dimensions of achievement. *Personality and Social Psychology Bulletin, 20,* 635-648.

Stevenson, H.W. & Stigler, J. (1992). *The learning gap: why our schools are failing and what we can learn from Japanese and Chinese education.* New York: Summit Books.

Sue, S. & Okazaki, S. (1990). Asian-American educational achievements: a phenomenon in search of an explanation. *American Psychologist, 44,* 349-359.

Tang, K.C.C. (1991). Effects of different assessment procedures on tertiary students' approaches to learning. The University of Hong Kong: Ph.D. Dissertation.

Tang, K.C.C. (1993). Spontaneous collaborative learning: a new dimension in student learning experience? *Higher Education Research and Development.*

Thomas, P.R. & Bain, J.D. (1984). Contextual dependance of learning approaches: the effects of assessments. *Human Learning, 3,* 227-240.

Volet, S.E. & Kee, J.P.P. (1993). Studying in Singapore - studying in Australia: a student perspective. Murdoch University Teaching Excellence Committee: Occasional Paper No. 1.

Volet, S.E., Renshaw, P.D. & Tietzel, K. (1994). A short-term longitudinal investigation of cross-cultural differences in study approaches using Biggs SPQ questionnaire. *British Journal of Educational Psychology, 64,* 801-318.

Wang, G.W. (1991). *The Chineseness of China: selected essays*. Hong Kong: Oxford University Press.

Watkins, D., Biggs, J. & Regmi, M. (1991). Does confidence in the language of instruction influence a student's approach to learning? *Instructional Science, 20*, 331-339.

Yang, K.S. (1986). Chinese personality and its change. In Bond, M.H. (Ed.), *The psychology of the Chinese people*. Hong Kong: Oxford University Press.

INDEX

assessing learning processes
  Approaches to Studying Inventory 7; 10-11
  cross-cultural validity 8-10; 20
  Inventory of Learning Processes 14; 16-17
  Learning Process Questionnaire 7; 10-19; 69-70
  Study Process Questionnaire 7; 10-19; 69-70; 146-147; 172; 207-210; 212; 216; 244-245; 251; 253

approaches to learning 5-8; 34-36; 45; 53-54; 69-70; 96-99; 114-116; 146-155; 165-166; 170; 174-179; 193-197; 207-210; 217-218; 243-245; 264

assessment 52; 63; 90; 153-174; 277
  assumptions about/conceptions of 155-157; 161; 165-166; 170-172; 176
  backwash effect of examinations 110-113; 153-154; 157-167; 169; 178-179
  SOLO taxonomy 169-173; 175-178; 199

attributions for success and failure 15-16; 30-33; 59-60; 92-95; 98-100; 113-117; 159; 275

Canada 124, 145, 278

China 26-27, 33, 38, 46-48, 50, 55, 60, 71, 88, 91, 93, 115, 145, 159, 188, 226, 228, 269, 274, 278-279

Chinese learners
  abroad 141-155; 205-208; 210-211; 213-218; 270; 272-273; 277-282
  achievement of 25; 48-49; 63; 70; 85; 206; 212-215
  docility (educability) of 28-30; 58-59; 86
  memorization by 36; 46-49; 75-82; 96-97; 109-116; 132; 167; 174-179; 196-197; 207-210; 217; 243; 270-273
  motivation of 33-34; 37-38; 87-89; 94-96; 99-100; 179; 212-214; 273-274
  the paradox of 18-19; 45-50; 63-64; 69-70; 82; 115-116; 160; 179; 243; 269
  Western misperceptions of 46-47; 55; 63; 205; 207-211; 215-217; 243; 264; 270-275; 277-279; 282

collectivism 33-34; 56; 86-88; 99-100; 183-184; 200; 225-227; 274-275

conceptions of learning 6; 25-26; 35; 70; 72-82; 108-116; 142; 211; 270-273

Confucius, teachings of 25-39

Confucian Heritage Cultures, learning in 25-28; 46-50; 53-57; 58-64; 160; 188; 269-271; 273-275; 277-280; 281-282

cue consciousness 60; 63; 160; 164; 176; 178-179; 278; 280; 282